Spanish

PHRASEBOOK & DICTIONARY

Language Writers Marta López, Cristina Hernández Montero
Cover Image Researcher Naomi Parker

Thanks
Sasha Baskett, James Hardy, Angela Tinson

Published by Lonely Planet Publications Pty Ltd
ABN 36 005 607 983

6th Edition – March 2015
ISBN 978 1 74321 442 8
Text © Lonely Planet 2015
Cover Image Paul Panayiotou – Corbis

Printed in China 10 9 8 7 6 5 4 3 2 1

Contact lonelyplanet.com/contact

Although the authors and Lonely Planet try to make the information as accurate as possible, we accept no responsibility for any loss, injury or inconvenience sustained by anyone using this book.

Paper in this book is certified against the Forest Stewardship Council™ standards. FSC™ promotes environmentally responsible, socially beneficial and economically viable management of the world's forests.

MIX
Paper from
responsible sources
FSC™ C021741

Look out for the following icons throughout the book:

'Shortcut' Phrase
Easy-to-remember alternative to the full phrase

Q&A Pair
Question-and-answer pair – we suggest a response to the question asked

Look For
Phrases you may see on signs, menus etc

Listen For
Phrases you may hear from officials, locals etc

Language Tip
An insight into the foreign language

Culture Tip
An insight into the local culture

How to read the phrases:
- Coloured words and phrases throughout the book are phonetic guides to help you pronounce the foreign language.
- Lists of phrases with tinted background are options you can choose to complete the phrase above them.

These abbreviations will help you choose the right words and phrases in this book:

a	adjective	m	masculine	sg	singular
f	feminine	n	noun	v	verb
inf	informal	pl	plural		
lit	literal	pol	polite		

Contents

PAGE 6

About Spanish
Learn about Spanish, build your own sentences and pronounce words correctly.

PAGE 31

Travel Phrases
Ready-made phrases for every situation –
buy a ticket, book a hotel and much more.

Basics — 31

Practical — 41

INTRO

Spanish

español es·pa·*nyol*

Who Speaks Spanish?
Official Language

NORTH & CENTRAL AMERICA
MEXICO
GUATEMALA
HONDURAS
NICARAGUA
EL SALVADOR
COSTA RICA
PANAMA

CARIBBEAN
CUBA
PUERTO RICO
DOMINICAN REPUBLIC

SOUTH AMERICA
ARGENTINA
CHILE • BOLIVIA
PARAGUAY
URUGUAY • PERU
VENEZUELA
COLOMBIA
ECUADOR

EUROPE & AFRICA
SPAIN
EQUATORIAL GUINEA

Widely Understood USA

Why Bother

You'll be seduced by this melodic language and have fun trying to roll your *rr*'s like the locals – not to mention ordering scrumptious tapas or engaging in all the shouting at the *fútbol*.

Distinctive Sounds

The strong and rolled r, harsh and guttural kh and, in European Spanish, 'lisping' th.

Spanish in the World

Over the last 500 years, Spanish in Latin America has evolved differently to the

300 MILLION
speak Spanish as their
first language

100 MILLION
speak Spanish as their
second language

Spanish of Europe. Among other differences, you'll easily recognise Latin Americans by the lack of lisp in their speech – ie *cerveza* (beer) is ther·*ve*·tha in Europe but ser·*ve*·sa across the Atlantic.

Spanish in Spain

Spanish, or Castilian (*castellano* ka·ste·*lya*·no) is primarily the language of Castille (covering the largest territory in Spain). However, Catalan, Galician and Basque are also official languages, and locals in these regions are very proud of their own language.

False Friends

Warning: many Spanish words look like English words but have a different

meaning altogether, eg *suburbio* soo·*boor*·byo is a slum district, not a suburb (which is *barrio* ba·ryo in Spanish).

Language Family

Romance (developed from Vulgar Latin spoken by Roman soldiers and merchants during the conquest from the 3rd to the 1st century BC). Close relatives include Portuguese, Italian, French and Romanian.

Must-Know Grammar

Spanish has a formal and informal word for 'you' (*Usted* oo·*ste* and *tú* too respectively). The verbs also have a different ending for each person, like the English 'I do' vs 'he/she do**es**'.

Donations to English

Thanks to Columbus' discovery of the New World in 1492, a large corpus of words from indigenous American languages has entered English via Spanish. You may recognise *canyon, guerrilla, ranch, tornado*...

5 Phrases to Learn Before You Go

1 **What time does it open/close?**
¿A qué hora abren/cierran? a ke o·ra *ab*·ren/*thye*·ran

The Spanish tend to observe the siesta (midday break), so opening times may surprise you.

2 **Are these complimentary?**
¿Son gratis? son *gra*·tees

Tapas (bar snacks) are available pretty much around the clock at Spanish bars. You'll find they're free in some places.

3 **When is admission free?**
¿Cuándo es la entrada gratuita?
kwan·do es la en·*tra*·da gra·*twee*·ta

Many museums and galleries in Spain have admission-free times, so check before buying tickets.

4 **Where can we go (salsa) dancing?**
¿Dónde podemos ir a bailar (salsa)?
don·de po·*de*·mos eer a bai·*lar* (*sal*·sa)

Flamenco may be the authentic viewing experience in Spain, but to actively enjoy the music you'll want to do some dancing.

5 **How do you say this in (Catalan/Galician/Basque)?**
¿Cómo se dice ésto en (catalán/gallego/euskera)?
ko·mo se *dee*·the es·to en (ka·ta·*lan*/ga·*lye*·go/e·oos·*ke*·ra)

Spain has four official languages, and people in these regions will appreciate it if you try to use their local language.

10 Phrases to Sound Like a Local

| What's up? | **¿Qué pasa?** | ke *pa*·sa |

| Great! | **¡Genial!** | khe·*nyal* |

| How cool! | **¡Qué guay!** | ke gwai |

| That's fantastic! | **¡Estupendo!** | es·too·*pen*·do |

| Really? | **¿En serio?** | en *se*·ryo |

| You don't say! | **¡No me digas!** | no me *dee*·gas |

| Sure. | **Seguro.** | se·*goo*·ro |

| OK. | **Vale.** | *va*·le |

| Of course! | **¡Por supuesto!** | por soo·*pwes*·to |

| Whatever. | **Lo que sea.** | lo ke *se*·a |

ABOUT Spanish

Pronunciation

Spanish pronunciation isn't difficult, as most sounds are similar to the sounds found in English. The relationship between Spanish sounds and their spelling is straightforward and consistent. There are some easy rules to follow and once you learn them you shouldn't have problems being understood. As in most languages, Spanish pronunciation can vary according to region – this book focuses on Castilian Spanish.

Vowel Sounds

SYMBOL	ENGLISH EQUIVALENT	SPANISH EXAMPLE	TRANSLITERATION
a	alms	agua	a·gwa
ai	aisle	bailar	bai·lar
e	red	número	noo·me·ro
ee	bee	día	dee·a
ey	hey	seis	seys
o	go	ojo	o·kho
oo	book	gusto	goo·sto
ow	cow	autobús	ow·to·boos
oy	boy	hoy	oy

Consonant Sounds

SYMBOL	ENGLISH EQUIVALENT	SPANISH EXAMPLE	TRANSLITERATION
b	big	barco	*bar*·ko
ch	chilli	chica	*chee*·ka
d	din	dinero	dee·*ne*·ro
f	fun	fiesta	*fye*·sta
g	go	gato	*ga*·to
k	kick	cabeza, queso	ka·*be*·tha, *ke*·so
kh	as in the Scottish *loch*	jardín, gente	khar·*deen*, *khen*·te
l	loud	lago	*la*·go
ly	million	llamada	lya·*ma*·da
m	man	mañana	ma·*nya*·na
n	no	nuevo	*nwe*·vo
ny	canyon	señora	se·*nyo*·ra
p	pig	padre	*pa*·dre
r	run (but stronger and rolled)	ritmo, burro, mariposa	*reet*·mo, *boo*·ro, ma·ree·*po*·sa
s	so	semana	se·*ma*·na
t	tin	tienda	*tyen*·da
th	thin	Barcelona, manzana	bar·the·*lo*·na, man·*tha*·na
v	soft 'b', between 'v' and 'b'	vaca	*va*·ka
w	win	guardia	*gwar*·dya
y	yes	viaje, ya	*vya*·khe, ya

Reading & Writing

There are some key things to remember about consonants in written Spanish:

» The letter *c* is pronounced with a lisp, eg *cerveza* ther·*ve*·tha, except when it comes before *a, o* and *u* or a consonant. Then, it's pronounced hard like the k in 'king'.
» When ending a word, the letter *d* is also pronounced soft, like a th, or is so slight that it hardly gets pronounced at all.
» The letter *j* stands for a harsh and guttural sound, and we use the kh symbol in our pronunciation guides.
» Try to roll your double *r*'s.
» The letter *q* is pronounced hard, like a k.
» The letter *v* sounds more like a b, said with the lips pressed together.
» There are a few letter combinations which you may find slightly unusual: *ch, ll* and *ñ*. The *ch* (che) and *ll* (e·lye) are no longer considered separate letters in the Spanish alphabet, so in dictionaries and the like, you'll find words starting with *ch* amongst the *c* listings, and those starting with *ll*, amongst the *l* listings. The letter *ñ* (e·nye) is considered a separate letter in the Spanish alphabet.

~ SPANISH ALPHABET ~

A	a	a	B	b	be	C	c	the
D	d	de	E	e	e	F	f	e·fe
G	g	khe	H	h	*a*·che	I	i	ee
J	j	*kho*·ta	K	k	ka	L	l	e·le
M	m	e·me	N	n	e·ne	Ñ	ñ	e·nye
O	o	o	P	p	pe	Q	q	koo
R	r	e·re	S	s	e·se	T	t	te
U	u	oo	V	v	oo·ve	W	w	oo·ve do·ble
X	x	e·kees	Y	y	ee·*grye*·ga	Z	z	*the*·ta

Word Stress

There is word stress in Spanish, which means you emphasise one syllable in a word over another. Rule of thumb: when a written word ends in *n, s* or a vowel, the stress falls on the second-last syllable, eg *lejos le*·khos (far), *casa ka*·sa (house). Otherwise, the final syllable is stressed, eg *hablar* a·*blar* (talk). If you see an accent mark over a syllable, it cancels out these rules and you just stress that syllable instead, eg *número noo*·me·ro (number).

LANGUAGE TIP

False Friends

Beware of false friends – those words that sound like familiar English, but could land you in a bit of trouble if you use them unwittingly in Spanish. Here are some mistakes that it's a little too easy to make:

el suburbio	el soo·*boor*·byo slum district, not 'suburb' which is *el barrio*, el *ba*·ryo
Estoy constipado/a. m/f	es·*toy* kons·tee·*pa*·do/a I have a cold, not 'I'm constipated', which is *estoy estreñido/a* m/f es·*toy* es·tre·*nyee*·do/a
Estoy embarazada.	es·*toy* em·ba·ra·*tha*·da I'm pregnant, not 'I'm embarassed', which is *estoy avergonzado/a* m/f es·*toy* a·ver·gon·*tha*·do/a
la injuria	la een·*khoo*·ree·a insult, not 'injury', which is *la herida*, la e·*ree*·da
los parientes	los pa·ree·*yen*·tes relatives, not 'parents', which is *los padres*, los *pa*·dres
sensible	sen·*see*·ble sensitive, not 'sensible', which is *prudente*, proo·*den*·te

ABOUT Spanish

Grammar

This chapter is designed to explain the main grammatical structures you need in order to make your own sentences. Look under each heading for information on functions which these grammatical categories express in a sentence. For example, demonstratives are used for giving instructions, so you'll need them to tell the taxi driver where your hotel is, etc. A glossary of grammatical terms is included at the end of this chapter to help you.

Adjectives & Adverbs

Describing People/Things • Doing Things

When using an adjective to describe a noun, you need to use a different ending depending on whether the noun is masculine or feminine, and singular or plural (see **gender** and **plurals**). Most adjectives use the following four endings:

~ ADJECTIVES ~

	singular		plural	
m	fantástico	fan·*tas*·tee·ko	fantásticos	fan·*tas*·tee·kos
f	fantástica	fan·*tas*·tee·ka	fantásticas	fan·*tas*·tee·kas

a fantastic hotel un hotel fantástico (lit: a-m-sg hotel fantastic-m-sg)
oon o·*tel* fan·*tas*·tee·ko

a fantastic meal	una comida fantástica (lit: a-f-sg meal fantastic-f-sg) *oo*·na ko·*mee*·da fan·*tas*·tee·ka
some fantastic books	unos libros fantásticos (lit: some-m-pl books fantastic-m-pl) *oo*·nos *lee*·bros fan·*tas*·tee·kos
some fantastic tapas	unas tapas fantásticas (lit: some-f-pl tapas fantastic-f-pl) *oo*·nas *ta*·pas fan·*tas*·tee·kas

Adjectives generally come after the noun in Spanish. However, adjectives expressing quantity (such as 'much', 'a lot', 'little', 'few', 'many') always precede the noun. See also **demonstratives** and **possessives**.

a comfortable hotel	un hotel cómodo (lit: a-m-sg hotel comfortable-m-sg) oon o·*tel* ko·mo·do
many tourists	muchos turistas (lit: many-m-pl tourists) *moo*·chos too·*rees*·tas

Most adverbs in Spanish are derived from adjectives by adding the ending -*mente* ·*men*·te to the singular feminine form of the adjective (ie the form ending in -*a*), just like you add the ending '-ly' to the adjective in English. In Spanish, adverbs are generally placed after the verb they refer to.

a slow train	un tren lento (lit: a-m-sg train slow-m-sg) oon tren *len*·to
to speak slowly	hablar lentamente (lit: to-speak slowly) ab·*lar* len·ta·*men*·te

Articles

Naming People/Things

There are four words for the definite article (ie equivalents of
'the' in English) in Spanish, used depending on the gender and
the number of the noun (see **gender** and **plurals**). The masculine singular form of the definite article is joined to some
prepositions when it's placed after them, so *a el* (to the-m-sg)
becomes *al* al and *de el* (of the-m-sg) becomes *del* del. See also
prepositions.

~ DEFINITE ARTICLES ~

m sg	**the car**	el coche	el *ko*·che
m pl	**the cars**	los coches	los *ko*·ches
f sg	**the shop**	la tienda	la *tyen*·da
f pl	**the shops**	las tiendas	las *tyen*·das

Similarly, Spanish has four words for the indefinite article (ie
'a/an' in English), depending on the gender and number of the
noun.

~ INDEFINITE ARTICLES ~

m sg	**an egg**	un huevo	oon *we*·vo
m pl	**some eggs**	unos huevos	oo·nos *we*·vos
f sg	**a house**	una casa	oo·na *ka*·sa
f pl	**some houses**	unas casas	oo·nas *ka*·sas

Be

Describing People/Things • Making Statements

Spanish has two words for the English verb 'be': *ser* ser and
estar es·tar, which are used depending on the context.

~ USE OF *SER* (TO BE) ~

permanent characteristics of persons/things	Liz es muy guapa. *leez es mooy gwa·pa*	Liz is very pretty.
occupations or nationality	Ana es de España. *a·na es de e·spa·nya*	Ana is from Spain.
time or location of events	Son las tres. *son las tres*	It's 3 o'clock.
possession	¿De quién es este bolso? *de kyen es es·te bol·so*	Whose bag is this?

~ USE OF *ESTAR* (TO BE) ~

temporary characteristics of persons/things	La sopa está fría. *la so·pa es·ta free·a*	The soup is cold.
time or location of persons/things	Estamos en Madrid. *es·ta·mos en ma·dreeth*	We're in Madrid.
mood of a person	Estoy contento/a. m/f *es·toy kon·ten·to/a*	I'm happy.

~ *SER* (TO BE) – PRESENT TENSE ~

I	am	yo	soy	yo	soy
you sg inf	are	tú	eres	too	e·res
you sg pol	are	Usted	es	oo·ste	es
he	is	él	es	el	es
she	is	ella	es	e·lya	es
we	are	nosotros m nosotras f	somos	no·so·tros no·so·tras	so·mos
you pl inf	are	vosotros m vosotras f	sois	vo·so·tros vo·so·tras	soys
you pl pol	are	Ustedes	son	oo·ste·des	son
they	are	ellos m ellas f	son	e·lyos e·lyas	son

~ ESTAR (TO BE) – PRESENT TENSE ~

I	am	yo	estoy	yo	es·*toy*
you sg inf	are	tú	estás	too	es·*tas*
you sg pol	are	Usted	está	oo·*ste*	es·*ta*
he	is	él	está	el	es·*ta*
she	is	ella	está	e·lya	es·*ta*
we	are	nosotros m nosotras f	estamos	no·so·tros no·so·tras	es·*ta*·mos
you pl inf	are	vosotros m vosotras f	estáis	vo·so·tros vo·so·tras	es·*tais*
you pl pol	are	Ustedes	están	oo·*ste*·des	es·*tan*
they	are	ellos m ellas f	están	e·lyos e·lyas	es·*tan*

Demonstratives

Giving Instructions • Indicating Location • Pointing Things Out

To point something out, the easiest phrases to use are *es* es (it is), *esto es* es·to es (this is) or *eso es* e·so es (that is).

It's a guide to Seville.   Es una guía de Sevilla.
(lit: is a-**f-sg** guide of Seville)
es oo·na *gee*·a de se·*vee*·lya

The Spanish words for 'this' and 'that' vary, depending on whether something is close (ie 'this'), away from you (ie 'that'), or even further away in time or space (ie 'that over there'). Each of these words changes form depending on the gender and number of the noun it refers to. See also **gender** and **plurals**.

~ DEMONSTRATIVES ~

	m sg		m pl	
this (close)	éste	e·ste	éstos	e·stos
that (away)	ése	e·se	ésos	e·sos
that (further away)	aquél	a·kel	aquéllos	a·ke·lyos

	f sg		f pl	
this (close)	ésta	e·sta	éstas	e·stas
that (away)	ésa	e·sa	ésas	e·sas
that (further away)	aquélla	a·ke·lya	aquéllas	a·ke·lyas

Gender

Naming People/Things

In Spanish, all nouns (words which denote a thing, person or idea) have either masculine or feminine gender. You can recognise the noun's gender by the article, demonstrative, possessive or any other adjective accompanying the noun, as they all change form to agree with the noun's gender (see **adjectives & adverbs**, **articles**, **demonstratives**, **possessives**). The gender of words is also indicated in the dictionary, but here are some general rules:

» a word is masculine/feminine if it refers to a man/woman
» words ending in -o or -or are generally masculine
» words ending in -a, -d, -z or -ión are usually feminine

The masculine and feminine forms of words are indicated with m and f throughout this book where relevant. See also p138.

20

Have

Possessing

Possession can be indicated in various ways in Spanish (see also **possessives**). One way is by using the verb *tener* te·*ner* (have). For negative forms with 'have', see **negatives**.

~ *TENER (TO HAVE)* ~

I	have	yo	tengo	yo	ten·go
you sg inf	have	tú	tienes	too	tye·nes
you sg pol	have	Usted	tiene	oo·ste	tye·ne
he	has	él	tiene	el	tye·ne
she	has	ella	tiene	e·lya	tye·ne
we	have	nosotros m nosotras f	ten-emos	no·so·tros no·so·tras	te·ne·mos
you pl inf	have	vosotros m vosotras f	tenéis	vo·so·tros vo·so·tras	te·neys
you pl pol	have	Ustedes	tienen	oo·ste·des	tye·nen
they	have	ellos m ellas f	tienen	e·lyos e·lyas	tye·nen

The word *hay* ai – which is the impersonal form of the verb *haber* ha·*ber* (have) – is used to mean 'there is/are' and in questions for 'is/are there ...?':

Is there hot water?   ¿Hay agua caliente?
(lit: is-there water hot-**f-sg**)
ai a·gwa ka·*lyen*·te

Negatives

Negating

To make a negative statement in Spanish, just add the word *no* no (not) before the main verb of the sentence:

I'm not going to try that.	No voy a probarlo. (lit: not I-go to to-try-it) no voy a pro·*bar*·lo

Contrary to English, Spanish uses double negatives:

I have nothing to declare.	No tengo nada que declarar. (lit: not I-have nothing that to-declare) no *ten*·go *na*·da ke dek·la·*rar*

Personal Pronouns

Making Statements • Naming People/Things

Personal pronouns ('I', 'you' etc) change form in Spanish depending on whether they're the subject or the object of a sentence. It's the same in English, which has 'I' and 'me' as subject and object pronouns (eg 'I see her' and 'She sees me'). Note, however, that the subject pronoun is usually omitted in Spanish as the subject is understood from the corresponding verb form (see **verbs**).

I'm a student.	Soy estudiante. (lit: I-am student-**m&f-sg**) soy es·too·*dyan*·te

ABOUT SPANISH · GRAMMAR

~ SUBJECT PRONOUNS ~

I	yo	yo	we	nosotros m nosotras f	no·so·tros no·so·tras
you sg inf	tú	too	**you** pl inf	vosotros m vosotras f	vo·so·tros vo·so·tras
you sg pol	Usted	oo·*ste*	**you** pl pol	Ustedes	oo·*ste*·des
he **she**	él ella	el e·lya	**they**	ellos m ellas f	e·lyos e·lyas

As the tables show, Spanish has two 'you' forms. With people familiar to you or younger than you, it's usual to use the informal form of 'you', *tú* too, rather than the polite form, *Usted* oo·*ste*. Phrases in this book use the form that is appropriate to the situation. Where both forms are used, they are indicated by pol and inf. See also the box **addressing people**, p95.

~ OBJECT PRONOUNS ~

me	me	me	**us**	nos	nos
you sg inf	te	te	**you** pl inf	vos	vos
you sg pol	lo/le m la/le f	lo/le la/le	**you** pl pol	los/les m las/les f	los/les las/les
him **it**	lo/le	lo/le	**them**	los/les m las/les f	los/les las/les
her **it**	la/le	la/le			

In this table, the forms separated by a slash are direct/indirect object pronouns.

The direct and indirect object pronouns differ only for the third person ('he', 'she', 'it', 'they') and the polite 'you' forms.

I don't know her.	No la conozco. (lit: not her I-know)
	no la ko·*noth*·ko
I'm talking to her.	Le hablo. (lit: to-her I-talk)
	le *a*·blo

The object pronouns generally come before the verb. The indirect object pronoun comes before the direct object pronoun.

I'll show it to you.	Te lo mostraré. (lit: to-you-**sg-inf**
	it-**m-sg** I-will-show)
	te lo mos·tra·*re*

Plurals

Naming People/Things

To form plurals in Spanish, add -*s* if the noun ends in a vowel and -*es* if it ends in a consonant. In this book singular and plural forms are shown with **sg** and **pl** respectively where needed.

~ SINGULAR ~			~ PLURAL ~		
bed	cama	*ka*·ma	**beds**	camas	*ka*·mas
woman	mujer	moo·*kher*	**women**	mujeres	moo·*khe*·res

Possessives

Possessing

A common way of indicating possession is by using possessive adjectives before the noun they refer to. Like other adjectives, they agree with the noun in number, and in case of 'our' and 'your' they also agree in gender (see also **gender** and **plurals**).

| our daughter | nuestra hija (lit: our-**f-sg** daughter) |
| | *nwes*·tra ee·kha |

~ POSSESSIVE ADJECTIVES ~

my	mi/mis	mee/mees	**our**	nuestro/ nuestros m nuestra/ nuestras f	nwes·tro/ nwes·tros nwes·tra/ nwes·tras
your sg inf	tu/tus	too/toos	**your** pl inf	vuestro/ vuestros m vuestra/ vuestras f	vwes·tro/ vwes·tros vwes·tra/ vwes·tras
your sg pol	su/sus	soo/soos	**your** pl pol	su/sus	soo/soos
his **her** **its**	su/sus	soo/soos	**their**	su/sus	soo/soos

Note that in the table above, the Spanish possessive adjective forms separated by a slash are used with a singular and plural noun respectively.

my child	mi hijo (lit: my-m-sg child) mee *ee*·kho
my children	mis hijos (lit: my-m-pl children) mees *ee*·khos

Another way to indicate possession is by using possessive pronouns (see the table opposite), which also agree in gender and number with the noun.

The book is mine.	El libro es mío. (lit: the-m-sg book is mine-m-sg) el *lee*·bro es *mee*·o

~ POSSESSIVE PRONOUNS ~

mine	mío/ míos m mía/ mías f	*mee·o/ mee·os mee·a/ mee·as*	ours	nuestro/ nuestros m nuestra/ nuestras f	*nwes·tro/ nwes·tros nwes·tra/ nwes·tras*
yours sg inf	tuyo/ tuyos m tuya/ tuyas f	*too·yo/ too·yos too·ya/ too·yas*	**yours** pl inf	vuestro/ vuestros m vuestra/ vuestras f	*vwes·tro/ vwes·tros vwes·tra/ vwes·tras*
yours sg pol	suyo/ suyos m suya/ suyas f	*soo·yo/ soo·yos soo·ya/ soo·yas*	**yours** pl pol	suyo/ suyos m suya/ suyas f	*soo·yo/ soo·yos soo·ya/ soo·yas*
his **hers** **its**			**theirs**		

The four alternatives in this table are used with m sg, m pl, f sg and f pl nouns.

Ownership can also be expressed in Spanish using the construction '*de* de (of) + noun', just like in English. See also **have**.

my friend's bag	el bolso de mi amigo (lit: the-m-sg bag of my friend-m-sg) el *bol*·so de mee a·*mee*·go

Prepositions

Giving Instructions • Indicating Location • Pointing Things Out

Like English, Spanish uses prepositions to explain where things are in time or space. Some common prepositions are listed in the table that follows. For more prepositions, see the **dictionary**.

When certain prepositions are followed by a definite article, they are contracted into a single word (see **articles**).

		~ PREPOSITIONS ~			
after	después de	des·*pwes* de	**from**	de	de
at (time)	a	a	**in (place)**	en	en
before	antes de	*an*·tes de	**to**	a	a

Questions

Asking Questions • Negating

The easiest way of forming 'yes/no' questions in Spanish is to add the phrase *verdad* ver·*da* (literally 'truth') to the end of a statement, similar to 'isn't it?' in English. You can also turn a statement into a question by putting the verb before the subject of the sentence, just like in English.

This is the right stop, isn't it?	¿Ésta es la parada, verdad? (lit: this-f-sg is the-f-sg stop truth) es·ta es la pa·*ra*·da ver·*da*
Is this the right stop?	¿Es ésta la parada? (lit: is this-f-sg the-f-sg stop) es es·ta la pa·*ra*·da

As in English, there are also question words for more specific questions. These words go at the start of the sentence.

		~ QUESTION WORDS ~			
how	cómo	*ko*·mo	**where**	dónde	*don*·de
what	qué	ke	**who**	quién sg	kyen
				quiénes pl	*kye*·nes
when	cuándo	*kwan*·do	**why**	por qué	por ke

Verbs

Doing Things

There are three verb categories in Spanish, depending on whether the infinitive ends in *-ar*, *-er* or *-ir*, eg *hablar* ab·*lar* (talk), *comer* ko·*mer* (eat), *vivir* vee·*veer* (live). Tenses are formed by adding various endings for each person to the verb stem (after removing *-ar*, *-er* or *-ir* from the infinitive) or to the infinitive, and for most verbs these endings follow regular patterns. The verb endings for the present, past and future tenses are presented in the tables on the following pages. For negative forms of verbs, see **negatives**.

~ PRESENT TENSE ~

		hablar	**comer**	**vivir**
I	yo	hablo	como	vivo
you sg inf	tú	hablas	comes	vives
you sg pol	Usted	habla	come	vive
he/she	él/ella	habla	come	vive
we	nosotros m nosotras f	hablamos	comemos	vivimos
you pl inf	vosotros m vosotras f	habláis	coméis	vivís
you pl pol	Ustedes	hablan	comen	viven
they	ellos m ellas f	hablan	comen	viven

See also **be** and **have**.

~ PAST TENSE ~

		hablar	comer	vivir
I	yo	hablé	comí	viví
you sg inf	tú	hablaste	comiste	viviste
you sg pol	Usted	habló	comió	vivió
he/she	él/ella	habló	comió	vivió
we	nosotros m nosotras f	hablamos	comimos	vivimos
you pl inf	vosotros m vosotras f	hablasteis	comisteis	vivisteis
you pl pol	Ustedes	hablaron	comieron	vivieron
they	ellos m ellas f	hablaron	comieron	vivieron

In case of the future tense, the endings follow the same pattern for all three verb categories, and they are simply added to the infinitive (dictionary form of the verb), not the verb stem:

~ FUTURE TENSE ~

		hablar	comer	vivir
I	yo	hablaré	comeré	viviré
you sg inf	tú	hablarás	comerás	vivirás
you sg pol	Usted	hablará	comerá	vivirá
he/she	él/ella	hablará	comerá	vivirá
we	nosotros m nosotras f	hablaremos	comeremos	viviremos
you pl inf	vosotros m vosotras f	hablaréis	comeréis	viviréis
you pl pol	Ustedes	hablarán	comerán	vivirán
they	ellos m ellas f	hablarán	comerán	vivirán

Word Order

Making Statements

Spanish has a basic word order of subject–verb–object, just like English. However, the subject pronoun is usually omitted in Spanish because the subject is understood from the corresponding verb form (see **verbs**). Both of the following examples are correct, but the second one is more common:

I study business.	Yo estudio comercio.
	(lit: I I-study business)
	yo es·*too*·dyo ko·*mer*·thyo
	Estudio comercio. (lit: I-study business)
	es·*too*·dyo ko·*mer*·thyo

See also **negatives** and **questions**.

CULTURE TIP — **Proverbs in Spain**

Proverbs are big in Spain. The Marqués de Santillana compiled a national collection in the second half of the 15th century, and one of the characters in *Don Quixote*, Sancho Panza, speaks almost entirely in proverbs. The novel's author, Cervantes, described these popular sayings as 'short sentences based on long experience'.

Ser como el perro del hortelano, que ni come las berzas, ni las deja comer al amo.	ser *ko*·mo el *pe*·ro del or·te·*la*·no ke nee *ko*·me las *ber*·thas nee las *de*·kha ko·*mer* al *a*·mo (lit: to be like the market gardener's dog, who doesn't eat the cabbages and won't let his master eat them either)

~ GRAMMAR GLOSSARY ~

adjective	a word that describes something – 'he was the **greatest** toreador of his time'
adverb	a word that explains how an action is done – 'he turned around **quickly**'
article	the words 'a', 'an' and 'the'
demonstrative	a word that means 'this' or 'that'
direct object	the thing or person in the sentence that has the action directed to it – 'and the bull missed **him**'
gender	classification of *nouns* into classes (like masculine and feminine), requiring other words (eg *adjectives*) to belong to the same class
indirect object	the person or thing in the sentence that is the recipient of the action – 'the public yelled to **him**'
infinitive	dictionary form of a verb – '**to be** careful'
noun	a thing, person or idea – 'the **fight** was exciting'
number	whether a word is singular or plural – 'and they sent in new **toreadors**'
personal pronoun	a word that means 'I', 'you' etc
possessive adjective	a word that means 'my', 'your' etc
possessive pronoun	a word that means 'mine', 'yours' etc
preposition	a word like 'for' or 'before' in English
subject	the thing or person in the sentence that does the action – '**his cape** fell on the ground'
tense	form of a *verb* that tells you whether the action is in the present, past or future – eg 'run' (present), 'ran' (past), 'will run' (future)
verb	a word that tells you what action happened – 'when the bull **charged** again'
verb stem	part of a *verb* that doesn't change – eg '**mov**e' in '**mov**ing' and '**mov**ed'

Basics

Understanding

KEY PHRASES

Do you speak English?	¿Habla inglés? **pol**	*ab*·la een·*gles*
I (don't) understand.	(No) Entiendo.	(no) en·*tyen*·do
What does ... mean?	¿Qué significa ...?	ke seeg·nee·*fee*·ka ...

There are two words for 'Spanish': *español* es·pa·*nyol* and *castellano* kas·te·*lya*·no. *Español* is used in Spain, whereas *castellano* is more likely to be used by Latin Americans.

Q Do you speak (English)?	¿Habla (inglés)? *ab*·la (een·*gles*)
Q Does anyone speak (English)?	¿Hay alguien que hable (inglés)? ai al·*gyen* ke *ab*·le een·*gles*
A I (don't) speak Spanish.	(No) Hablo español. (no) *ab*·lo es·pa·*nyol*
A I speak a little (Spanish).	Hablo un poco de (español). *ab*·lo oon *po*·ko de (es·pa·*nyol*)
I'd like to practise Spanish.	Me gustaría practicar español. me goos·ta·*ree*·a prak·tee·*kar* es·pa·*nyol*
I need an interpreter who speaks (English).	Necesito un intérprete que hable (inglés). ne·the·*see*·to oon in·*ter*·pre·te ke *ab*·le (een·*gles*)

🔊 **LISTEN FOR**

¿Cómo?	ko·mo	Pardon?
No.	no	No.
Sí.	see	Yes.

BASICS — UNDERSTANDING

Would you like me to teach you some English?	¿Quieres que te enseñe algo de inglés? **inf** *kye·res ke te en·se·nye al·go de een·gles*
🇶 Do you understand?	¿Me entiende/entiendes? **pol/inf** *me en·tyen·de/en·tyen·des*
🇦 I (don't) understand.	(No) Entiendo. *(no) en·tyen·do*
How do you pronounce this word?	¿Cómo se pronuncia esta palabra? *ko·mo se pro·noon·thya es·ta pa·lab·ra*
How do you write 'ciudad'?	¿Cómo se escribe 'ciudad'? *ko·mo se es·kree·be thyu·da*
What does ... mean?	¿Qué significa ...? *ke seeg·nee·fee·ka ...*
Could you repeat that?	¿Puede repetirlo? *pwe·de re·pe·teer·lo*
Could you please write it down?	¿Puede escribirlo, por favor? *pwe·de es·kree·beer·lo por fa·vor*
Could you please speak more slowly?	¿Puede hablar más despacio, por favor? *pwe·de ab·lar mas des·pa·thyo por fa·vor*

✂		
Slowly, please!	Más despacio, por favor.	*mas des·pa·thyo por fa·vor*

Numbers & Amounts

KEY PHRASES

How much?	¿Cuánto?	*kwan·to*
a little	un poquito	oon po·*kee*·to
some	algunos/as m/f	al·*goo*·nos/as

Cardinal Numbers

0	cero	*the*·ro
1	uno	*oo*·no
2	dos	dos
3	tres	tres
4	cuatro	*kwa*·tro
5	cinco	*theen*·ko
6	seis	seys
7	siete	*sye*·te
8	ocho	*o*·cho
9	nueve	*nwe*·ve
10	diez	dyeth
11	once	*on*·the
12	doce	*do*·the
13	trece	*tre*·the
14	catorce	ka·*tor*·the
15	quince	*keen*·the
16	dieciséis	dye·thee·*seys*
17	diecisiete	dye·thee·*sye*·te
20	veinte	*veyn*·te

21	veintiuno	veyn·tee·oo·no
22	veintidós	veyn·tee·dos
30	treinta	treyn·ta
40	cuarenta	kwa·ren·ta
50	cincuenta	theen·kwen·ta
60	sesenta	se·sen·ta
70	setenta	se·ten·ta
80	ochenta	o·chen·ta
90	noventa	no·ven·ta
100	cien	thyen
101	ciento uno	thyen·to oo·no
500	quinientos	kee·nyen·tos
1000	mil	mil
1,000,000	un millón	oon mee·lyon

Ordinal Numbers

1st	primero/a m/f	pree·me·ro/a
2nd	segundo/a m/f	se·goon·do/a
3rd	tercero/a m/f	ter·the·ro/a

Amounts

How much?	¿Cuánto?	kwan·to
a little	un poquito	oon po·kee·to
many	muchos/as m/f	moo·chos/as
some	algunos/as m/f	al·goo·nos/as
more/less	más/menos	mas/me·nos
a quarter/half	un cuarto/medio	oon kwar·to/me·dyo
a third	un tercio	oon ter·thyo
all/none	todo/nada	to·do/na·da

For other amounts, see **self-catering** (p184).

BASICS

TIMES & DATES

Times & Dates

KEY PHRASES

What time is it?	¿Qué hora es?	ke o·ra es
At what time ...?	¿A qué hora ...?	a ke o·ra ...
What date?	¿Qué día?	ke dee·a

Telling the Time

Q **What time is it?**	¿Qué hora es? ke o·ra es
A **It's one o'clock.**	Es la una. es la oo·na
A **It's (10) o'clock.**	Son las (diez). son las (dyeth)
Quarter past one.	Es la una y cuarto. es la oo·na ee kwar·to
Twenty past one.	Es la una y veinte. es la oo·na ee veyn·te
Half past one.	Es la una y media. es la oo·na ee me·dya
Twenty to one.	Es la una menos veinte. es la oo·na me·nos veyn·te
Quarter to one.	Es la una menos cuarto. es la oo·na me·nos kwar·to
It's early.	Es temprano. es tem·pra·no
It's late.	Es tarde. es tar·de

Q At what time?	¿A qué hora? a ke o·ra	
A At ...	A las ... a las ...	
am	de la mañana de la ma·nya·na	
pm	de la tarde de la tar·de	

The Calendar

Monday	lunes m	loo·nes
Tuesday	martes m	mar·tes
Wednesday	miércoles m	myer·ko·les
Thursday	jueves m	khwe·ves
Friday	viernes m	vyer·nes
Saturday	sábado m	sa·ba·do
Sunday	domingo m	do·meen·go
January	enero m	e·ne·ro
February	febrero m	fe·bre·ro
March	marzo m	mar·tho
April	abril m	a·breel
May	mayo m	ma·yo
June	junio m	khoo·nyo
July	julio m	khoo·lyo
August	agosto m	a·gos·to
September	septiembre m	sep·tyem·bre
October	octubre m	ok·too·bre
November	noviembre m	no·vyem·bre
December	diciembre m	dee·thyem·bre

summer	verano m	ve·*ra*·no
autumn	otoño m	o·*to*·nyo
winter	invierno m	een·*vyer*·no
spring	primavera f	pree·ma·ve·ra

What date?	¿Qué día? ke *dee*·a	
🇶 **What date is it today?**	¿Qué día es hoy? ke *dee*·a es oy	
🇦 **It's (18 October).**	Es (el dieciocho de octubre). es (el dye·thee·o·cho de ok·*too*·bre)	

Present

now	ahora	a·*o*·ra
right now	ahora mismo	a·*o*·ra *mees*·mo
this afternoon	esta tarde	es·ta *tar*·de
this month	este mes	*es*·te mes
this morning	esta manana	es·ta ma·*nya*·na
this week	esta semana	es·ta se·*ma*·na
this year	este año	*es*·te *a*·nyo
today	hoy	oy
tonight	esta noche	es·ta *no*·che

Past

(three) days ago	hace (tres) días	a·the (tres) *dee*·as
half an hour ago	hace media hora	a·the *me*·dya o·ra
a while ago	hace un rato	a·the un *ra*·to
(five) years ago	hace (cinco) años	a·the (*theen*·ko) *a*·nyos

day before yesterday	anteayer	an·te·a·*yer*
last month	el mes pasado	el mes pa·*sa*·do
last night	anoche	a·*no*·che
last week	la semana pasada	la se·*ma*·na pa·*sa*·da
last year	el año pasado	el *a*·nyo pa·*sa*·do
since (May)	desde (mayo)	*des*·de (*ma*·yo)
yesterday	ayer	a·*yer*
yesterday afternoon	ayer por la tarde	a·*yer* por la *tar*·de
yesterday evening	ayer por la noche	a·*yer* por la *no*·che
yesterday morning	ayer por la mañana	a·*yer* por la ma·*nya*·na

Future

in (six) days	dentro de (seis) días	*den*·tro de (seys) *dee*·as
in an hour	dentro de una hora	*den*·tro de *oo*·na *o*·ra
in (five) minutes	dentro de (cinco) minutos	*den*·tro de (*theen*·ko) mee·*noo*·tos
in a month	dentro de un mes	*den*·tro de oon mes
next month	el mes que viene	el mes ke *vye*·ne
next week	la semana que viene	la se·*ma*·na ke *vye*·ne
next year	el año que viene	el *a*·nyo ke *vye*·ne
tomorrow	manana	ma·*nya*·na
tomorrow morning	mañana por la mañana	ma·*nya*·na por la ma·*nya*·na

tomorrow afternoon	mañana por la tarde	ma·*nya*·na por la *tar*·de
tomorrow evening	mañana por la noche	ma·*nya*·na por la *no*·che
day after tomorrow	pasado manana	pa·*sa*·do ma·*nya*·na
until (June)	hasta (junio)	*as*·ta (*khoo*·nyo)

During the Day

afternoon	tarde f	*tar*·de
day	día m	*dee*·a
evening	noche f	*no*·che
midday	mediodía m	me·dyo·*dee*·a
midnight	medianoche f	me·dya·*no*·che
early morning (midnight to 5am)	madrugada f	ma·droo·*ga*·da
morning	mañana f	ma·*nya*·na
night	noche f	*no*·che
sunrise	amanecer m	a·ma·ne·*ther*
sunset	puesta f del sol	*pwes*·ta del sol

Practical

Transport

KEY PHRASES

At what time's the next bus?	¿A qué hora es el próximo autobús?	a ke o·ra es el *prok*·see·mo ow·to·*boos*
One ... ticket, please.	Un ... billete, por favor.	oon ... bee·*lye*·te, por fa·vor
Can you tell me when we get to (Valladolid)?	¿Puede avisarme cuando lleguemos a (Valladolid)?	*pwe*·de a·vee·*sar*·me *kwan*·do lye·*ge*·mos a (va·lya·do·*leeth*)
Please take me to this address.	Por favor, lléveme a esta dirección.	por fa·*vor* *lye*·ve·me a *es*·ta dee·rek·*thyon*
I'd like to hire a car.	Quisiera alquilar un coche.	kee·*sye*·ra al·kee·*lar* oon *ko*·che

Getting Around

At what time does the ... leave/arrive?	¿A qué hora sale/llega el ...? a ke o·ra sa·le/*lye*·ga el ...	
boat	barco	*bar*·ko
bus (city)	autobús	ow·to·*boos*
bus (intercity)	autocar	ow·to·*kar*
plane	avión	a·*vyon*
train	tren	tren
tram	tranvía	tran·*vee*·a

At what time's the first (bus)?	¿A qué hora es el primer (autobús)? a ke *o*·ra es el pree·*mer* (ow·to·*boos*)
At what time's the last (train)?	¿A qué hora es el último (tren)? a ke *o*·ra es el *ool*·tee·mo (tren)
At what time's the next (boat)?	¿A qué hora es el próximo (barco)? a ke *o*·ra es el *prok*·see·mo (*bar*·ko)
How long will it be delayed?	¿Cuánto tiempo se retrasará? *kwan*·to *tyem*·po se re·tra·sa·*ra*
Is this seat free?	¿Está libre este asiento? es·*ta lee*·bre es·te a·*syen*·to
✂ **Is it free?**	¿Está libre? es·*ta lee*·bre
That's my seat.	Ése es mi asiento. *e*·se es mee a·*syen*·to
I'd like to get off at (Aranjuez).	Me gustaría bajarme en (Aranjuez). me goos·ta·*ree*·a ba·*khar*·me en (a·ran·*khweth*)
I want to get off here!	¡Quiero bajarme aquí! *kye*·ro ba·*khar*·me a·*kee*
I'd prefer to walk there.	Prefiero ir a pie. pre·*fye*·ro eer a pye
Can we get there by public transport?	¿Se puede ir en transporte público? se *pwe*·de eer en trans·*por*·te *poo*·blee·ko

Buying Tickets

Do I need to book?	¿Tengo que reservar? *ten*·go ke re·ser·*var*
How much is it?	¿Cuánto cuesta? *kwan*·to *kwes*·ta
Where can I buy a ticket?	¿Dónde puedo comprar un billete? *don*·de *pwe*·do kom·*prar* oon bee·*lye*·te
Is it a direct route?	¿Es un viaje directo? es oon *vya*·khe dee·*rek*·to
Is there a toilet?	¿Hay servicios? ai ser·*vee*·thyos
How long does the trip take?	¿Cuánto se tarda? *kwan*·to se *tar*·da
Can I get a stand-by ticket?	¿Puede ponerme en la lista de espera? *pwe*·de po·*ner*·me en la *lees*·ta de es·*pe*·ra
I'd like an aisle seat.	Quisiera un asiento de pasillo. kee·*sye*·ra oon a·*syen*·to de pa·*see*·lyo
I'd like a window seat.	Quisiera un asiento junto a la ventana. kee·*sye*·ra oon a·*syen*·to *khoon*·to a la ven·*ta*·na
I'd like a (non)smoking seat.	Quisiera un asiento de (no) fumadores. kee·*sye*·ra oon a·*syen*·to de (no) foo·ma·*do*·res

Buying a Ticket

What time is the next ...?

¿A qué hora sale el próximo ...?

a ke o·ra sa·le el prok·see·mo ...

boat
barco
bar·ko

bus
autobús
ow·to·boos

train
tren
tren

One ... ticket, please.

Un billete ..., por favor.

oon bee·lye·te ... por fa·vor

one-way
sencillo
sen·thee·lyo

return
de ida y vuelta
de ee·da ee vwel·ta

I'd like a/an ... seat.

Quisiera un asiento ...

kee·sye·ra oon a·syen·to ...

aisle
de pasillo
de pa·see·lyo

window
junto a la
ventana
*khoon·to a la
ven·ta·na*

Which platform does it depart from?

¿De cuál andén sale?

de kwal an·den sa·le

I'd like to ... my ticket.		Me gustaría ... mi billete. me goos·ta·*ree*·a ... mee bee·*lye*·te
cancel	cancelar	kan·the·*lar*
change	cambiar	kam·*byar*
collect	recoger	re·ko·*kher*
confirm	confirmer	kon·feer·*mar*

(Two) ... tickets, please.		(Dos) billetes ..., por favor. (dos) bee·*lye*·tes ... por fa·*vor*
1st-class	de primera clase	de pree·*me*·ra *kla*·se
2nd-class	de segunda clase	de se·*goon*·da *kla*·se
child's	infantil	een·fan·*teel*
return	de ida y vuelta	de ee·da ee *vwel*·ta
student's	de estudiante	de es·too·*dyan*·te

A one-way ticket to (Barcelona).	Un billete sencillo a (Barcelona). oon bee·*lye*·te sen·*thee*·lyo a (bar·the·*lo*·na)

Luggage

My luggage has been damaged/lost.	Mis maletas han sido dañadas/perdidas. mees ma·*le*·tas an *see*·do da·*nya*·das/per·*dee*·das

🔊 LISTEN FOR

Esta parada es ...	es·ta pa·ra·da es ... This stop is ...
La próxima parada es ...	la prok·see·ma pa·ra·da es ... The next stop is ...
Está completo.	es·ta kom·ple·to It's full.
El ... está retrasado/ cancelado.	el ... es·ta re·tra·sa·do/ kan·the·la·do The ... is delayed/ cancelled.

My luggage has been stolen.	Mis maletas han sido robadas. mees ma·le·tas an see·do ro·ba·das
I'd like a luggage locker.	Quisiera un casillero de consigna. kee·sye·ra oon ka·see·lye·ro de kon·seeg·na

Bus

Which bus goes to (Madrid)?	¿Qué autobús va a (Madrid)? ke ow·to·boos va a (ma·dreeth)
Where's the bus stop?	¿Dónde está la parada del autobús? don·de es·ta la pa·ra·da del ow·to·boos
What's the next stop?	¿Cuál es la próxima parada? kwal es la prok·see·ma pa·ra·da

Please tell me when we get to (Valladolid).	¿Puede avisarme cuando lleguemos a (Valladolid)? *pwe*·de a·vee·*sar*·me *kwan*·do lye·*ge*·mos a (va·lya·do·*leeth*)
Bus number ...	El autobús número ... el ow·to·*boos noo*·me·ro ...

For bus numbers, see **numbers & amounts**, p34.

Train

What station is this?	¿Cuál es esta estación? kwal es *es*·ta es·ta·*thyon*
What's the next station?	¿Cuál es la próxima estación? kwal es la *prok*·see·ma es·ta·*thyon*
Does this train stop at (Valencia)?	¿Para el tren en (Valencia)? *pa*·ra el tren en (va·*len*·thya)
Do I need to change trains?	¿Tengo que cambiar de tren? *ten*·go ke kam·*byar* de tren
Which carriage is for (Bilbao)?	¿Cuál es el coche para (Bilbao)? kwal es el *ko*·che *pa*·ra (beel·*bow*)

Boat

Are there life jackets?	¿Hay chalecos salvavidas? ai cha·*le*·kos sal·va·*vee*·das
What's the sea like today?	¿Cómo está el mar hoy? *ko*·mo es·*ta* el mar oy
I feel seasick.	Estoy mareado/a. **m/f** es·*toy* ma·re·*a*·do/a

Taxi

I'd like a taxi at (9am).	Quisiera un taxi a (las nueve de la mañana). kee·*sye*·ra oon *tak*·see a (las *nwe*·ve de la ma·*nya*·na)
I'd like a taxi tomorrow.	Quisiera un taxi manana. kee·*sye*·ra oon *tak*·see ma·*nya*·na
Where's the taxi stand?	¿Dónde está la parada de taxis? *don*·de es·*ta* la pa·*ra*·da de *tak*·sees

PRACTICAL TRANSPORT

Where's the bus stop?
don·de es·*ta* la pa·*ra*·da del ow·to·*boos*
¿Dónde está la parada del autobús?

Is this taxi free?	¿Está libre este taxi? es·ta lee·bre es·te tak·see
✂ Is it free?	¿Está libre? es·ta lee·bre
How much is the flag fall/ hiring charge?	¿Cuánto es la tasa de alquiler? kwan·to es la ta·sa de al·kee·ler
Please put the meter on.	Por favor, ponga el taxímetro. por fa·vor pon·ga el tak·see·me·tro
How much is it to (the Prado)?	¿Cuánto cuesta ir (al Prado)? kwan·to kwes·ta eer (al pra·do)
Please take me to (this address).	Por favor, lléveme a (esta dirección). por fa·vor lye·ve·me a (es·ta dee·rek·thyon)
✂ To ...	A ... a ...
How much is the final fare?	¿Cuánto es en total? kwan·to es en to·tal
Please slow down.	Por favor vaya más despacio. por fa·vor va·ya mas des·pa·thyo
Please wait here.	Por favor espere aquí. por fa·vor es·pe·re a·kee
Stop here!	¡Pare aquí! pa·re a·kee

For other useful phrases, see **directions**, p57.

Car & Motorbike

Where can I hire a ...?	¿Dónde se puede alquilar ...? *don·de se pwe·de al·kee·lar ...*
Does that include insurance/mileage?	¿Incluye el seguro/ kilometraje? *een·kloo·ye el se·goo·ro/ kee·lo·me·tra·khe*
I'd like to hire a/an ...	Quisiera alquilar ... *kee·sye·ra al·kee·lar ...*

4WD	un todoterreno	oon to·do·te·*re*·no
automatic car	un coche automático	oon *ko*·che ow·to·*ma*·tee·ko
manual car	un coche manual	oon *ko*·che man·*wal*
motorbike	una moto	*oo*·na *mo*·to

How much for hourly/ daily hire?	¿Cuánto cuesta el alquiler por hora/día? *kwan·to kwes·ta el al·kee·ler por o·ra/dee·a*
How much for weekly hire?	¿Cuánto cuesta el alquiler por semana? *kwan·to kwes·ta el al·kee·ler por se·ma·na*
Is this the road to (Seville)?	¿Se va a (Sevilla) por esta carretera? *se va a (se·vee·lya) por es·ta ka·re·te·ra*
Where's a petrol station?	¿Dónde hay una gasolinera? *don·de ai oo·na ga·so·lee·ne·ra*

PRACTICAL TRANSPORT

🔍 LOOK FOR

Acceso	ak·*the*·so	Entrance
Aparcamiento	a·par·ka·*myen*·to	Parking
Ceda el Paso	*the*·da el *pa*·so	Give Way
Desvío	des·*vee*·o	Detour
Dirección Única	dee·rek·*thyon* oo·nee·ka	One Way
Frene	*fre*·ne	Slow Down
Peaje	pe·*a*·khe	Toll
Peligro	pe·*lee*·gro	Danger
Prohibido Aparcar	pro·ee·*bee*·do a·par·*kar*	No Parking
Prohibido el Paso	pro·ee·*bee*·do el *pa*·so	No Entry
Stop	es·*top*	Stop
Vía de Acceso	*vee*·a de ak·*the*·so	Exit Freeway

What's the (city) speed limit?	¿Cuál es el límite de velocidad (en la ciudad)? kwal es el *lee*·mee·te de ve·lo·thee·*da* (en la thyu·*da*)
Please fill it up.	Por favor, lléneme el depósito. por fa·*vor lye*·ne·me el de·*po*·see·to
I'd like (20) litres of ...	Quiero (veinte) litros de ... *kye*·ro (*veyn*·te) *lee*·tros de ...
Please check the oil/water.	Por favor, revise el nivel del aceite/agua. por fa·*vor* re·*vee*·se el nee·*vel* del a·*they*·te/*a*·gwa

windscreen
parabrisas m
pa·ra·*bree*·sas

petrol
gasolina f
ga·so·*lee*·na

battery
batería f
ba·ta·*ree*·a

engine
motor m
mo·*tor*

headlight
faro m
fa·ro

tyre
rueda f
rwe·da

Please check the tyre pressure.	Por favor, revise la presión de los neumáticos. por fa·*vor* re·*vee*·se la pre·*syon* de los ne·oo·*ma*·tee·kos
(How long) Can I park here?	¿(Por cuánto tiempo) Puedo aparcar aquí? (por *kwan*·to *tyem*·po) *pwe*·do a·par·*kar* a·*kee*
I need a mechanic.	Necesito un/una mecánico/a. **m/f** ne·the·*see*·to oon/*oo*·na me·*ka*·nee·ko/a
The car has broken down (at Salamanca).	El coche se ha averiado (en Salamanca). el *ko*·che se a a·ve·*rya*·do (en sa·la·*man*·ka)
I had an accident.	He tenido un accidente. e te·*nee*·do oon ak·thee·*den*·te

Bicycle

Can we get there by bike?	¿Se puede ir en bici? se *pwe*·de eer en *bee*·thee
Where can I hire a bicycle?	¿Dónde se puede alquilar una bicicleta? *don*·de se *pwe*·de al·kee·*lar* *oo*·na bee·thee·*kle*·ta
Where can I buy a (secondhand) bike?	¿Dónde se puede comprar una bicicleta (de segunda mano)? *don*·de se *pwe*·de kom·*prar* *oo*·na bee·thee·*kle*·ta (de se·*goon*·da *ma*·no)
How much is it per day?	¿Cuánto cuesta por un día? *kwan*·to *kwes*·ta por oon *dee*·a
How much is it per hour?	¿Cuánto cuesta por una hora? *kwan*·to *kwes*·ta por *oo*·na *o*·ra
I have a puncture.	Se me ha pinchado una rueda. se me a peen·*cha*·do *oo*·na *rwe*·da
I'd like to have my bicycle repaired.	Me gustaría arreglar mi bicicleta. me goo·sta·*ree*·a a·reg·*lar* mee bee·thee·*kle*·ta
Are there cycling paths?	¿Hay carril bicicleta? ai ka·*reel* bee·thee·*kle*·ta
Is there bicycle parking?	¿Hay aparcamiento de bicicletas? ai a·par·ka·*myen*·to de bee·thee·*kle*·tas
Can I take my bike on the train?	¿Puedo llevar mi bicicleta en el tren? *pwe*·do lye·*var* mee bee·thee·*kle*·ta en el tren

Border Crossing

KEY PHRASES

I'm here for ... days.	Estoy aquí por ... días.	es·*toy* a·*kee* por ... *dee*·as
I'm staying at ...	Me estoy alojando en ...	me es·*toy* a·lo·*khan*·do en ...
I have nothing to declare.	No tengo nada que declarar.	no *ten*·go *na*·da ke de·kla·*rar*

Passport Control

I'm here on business.	Estoy aquí de negocios. es·*toy* a·*kee* de ne·*go*·thyos
I'm here on holiday.	Estoy aquí de vacaciones. es·*toy* a·*kee* de va·ka·*thyo*·nes
I'm here in transit.	Estoy aquí en tránsito. es·*toy* a·*kee* en *tran*·see·to
I'm here for ... days.	Estoy aquí por ... días. es·*toy* a·*kee* por ... *dee*·as
I'm here for ... weeks.	Estoy aquí por ... semanas. es·*toy* a·*kee* por ... se·*ma*·nas
I'm here for ... months.	Estoy aquí por ... meses. es·*toy* a·*kee* por ... *me*·ses
I'm going to (Salamanca).	Voy a (Salamanca). voy a (sa·la·*man*·ka)
I'm staying at ...	Me estoy alojando en ... me es·*toy* a·lo·*khan*·do en ...

PRACTICAL BORDER CROSSING

Su pasaporte, por favor.	soo pa·sa·*por*·te por fa·*vor* Your passport, please.
Su visado, por favor.	soo vee·*sa*·do por fa·*vor* Your visa, please.
¿Está viajando en un grupo?	es·*ta* vya·*khan*·do en oon *groo*·po Are you travelling in a group?
¿Está viajando con familia?	es·*ta* vya·*khan*·do kon fa·*mee*·lya Are you travelling with family?
¿Está viajando solo/a? m/f	es·*ta* vya·*khan*·do *so*·lo/a Are you travelling on your own?

Customs

I have nothing to declare.	No tengo nada que declarar. no *ten*·go *na*·da ke de·kla·*rar*
I have something to declare.	Quisiera declarar algo. kee·*sye*·ra de·kla·*rar* al·go
That's (not) mine.	Eso (no) es mío. e·so (no) es *mee*·o
I didn't know I had to declare it.	No sabía que tenía que declararlo. no sa·*bee*·a ke te·*nee*·a ke de·kla·*rar*·lo

For phrases on payments and receipts, see **money & banking**, p91.

Directions

KEY PHRASES

Where's ...?	¿Dónde está ...?	don·de es·ta ...
What's the address?	¿Cuál es la direc-ción?	kwal es la dee·rek·thyon
How far is it?	¿A cuánta distancia está?	a kwan·ta dees·tan·thya es·ta

Excuse me.	Perdón. per·don
Could you help me, please?	¿Perdón, puede ayudarme, por favor? per·don pwe·de a·yoo·dar·me por fa·vor
Where's ...?	¿Dónde está ...? don·de es·ta ...
I'm looking for ...	Busco ... boos·ko ...
Which way is ...?	¿Por dónde se va a ...? por don·de se va a ...
How can I get there?	¿Cómo se puede ir? ko·mo se pwe·de eer
How far is it?	¿A cuánta distancia está? a kwan·ta dees·tan·thya es·ta
What's the address?	¿Cuál es la dirección? kwal es la dee·rek·thyon

Can you show me (on the map)?	¿Me lo puede indicar (en el mapa)? me lo *pwe*·de een·dee·*kar* (en el *ma*·pa)

It's ...	Está ... es·*ta* ...

behind ...	detrás de ...	de·*tras* de ...
far away	lejos	*le*·khos
here	aquí	a·*kee*
in front of ...	enfrente de ...	en·*fren*·te de ...
left	por la izquierda	por la eeth·*kyer*·da
near	cerca	*ther*·ka
next to ...	al lado de ...	al *la*·do de ...
opposite ...	frente a ...	*fren*·te a ...
right	por la derecha	por la de·*re*·cha
straight ahead	todo recto	*to*·do *rek*·to
there	ahí	a·*ee*

Turn at the corner.	Doble en la esquina. *do*·ble en la es·*kee*·na

Turn at the traffic lights.	Doble en el semáforo. *do*·ble en el se·*ma*·fo·ro

Turn left/right.	Doble a la izquierda/derecha. *do*·ble a la eeth·*kyer*·da/ de·*re*·cha

(two) kilometres	(dos) kilómetros (dos) kee·*lo*·me·tros

(three) metres	(tres) metros (tres) *me*·tros

(six) minutes	(seis) minutos (seys) mee·*noo*·tos

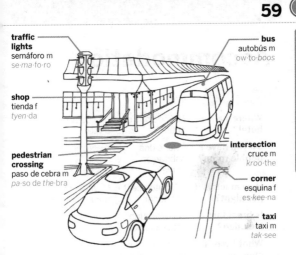

traffic lights
semáforo m
se·ma·fo·ro

shop
tienda f
tyen·da

pedestrian crossing
paso de cebra m
pa·so de the·bra

bus
autobús m
ow·to·boos

intersection
cruce m
kroo·the

corner
esquina f
es·kee·na

taxi
taxi m
tak·see

by bus	por autobús por ow·to·boos
by taxi	por taxi por tak·see
by train	por tren por tren
on foot	a pie a pye
avenue	avenida f a·ve·nee·da
lane	callejón m ka·lye·khon
street	calle f ka·lye

For locations and compass directions, see the **dictionary**.

Accommodation

KEY PHRASES

Where's a hotel?	¿Dónde hay un hotel?	*don·de ai on o·tel*
Do you have a double room?	¿Tiene una habitación doble?	*tye·ne oo·na a·bee·ta·thyon do·ble*
How much is it per night?	¿Cuánto cuesta por noche?	*kwan·to kwes·ta por no·che*
Is breakfast included?	¿El desayuno está incluído?	*el de·sa·yoo·no es·ta een·kloo·ee·do*
What time is checkout?	¿A qué hora hay que dejar libre la habitación?	*a ke o·ra ai ke de·khar lee·bre la a·bee·ta·thyon*

Finding Accommodation

Where's a ...?　　　　　¿Dónde hay ...?
　　　　　　　　　　　　　don·de ai ...

bed & breakfast	una pensión con desayuno	*oo·na pen·syon kon de·sa·yoo·no*
camping ground	terreno de cámping	*te·re·no de kam·peeng*
guesthouse	una pensión	*oo·na pen·syon*
hotel	un hotel	*oon o·tel*
youth hostel	un albergue juvenil	*oon al·ber·ge khoo·ve·neel*

Can you recommend somewhere (cheap)?	¿Puede recomendar algún sitio (barato)? *pwe·de re·ko·men·dar al·goon see·tyo (ba·ra·to)*
Can you recommend somewhere (nearby)?	¿Puede recomendar algún sitio (cercano)? *pwe·de re·ko·men·dar al·goon see·tyo (ther·ka·no)*
Can you recommend somewhere (luxurious)?	¿Puede recomendar algún sitio (de lujo)? *pwe·de re·ko·men·dar al·goon see·tyo (de loo·kho)*
What's the address?	¿Cuál es la dirección? *kwal es la dee·rek·thyon*

For more on how to get there, see **directions** (p57).

Booking Ahead & Checking In

I'd like to book a room, please.	Quisiera reservar una habitación. *kee·sye·ra re·ser·var oo·na a·bee·ta·thyon*

✂	**Are there rooms?**	¿Hay habitaciones?	ai a·bee·ta·thyo·nes

I have a reservation.	He hecho una reserva. *e e·cho oo·na re·ser·va*
My name's ...	Me llamo ... *me lya·mo ...*
For (three) nights/weeks.	Por (tres) noches/semanas. *por (tres) no·ches/se·ma·nas*
From (July 2) to (July 6).	Desde (el dos de julio) hasta (el seis de julio). *des·de (el dos de khoo·lyo) as·ta (el seys de khoo·lyo)*

PRACTICAL ACCOMMODATION

Do I need to pay upfront?	¿Necesito pagar por adelantado? ne·the·*see*·to pa·*gar* por a·de·lan·*ta*·do
Do you offer (long-stay) discounts?	¿Ofrecen descuentos (por larga estancia)? of·*re*·then des·*kwen*·tos (por *lar*·ga es·*tan*·thya)
Is breakfast included?	¿El desayuno está incluído? el de·sa·*yoo*·no es·*ta* een·kloo·ee·do
Is there parking?	¿Hay aparcamiento? ai a·par·ka·*myen*·to
Is there wireless internet access here?	¿Hay acceso inalámbrico a internet aquí? ai ak·*the*·so een·a·*lam*·bree·ko a een·ter·net a·*kee*
How much is it per person?	¿Cuánto cuesta por persona? *kwan*·to *kwes*·ta por per·*so*·na
How much is it per night/ week?	¿Cuánto cuesta por noche/ semana? *kwan*·to *kwes*·ta por *no*·che/ se·*ma*·na

Finding a Room

Do you have a ... room?
¿Tiene una habitación ...?
tye·ne oo·na a·bee·ta·thyon ...

double
doble
do·ble

single
individual
een·dee·vee·dwal

How much is it per ...?
¿Cuánto cuesta por ...?
kwan·to kwes·ta por ...

night
noche
no·che

person
persona
per·so·na

Is breakfast included?
¿El desayuno está incluído?
el de·sa·yoo·no es·ta een·kloo·ee·do

Can I see the room?
¿Puedo verla?
pwe·do ver·la

I'll take it.
La alquilo.
la al·kee·lo

I won't take it.
No la alquilo.
no la al·kee·lo

Can I pay by credit card?	¿Puedo pagar con tarjeta de crédito? *pwe·do pa·gar con tar·khe·ta de kre·dee·to*

For other methods of payment, see **money & banking**, p91.

Do you have a double room?	¿Tiene una habitación doble? *tye·ne oo·na a·bee·ta·thyon do·ble*
Do you have a single room?	¿Tiene una habitación individual? *tye·ne oo·na a·bee·ta·thyon een·dee·vee·dwal*
Do you have a twin room?	¿Tiene una habitación con dos camas? *tye·ne oo·na a·bee·ta·thyon con dos ka·mas*
Do you have a room with/ without (a) ...?	¿Tiene una habitación con/sin ...? *tye·ne oo·na a·bee·ta·thyon kon/seen ...*
Can I see it?	¿Puedo verla? *pwe·do ver·la*
It's fine, I'll take it.	Vale, la alquilo. *va·le la al·kee·lo*

Requests & Queries

When/Where's breakfast served?	¿Cuándo/Dónde se sirve el desayuno? *kwan·do/don·de se seer·ve el de·sa·yoo·no*
Please wake me at (seven).	Por favor, despiérteme a (las siete). *por fa·vor des·pyer·te·me a (las sye·te)*

| Can I get another ...? | ¿Puede darme otro/a ...? m/f |
| | pwe·de dar·me o·tro/a ... |

| Can I use the ...? | ¿Puedo usar ...? |
| | pwe·do oo·sar ... |

internet	el internet	el een·ter·net
kitchen	la cocina	la ko·thee·na
laundry	el lavadero	el la·va·de·ro
telephone	el teléfono	el te·le·fo·no

| Is there a/an ...? | ¿Hay ...? |
| | ai ... |

lift (elevator)	ascensor	as·then·sor
message board	tablón de anuncios	ta·blon de a·noon·thyos
safe	una caja fuerte	oo·na ka·kha fwer·te
swimming pool	piscina	pees·thee·na

| Do you arrange tours here? | ¿Aquí organizan recorridos? |
| | a·kee or·ga·nee·than re·ko·ree·dos |

| Do you change money here? | ¿Aquí cambian dinero? |
| | a·kee kam·byan dee·ne·ro |

| Is there a message for me? | ¿Tiene un mensaje para mí? |
| | tye·ne oon men·sa·khe pa·ra mee |

| I'm locked out of my room. | Cerré la puerta y se me olvidaron las llaves dentro. |
| | the·re la pwer·ta y se me ol·vee·da·ron las lya·ves den·tro |

The (bathroom) door is locked.	La puerta (del baño) está cerrada. la *pwer*·ta (del *ba*·nyo) es·*ta* the·*ra*·da
There's no need to change my sheets.	No hace falta cambiar las sábanas. no *a*·the *fal*·ta kam·*byar* las *sa*·ba·nas

Complaints

It's too ...	Es demasiado ... es de·ma·*sya*·do ...	
cold	fría f	*free*·a
dark	oscura f	os·*koo*·ra
light/bright	clara f	*kla*·ra
noisy	ruidosa f	rwee·*do*·sa
small	pequeña f	pe·*ke*·nya

The ... doesn't work.	No funciona ... no foon·*thyo*·na ...	
air-conditioning	el aire acondicionado	el *ai*·re a·kon·dee·thyo·*na*·do
fan	el ventilador	el ven·tee·la·*dor*
heater	la estufa	la es·*too*·fa
toilet	el retrete	el re·*tre*·te
window	la ventana	la ven·*ta*·na

This ... isn't clean.	Éste/Ésta ... no está limpio/a. m/f *es*·te/*es*·ta ... no es·*ta leem*·pyo/a
There's no hot water.	No hay agua caliente. no ai *a*·gwa ka·*lyen*·te

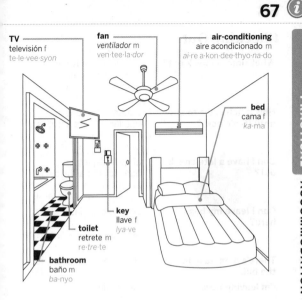

TV
televisión f
te·le·vee·*syon*

fan
ventilador m
ven·tee·la·*dor*

air-conditioning
aire acondicionado m
ai·re a·kon·dee·*thyo*·na·do

bed
cama f
ka·ma

key
llave f
lya·ve

toilet
retrete m
re·*tre*·te

bathroom
baño m
ba·nyo

Answering the Door

Who is it?	¿Quién es? kyen es
Just a moment.	Un momento. oon mo·*men*·to
Come in.	Adelante. a·de·*lan*·te
Can you come back later, please?	¿Puede volver más tarde, por favor? *pwe*·de vol·*ver* mas *tar*·de por fa·*vor*

Checking Out

What time is check out?	¿A qué hora hay que dejar libre la habitación? a ke o·ra ai ke de·*khar* *lee*·bre la a·bee·ta·*thyon*
How much extra to stay until (6 o'clock)?	¿Cuánto más cuesta quedarse hasta (las seis)? *kwan*·to mas *kwes*·ta ke·*dar*·se *as*·ta (las seys)
Can I have a late check out?	¿Puedo dejar la habitación más tarde? *pwe*·do de·*khar* la a·bee·ta·*thyon* mas *tar*·de
Can I leave my bags here?	¿Puedo dejar las maletas aquí? *pwe*·do de·*khar* las ma·*le*·tas a·*kee*
There's a mistake in the bill.	Hay un error en la cuenta. ai oon e·*ror* en la *kwen*·ta
I'm leaving now.	Me voy ahora. me voy a·o·ra
Can you call a taxi for me (for 11 o'clock)?	¿Me puede pedir un taxi (para las once)? me *pwe*·de pe·*deer* oon *tak*·see (*pa*·ra las *on*·the)
Could I have my deposit, please?	¿Me puede dar mi depósito, por favor? me *pwe*·de dar mee de·*po*·see·to por fa·*vor*

Could I have my passport, please?	¿Me puede dar mi pasaporte, por favor? me *pwe*·de dar mee pa·sa·*por*·te por fa·*vor*
Could I have my valuables, please?	¿Me puede dar mis objetos de valor, por favor? me *pwe*·de dar mees ob·*khe*·tos de va·*lor* por fa·*vor*
I'll be back on (Tuesday).	Volveré el (martes). vol·ve·*re* el (*mar*·tes)
I'll be back in (three) days.	Volveré en (tres) días. vol·ve·*re* en (tres) *dee*·as

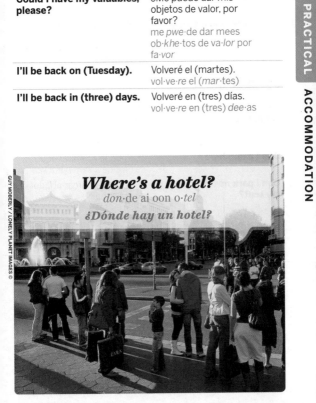

Where's a hotel?
don·de ai oon o·*tel*

¿Dónde hay un hotel?

I had a great stay, thank you.	He tenido una estancia muy agradable, gracias. e te·*nee*·do *oo*·na es·*tan*·thya mooy a·gra·*da*·ble *gra*·thyas
You've been terrific.	Han sido estupendos. an *see*·do es·too·*pen*·dos
I'll recommend it to my friends.	Se lo recomendaré a mis amigos. se lo re·ko·men·da·*re* a mees a·*mee*·gos

Camping

Where's the nearest camp site?	¿Dónde está el terreno de cámping más cercano? *don*·de es·*ta* el te·*re*·no de *kam*·peeng mas ther·*ka*·no
Can I camp here?	¿Se puede acampar aquí? se *pwe*·de a·kam·*par* a·*kee*
Can I park next to my tent?	¿Se puede aparcar al lado de la tienda? se *pwe*·de a·par·*kar* al *la*·do de la *tyen*·da
Do you have ...?	¿Tiene ...? *tye*·ne ...

electricity	electricidad	e·lek·tree·thee·*da*
shower facilities	duchas	*doo*·chas
a site	un sitio	oon *see*·tyo
tents for hire	tiendas de campaña para alquilar	*tyen*·das de kam·*pa*·nya *pa*·ra al·kee·*lar*

How much is it per ...?	¿Cuánto vale por ...? *kwan·*to *va·*le por ...	
caravan	caravana	ka·ra·*va·*na
person	persona	per·*so·*na
tent	tienda	*tyen·*da
vehicle	vehículo	ve·*ee·*koo·lo

Is the water drinkable?	¿Se puede beber el agua? se *pwe·*de *be·*ber el *a·*gwa
I'm looking for the nearest showers.	Estoy buscando las duchas más cercanas. es·*toy* boos·*kan·*do las *doo·*chas mas ther·*ka·*nas
I'm looking for the nearest toilet block.	Estoy buscando los servicios más cercanos. es·*toy* boos·*kan·*do los ser·*vee·*thyos mas ther·*ka·*nos
Could I borrow ...?	¿Me puede prestar ...? me *pwe·*de pres·*tar* ...

For cooking utensils, see **self-catering** (p186) and the **dictionary**.

🔍 LOOK FOR

Caballeros	ka·ba·*lye·*ros	Men
Caliente	ka·*lyen·*te	Hot
Dirección Prohibida	dee·rek·*thyon* pro·hee·*bee·*da	No Entry
Frío	*free·*o	Cold
Señoras	se·*nyo·*ras	Women

PRACTICAL ACCOMMODATION

Renting

Do you have a/an ... for rent?	¿Tiene ... para alquilar? *tye*·ne ... *pa*·ra al·kee·*lar*	
apartment	un piso	oon *pee*·so
cabin	una cabaña	oo·na ka·*ba*·nya
house	una casa	oo·na *ka*·sa
room	una habitación	oo·na a·bee·ta·*thyon*
villa	un chalet	oon cha·*le*

furnished	amueblado/a m/f a·mwe·*bla*·do/a
partly furnished	semi amueblado/a m/f *se*·mee a·mwe·*bla*·do/a
unfurnished	sin amueblar seen a·mwe·*blar*

Staying with Locals

Can I stay at your place?	¿Me puedo quedar en su/tu casa? pol/inf me *pwe*·do ke·*dar* en soo/too *ka*·sa
Thanks for your hospitality.	Gracias por su/tu hospitalidad. pol/inf *gra*·thyas por soo/too os·pee·ta·lee·*da*
I have my own mattress.	Tengo mi propio colchón. *ten*·go mee *pro*·pyo kol·*chon*
I have my own sleeping bag.	Tengo mi propio saco de dormir. *ten*·go mee *pro*·pyo *sa*·ko de dor·*meer*

Can I bring anything for the meal?	¿Puedo traer algo para la comida? *pwe·do tra·er al·go pa·ra la ko·mee·da*
Can I use your telephone?	¿Puedo usar su/tu teléfono? **pol/inf** *pwe·do oo·sar soo/too te·le·fo·no*
Can I help?	¿Puedo ayudar? *pwe·do a·yoo·dar*
Can I set/clear the table?	¿Puedo poner/quitar la mesa? *pwe·do po·ner/kee·tar la me·sa*
Can I do the dishes?	¿Puedo lavar los platos? *pwe·do la·var los pla·tos*
Can I take out the rubbish?	¿Puedo sacar la basura? *pwe·do sa·kar la ba·soo·ra*

For compliments to the chef, see **eating out** (p174).

Shopping

KEY PHRASES

I'd like to buy ...	Quisiera comprar ...	kee·sye·ra kom·prar ...
Can I look at it?	¿Puedo verlo?	pwe·do ver·lo
Can I try it on?	¿Me lo puedo probar?	me lo pwe·do pro·bar
How much?	¿Cuánto cuesta?	kwan·to kwes·ta
That's too expensive.	Es muy caro.	es mooy ka·ro

Looking For ...

Where's a (super)market?	¿Dónde está un (super)mercado? don·de es·ta oon (soo·per·)mer·ka·do
Where's a camping store?	¿Dónde está una tienda de camping? don·de es·ta oo·na tyen·da de kam·peeng
Where can I buy locally produced goods/souvenirs?	¿Dónde puedo comprar recuerdos de la zona? don·de pwe·do kom·prar re·kwer·dos de la tho·na
Where can I buy ...?	¿Dónde puedo comprar ...? don·de pwe·do kom·prar ...

For more on shops and how to get there, see **directions** (p57) and the **dictionary**.

Making a Purchase

How much is this?	¿Cuánto cuesta esto? *kwan·to kwes·ta es·to*	
✂ **How much?**	¿Cuánto cuesta?	*kwan·to kwes·ta*
I'd like to buy ...	Quisiera comprar ... *kee·sye·ra kom·prar ...*	
I'm just looking.	Sólo estoy mirando. *so·lo es·toy mee·ran·do*	
Can I look at it?	¿Puedo verlo? *pwe·do ver·lo*	
Do you have any others?	¿Tiene otros? *tye·ne o·tros*	
What is this made from?	¿De qué está hecho? *de ke es·ta e·cho*	
Do you accept credit/debit cards?	¿Aceptan tarjetas de crédito/débito? *a·thep·tan tar·khe·tas de kre·dee·to/de·bee·to*	
Could I have a bag, please?	¿Podría darme una bolsa, por favor? *po·dree·a dar·me oo·na bol·sa por fa·vor*	
Could I have a receipt, please?	¿Podría darme un recibo, por favor? *po·dree·a dar·me oon re·thee·bo por fa·vor*	
✂ **Receipt, please.**	El recibo, por favor.	el re·thee·bo por fa·vor

🔊 LISTEN FOR

¿En qué le puedo servir?	en ke le *pwe*·do ser·*veer* Can I help you?
No tengo.	no *ten*·go I don't have any.
¿Algo más?	*al*·go mas Anything else?

I don't need a bag, thanks.	No necesito bolsa, gracias. no ne·the·*see*·to *bol*·sa *gra*·thyas
Can you write down the price?	¿Puede escribir el precio? *pwe*·de es·kree·*beer* el *pre*·thyo
Could I have it wrapped?	¿Me lo podría envolver? me lo po·*dree*·a en·vol·*ver*
Does it have a guarantee?	¿Tiene garantía? *tye*·ne ga·ran·*tee*·a
Can I pick it up later?	¿Puedo recogerlo más tarde? *pwe*·do re·ko·*kher*·lo mas *tar*·de
Can I have it sent overseas?	¿Pueden enviarlo por correo a otro país? *pwe*·den en·vee·*ar*·lo por ko·*re*·o a *o*·tro pa·*ees*
It's faulty.	Es defectuoso. es de·fek·*two*·so
I'd like my change, please.	Quisiera mi cambio, por favor. kee·*sye*·ra mee *kam*·byo por fa·*vor*

Making a Purchase

I'd like to buy ...
Quisiera comprar ...
kee·sye·ra kom·prar ...

How much is it?
¿Cuánto cuesta esto?
kwan·to kwes·ta es·to

--- OR ---

Can you write down the price?
¿Puede escribir el precio?
pwe·de es·kree·beer el pre·thyo

Do you accept credit cards?
¿Aceptan tarjetas de crédito?
a·thep·tan tar·khe·tas de kre·dee·to

Could I have a ..., please?
¿Podría darme ..., por favor?
po·dree·a dar·me ... por fa·vor

receipt
un recibo
oon re·thee·bo

bag
una bolsa
oo·na bol·sa

🔊 LISTEN FOR

cazador m de ofertas	ka·tha·*dor* de o·*fer*·tas	bargain hunter
estafa f	es·*ta*·fa	rip-off
ganga f	*gan*·ga	bargain
rebajas f pl	re·*ba*·khas	specials
ventas f pl	*ven*·tas	sale

I'd like my money back, please.	Quisiera que me devuelva el dinero, por favor. kee·*sye*·ra ke me de·*vwel*·va el dee·*ne*·ro por fa·*vor*
I'd like to return this, please.	Quisiera devolver esto, por favor. kee·*sye*·ra de·vol·*ver* es·to por fa·*vor*

Bargaining

That's too expensive.	Es muy caro. es mooy *ka*·ro
Do you have something cheaper?	¿Tiene algo más barato? *tye*·ne *al*·go mas ba·*ra*·to
Can you lower the price?	¿Podría bajar un poco el precio? po·*dree*·a ba·*khar* oon *po*·ko el *pre*·thyo
I'll give you ...	Le/Te daré ... pol/inf le/te da·*re* ...

Clothes

Can I try it on?	¿Me lo puedo probar? me lo *pwe*·do *pro*·bar
My size is ...	Uso la talla ... *oo*·so la *ta*·lya ...
It doesn't fit.	No me queda bien. no me *ke*·da byen
small	pequeño/a **m/f** pe·*ke*·nyo/a
medium	mediano/a **m/f** me·*dya*·no/a
large	grande **m&f** *gran*·de

For clothing items, see the **dictionary**. For sizes, see **numbers & amounts** (p34).

I'm just looking.
so·lo es·*toy* mee·*ran*·do
Sólo estoy mirando.

PRACTICAL SHOPPING

Repairs

Can I have my (camera) repaired here?	¿Puede reparar mi (cámara) aquí? *pwe·de re·pa·rar mee (ka·ma·ra) a·kee*
When will my (sun)glasses be ready?	¿Cuándo estarán listas mis gafas (de sol)? *kwan·do es·ta·ran lees·tas mees ga·fas (de sol)*
When will my shoes be ready?	¿Cuándo estarán listos mis zapatos? *kwan·do es·ta·ran lees·tos mees tha·pa·tos*

Books & Reading

Is there a/an (English-language) bookshop?	¿Hay una librería (en inglés)? *ai oo·na lee·bre·ree·a (en een·gles)*
Is there a/an (English-language) section?	¿Hay una sección (en inglés)? *ai oo·na sek·thyon (en een·gles)*
I (don't) like ...	(No) Me gusta/gustan ... **sg/pl** *(no) me goos·ta/goos·tan ...*
I'm looking for something by (Javier Marías).	Estoy buscando algo de (Javier Marías). *es·toy boos·kan·do al·go de (kha·vyer ma·ree·as)*

For more on books and reading, see **interests** (p124).

> **CULTURE TIP**
>
> **Hispanic Literature**
> Spanish-language literature has a long history, dating from the 12th century and written across the Spanish-speaking world. Today's thriving industry includes such authors as Ana María Matute, Isabel Allende, Jorge Luis Borges, Miguel de Unamuno, Carmen Martín Gaite, Juan Goytisolo, Miguel Delibes, 1982 Nobel Prize winner Gabriel García Márquez and the 1989 Nobel Prize winner, Camilo José Cela.

Music & DVD

I heard a band called ...	Escuché a un grupo que se llama ... es·koo·*che* a oon *groo*·po ke se *lya*·ma ...
What's their best recording?	¿Cuál es su mejor disco? kwal es soo me·*khor dees*·ko
Can I listen to this?	¿Puedo escuchar esto? *pwe*·do es·koo·*char es*·to
What region is this DVD for?	¿Para qué región es este DVD? *pa*·ra ke re·*khyon* es *es*·te de·oo·ve·de
I'd like a CD/DVD.	Quisiera un compact/DVD. kee·*sye*·ra oon *kom*·pak/de·oo·ve·de
Is this a pirated copy?	¿Es copia pirata? es *ko*·pya pee·*ra*·ta
I'd like some headphones.	Quisiera unos auriculares. kee·*sye*·ra *oo*·nos ow·ree·koo·*la*·res

Video & Photography

Can you print digital photos?	¿Podría imprimir fotos digitales? po·*dree*·a eem·pree·*meer* *fo*·tos dee·khee·*ta*·les
Can you transfer my photos from camera to CD?	¿Podría pasar las fotos de mi cámara a un compact? po·*dree*·a pa·*sar* las *fo*·tos de mee *ka*·ma·ra a oon *kom*·pak
How much is it to develop this film?	¿Cuánto cuesta revelar este carrete? *kwan*·to *kwes*·ta re·ve·*lar* *es*·te ka·*re*·te
Do you have slide film?	¿Tiene diapositivas? *tye*·ne dee·a·po·see·*tee*·vas
I need a cable to connect my camera to a computer.	Necesito un cable para conectar mi cámara al ordenador. ne·the·*see*·to oon *ka*·ble *pa*·ra ko·nek·*tar* mee *ka*·ma·ra al or·de·na·*dor*
I need a cable to recharge this battery.	Necesito un cable para recargar esta batería. ne·the·*see*·to oon *ka*·ble *pa*·ra re·kar·*gar* *es*·ta ba·te·*ree*·a
Do you have batteries for this camera?	¿Tiene pilas para esta cámara? *tye*·ne *pee*·las *pa*·ra *es*·ta *ka*·ma·ra
Do you have memory cards for this camera?	¿Tiene tarjetas de memoria para esta cámara? *tye*·ne tar·*khe*·tas de me·*mo*·rya *pa*·ra *es*·ta *ka*·ma·ra

> **CULTURE TIP**
>
> **The Spanish Lisp**
>
> According to a popular legend, one Spanish king – some say Felipe IV, others Ferdinand I – was unable to pronounce the *s* sound properly and his court, and eventually all of Spain, mimicked his lisp. Of course, the tale is a myth. Indeed, only the letters *c* and *z* are pronounced th (when they precede an *i* or an *e*), while the letter *s* remains the same as in English – a selectiveness due to the way Spanish evolved from Latin. So when you hear someone say *gracias* gra·thyas, they are no more lisping than when you say 'thank you' in English.

Do you have (a) ... for this camera?	¿Tiene ... para esta cámara? *tye·*ne ... *pa·*ra es·ta *ka·*ma·ra
I need a B&W film for this camera.	Necesito película en blanco y negro para esta cámara. ne·the·*see·*to pe·*lee·*koo·la en *blan·*ko y *ne·*gro *pa·*ra es·ta *ka·*ma·ra
I need a colour film for this camera.	Necesito película en color para esta cámara. ne·the·*see·*to pe·*lee·*koo·la en ko·*lor pa·*ra es·ta *ka·*ma·ra
I need a (400) speed film for this camera.	Necesito película de sensibilidad (cuatrocientos) para esta cámara. ne·the·*see·*to pe·*lee·*koo·la de sen·see·bee·lee·*da (kwa·tro·*thyen·*tos) *pa·*ra es·ta *ka·*ma·ra
I need a passport photo taken.	Necesito fotos de pasaporte. ne·the·*see·*to *fo·*tos de pa·sa·*por·*te

Communications

KEY PHRASES

Where's the local internet cafe?	¿Dónde hay un cibercafé cercano?	don·de ai oon thee·ber·ka·fe ther·ka·no
I'd like to check my email.	Quisiera revisar mi correo electrónico.	kee·sye·ra re·vee·sar mee ko·re·o e·lek·tro·nee·ko
I want to send a parcel.	Quisiera enviar un paquete.	kee·sye·ra en·vee·ar oon pa·ke·te
I'd like a SIM card.	Quisiera una tarjeta SIM.	kee·sye·ra oo·na tar·khe·ta seem

Post Office

I want to send a parcel.	Quisiera enviar un paquete. kee·sye·ra en·vee·ar oon pa·ke·te
I want to send a postcard.	Quisiera enviar una postal. kee·sye·ra en·vee·ar oo·na pos·tal
I want to buy an envelope.	Quisiera comprar un sobre. kee·sye·ra kom·prar oon so·bre
I want to buy stamps.	Quisiera comprar sellos. kee·sye·ra kom·prar se·lyos
Please send it by air/ surface mail to ...	Por favor, mándelo por vía aérea/terrestre a ... por fa·vor man·de·lo por vee·a a·e·re·a/te·res·tre a ...

🔊 LISTEN FOR

buzón m	boo·*thon*	mail box
código m **postal**	*ko*·dee·go pos·*tal*	postcode
correo m **certificado**	ko·*re*·o ther·tee·fee·*ka*·do	registered mail
por vía aérea	por *vee*·a a·*e*·re·a	airmail
correo m **urgente**	ko·*re*·o oor·*khen*·te	express mail
declaración f **de aduana**	de·kla·ra·*thyon* de a·*dwa*·na	customs declaration
frágil	*fra*·kheel	fragile
internacional	een·ter·na·thyo·*nal*	international
nacional	na·thyo·*nal*	domestic

It contains ...	Contiene ... kon·*tye*·ne ...
Where's the poste restante section?	¿Dónde está la lista de correos? *don*·de es·*ta* la *lees*·ta de ko·*re*·os
Is there any mail for me?	¿Hay alguna carta para mí? ai al·*goo*·na *kar*·ta *pa*·ra mee

Phone

Q What's your phone number?	¿Cuál es su/tu número de teléfono? pol/inf kwal es soo/too *noo*·me·ro de te·*le*·fo·no
A The number is ...	El número es ... el *noo*·me·ro es ...

Where's the nearest public phone?	¿Dónde hay una cabina telefónica?	
	don·de ai oo·na ka·bee·na te·le·fo·nee·ka	
Can I look at a phone book?	¿Puedo mirar la guía de teléfonos?	
	pwe·do mee·rar la gee·a de te·le·fo·nos	
What's the area code for ...?	¿Cuál es el prefijo de la zona de ...?	
	kwal es el pre·fee·kho de la tho·na de ...	
What's the country code for ...?	¿Cuál es el prefijo del país de ...?	
	kwal es el pre·fee·kho del pa·ees de ...	

For telephone numbers, see **numbers & amounts**, page 34.

I want to...	Quiero ...	
	kye·ro ...	

make a call to (Singapore)	hacer una llamada a (Singapur)	*a·ther oo·na lya·ma·da a (seen·ga·poor)*
make a local call	hacer una llamada local	*a·ther oo·na lya·ma·da lo·kal*
a reverse-charge/ collect call	una llamada a cobro revertido	*oo·na lya·ma·da a ko·bro re·ver·tee·do*
buy a phone card	comprar una tarjeta telefónica	*kom·prar oo·na tar·khe·ta te·le·fo·nee·ka*

It's engaged.	Está comunicando.	
	es·ta ko·moo·nee·kan·do	

🔊 LISTEN FOR

¿De parte de quién?	de *par*·te de kyen	Who's calling?
¿Con quién quiere hablar?	kon kyen *kye*·re a·*blar*	Who do you want to speak to?
Lo siento, pero ahora no está.	lo *syen*·to *pe*·ro a·*o*·ra no es·*ta*	I'm sorry, he/she is not here.
Lo siento, tiene el numero equivocado.	lo *syen*·to *tye*·ne el *noo*·me·ro e·kee·vo·*ka*·do	Sorry, you have got the wrong number.

The connection's bad.	Es mala conexión. es *ma*·la ko·nek·*syon*
Hello. (calling)	Hola. o·la
Hello? (answering)	¿Diga? *dee*·ga
Can I speak to ...?	¿Está ...? es·*ta* ...
It's (Julio) ...	Soy (Julio) ... soy (Julio) ...
I've been cut off.	Me han cortado. me an kor·*ta*·do
Can I leave a message?	¿Puedo dejar un mensaje? *pwe*·do de·*khar* oon men·*sa*·khe
Please tell him/her I called.	Sí, por favor, dile que he llamado. see por fa·*vor dee*·le ke e lya·*ma*·do
I'll call back later.	Ya llamaré más tarde. ya lya·ma·*re* mas *tar*·de

Mobile/Cell Phone

I'd like a/an ...
Quisiera ...
kee·*sye*·ra ...

charger for my phone	un cargador para mi teléfono	oon kar·ga·*dor* *pa*·ra mee te·*le*·fo·no
mobile/cell phone for hire	un móvil para alquilar	oon *mo*·veel *pa*·ra al·kee·*lar*
prepaid phone	una tarjeta prepagada	oo·na tar·*khe*·ta pre·pa·ga·da
SIM card (for your network)	una tarjeta SIM (para su red)	oo·na tar·*khe*·ta seem (*pa*·ra soo red)

What are the rates?
¿Cuál es la tarifa?
kwal es la ta·*ree*·fa

The Internet

Where's the local internet cafe?
¿Dónde hay un cibercafé cercano?
don·de ai oon thee·ber·ka·*fe* ther·*ka*·no

Do you have public internet access here?
¿Tiene acceso público a internet?
tye·ne ak·*the*·so *poo*·blee·ko a *een*·ter·net

Is there wireless internet access here?
¿Hay acceso inalámbrico a internet aquí?
ai ak·*the*·so een·a·*lam*·bree·ko a *een*·ter·net a·*kee*

Can I connect my laptop here?	¿Puedo conectar mi ordenador portátil aquí? *pwe·*do ko·nek·*tar* mee or·de·na·*dor* por·ta·teel a·*kee*
Do you have headphones (with a microphone)?	¿Tiene auriculares (con micrófono)? *tye*·ne ow·ree·koo·*la*·res (kon mee·*kro*·fo·no)
I'd like to buy a card/ USB for prepaid mobile internet.	Quisiera comprar una tarjeta/USB para internet móvil de prepago. kee·*sye*·ra kom·*prar* oo·na tar·*khe*·ta/oo·e·se·be *pa*·ra *een*·ter·net *mo*·veel de pre·*pa*·go

🔍 LOOK FOR

Here are some Spanish substitutes for common internet-related terms.

charlar	char·lar	chat
ciberespacio m	thee·ber·e·*spa*·thyo	cyberspace
correr tabla por la red	ko·*rer* ta·bla por la re	surf
descargar	des·kar·*gar*	download
en línea	en *lee*·ne·a	online
nombre m **de usuario**	*nom*·bre de oo·*swa*·ryo	username
página f **Web inicial**	*pa*·khe·na web ee·nee·*thyal*	homepage
sistema f **de búsqueda**	sees·*te*·ma de *boos*·ke·da	search engine
sitio m **Web**	*see*·tyo web	website

I'd like to ...	Quisiera ... kee·sye·ra ...	
burn a CD	copiar un disco	ko·pyar oon dees·ko
check my email	revisar mi correo electrónico	re·vee·sar mee ko·re·o e·lek·tro·nee·ko
download my photos	descargar mis fotos	des·kar·gar mees fo·tos
use a printer	usar una impresora	oo·sar oo·na eem·pre·so·ra
use a scanner	usar un escáner	oo·sar oon es·ka·ner
use Skype	usar Skype	oo·sar es·kaip

How much per hour/page?	¿Cuánto cuesta por hora/página? kwan·to kwes·ta por o·ra/pa·khee·na
How do I log on?	¿Cómo entro al sistema? ko·mo en·tro al sees·te·ma
It's crashed.	Se ha quedado colgado. se a ke·da·do kol·ga·do
I've finished.	He terminado. e ter·mee·na·do
media player (MP3)	equipo m MP3 e·kee·po e·me·pe·tres
portable hard drive	disco duro m portátil dees·ko doo·ro por·ta·teel
PSP	PSP m pe·e·se·pe
USB flash drive (memory stick)	memoria f USB me·mo·rya oo·e·se·be

Money & Banking

KEY PHRASES

How much is it?	¿Cuánto cuesta esto?	*kwan*·to *kwes*·ta *es*·to
What's the exchange rate?	¿Cuál es el tipo de cambio?	kwal es el *tee*·po de *kam*·byo
Where's the nearest ATM?	¿Dónde está el cajero automático más cercano?	*don*·de es·*ta* el ka·*khe*·ro ow·to·*ma*·tee·ko mas ther·*ka*·no

Paying the Bill

Q How much is it?	¿Cuánto cuesta esto? *kwan*·to *kwes*·ta *es*·to
A It's (12) euros.	Son (doce) euros. son (*do*·the) e·oo·ros
A It's free.	Es gratis. es *gra*·tees
There's a mistake in the bill.	Hay un error en la cuenta. ai oon e·*ror* en la *kwen*·ta
Do you accept credit/ debit cards?	¿Aceptan tarjetas de crédito/débito? a·*thep*·tan tar·*khe*·tas de *kre*·dee·to/*de*·bee·to
Do you accept travellers cheques?	¿Aceptan cheques de viajero? a·*thep*·tan *che*·kes de vya·*khe*·ro

I'd like my change, please.	Quisiera mi cambio, por favor.	kee·sye·ra mee kam·byo por fa·vor
Could I have a receipt, please?	¿Podría darme un recibo, por favor?	po·dree·a dar·me oon re·thee·bo por fa·vor

See also **bargaining** (p78).

Banking

Where can I ...?	¿Dónde puedo ...?	don·de pwe·do ...
I'd like to ...	Me gustaría ...	me goos·ta·ree·a ...

arrange a transfer	hacer una transferencia	ha·ther oo·na trans·fe·ren·thee·ya
get a cash advance	obtener un adelanto	ob·te·ner on a·de·lan·to
change money	cambiar dinero	kam·byar dee·ne·ro
change a travellers cheque	cambiar un cheque de viajero	kam·byar oon che·ke de vya·khe·ro
get change for this note	conseguir cambio para este billete	kon·se·geer kam·byo pa·ra es·te bee·lye·te
withdraw money	sacar dinero	sa·kar dee·ne·ro

Where's the nearest ATM?	¿Dónde está el cajero automático más cercano?	don·de es·ta el ka·khe·ro ow·to·ma·tee·ko mas ther·ka·no

◀)) **LISTEN FOR**

No le quedan fondos.	no le *ke*·dan *fon*·dos You have no money left.
Hay un problema con su cuenta.	ai oon pro·*ble*·ma kon soo *kwen*·ta There's a problem with your account.
¿Puedo ver su identificación, por favor?	*pwe*·do ver soo ee·den·tee·fee·ka·*thyon* por fa·*vor* Can I see your ID, please?
Por favor firme aquí.	por fa·*vor* *feer*·me a·*kee* Please sign here.

Where's the nearest foreign exchange office?	¿Dónde está la oficina de cambio más cercano? *don*·de es·*ta* la o·fee·*thee*·na de *kam*·byo mas ther·*ka*·no
What's the exchange rate?	¿Cuál es el tipo de cambio? kwal es el *tee*·po de *kam*·byo
What's the charge for that?	¿Cuánto hay que pagar por eso? *kwan*·to ai ke pa·*gar* por e·so
The ATM took my card.	El cajero automático se ha tragado mi tarjeta. el ka·*khe*·ro ow·to·*ma*·tee·ko se a *tra*·ga·do mee tar·*khe*·ta
I've forgotten my PIN.	Me he olvidado del NPI. me e ol·vee·*da*·do del e·ne·pe·ee
Has my money arrived yet?	¿Ya ha llegado mi dinero? ya a lye·*ga*·do mee dee·*ne*·ro
How long will it take to arrive?	¿Cuánto tiempo tardará en llegar? *kwan*·to *tyem*·po tar·da·*ra* en lye·*gar*

Business

KEY PHRASES

I'm attending a conference.	Asisto a un congreso.	a·sees·to a oon kon·gre·so
I have an appointment with ...	Tengo una cita con ...	ten·go oo·na thee·ta kon ...
Can I have your business card?	¿Puede darme su tarjeta de visita?	pwe·de dar·me soo tar·khe·ta de vee·see·ta

People usually chit-chat for a while before they get down to business.
For titles and greetings, see **meeting people** (p106).

I'm attending a ...	Asisto a ... a·sees·to a ...

conference	un congreso	oon kon·gre·so
course	un curso	oon koor·so
meeting	una reunión	oo·na re·oo·nyon
trade fair	una feria de muestras	oo·na fe·rya de mwes·tras

I'm with my colleagues.	Estoy con mis colegas. m&f es·toy kon mees ko·le·gas

I'm alone.	Estoy solo/a. m/f es·toy so·lo/a

Where's the business district?	¿Dónde está el centro financiero? don·de es·ta el then·tro fee·nan·thye·ro

LANGUAGE TIP

Addressing People
To show formality or respect, you should use the polite form of address *Usted* sg pol oo·*ste* or *Ustedes* pl pol oo·*ste*·des in business and with any service providers (be they kiosk attendants or doctors). It's best to take the lead from how people address you, and respond in the same way. For more on polite forms, see **personal pronouns** in the **grammar** chapter, p21.

Where's the conference?	¿Dónde está el congreso? *don*·de es·*ta* el kon·*gre*·so
Where's the meeting?	¿Dónde es la reunión? *don*·de es la re·oo·*nyon*
I have an appointment with ...	Tengo una cita con ... *ten*·go oo·na *thee*·ta kon ...
Q Can I have your business card?	¿Puede darme su tarjeta de visita? *pwe*·de *dar*·me soo tar·*khe*·ta de vee·*see*·ta
A Here's my business card.	Aquí tiene mi tarjeta de visita. a·*kee tye*·ne mee tar·*khe*·ta de vee·*see*·ta
That went very well.	Eso fue muy bien. *e*·so fwe mooy byen
Thank you for your interest/time.	Gracias por su interés/tiempo. *gra*·thyas por soo een·te·*res*/*tyem*·po
Shall we go for a drink/meal?	¿Vamos a tomar/comer algo? *va*·mos a to·*mar*/ko·*mer al*·go
It's on me.	Invito yo. een·*vee*·to yo

Sightseeing

KEY PHRASES

Can we hire a guide?	¿Podemos alquilar un guía?	po·de·mos al·kee·lar oon gee·a
Can I take photographs?	¿Puedo tomar fotos?	pwe·do to·mar fo·tos
When's the museum open?	¿A qué hora abren el museo?	a ke o·ra ab·ren el moo·se·o

Requests & Queries

I'd like a/an ...   Quisiera ...
kee·sye·ra ...

audio set	un equipo audio	oon e·kee·po ow·dyo
catalogue	un catálogo	oon ka·ta·lo·go
guidebook in English	una guía turística en inglés	oo·na gee·a too·rees·tee·ka en een·gles
(local) map	un mapa (de la zona)	oon ma·pa (de la tho·na)

I'd like to see ...   Me gustaría ver ...
me goos·ta·ree·a ver ...

Do you have information on local sights?	¿Tiene información sobre los lugares de interés local? *tye·ne een·for·ma·thyon so·bre los loo·ga·res de een·te·res lo·kal*
Do you have information on historical sights?	¿Tiene información sobre los lugares de interés histórico? *tye·ne een·for·ma·thyon so·bre los loo·ga·res de een·te·res ees·to·ree·ko*
Do you have information on religious sights?	¿Tiene información sobre los lugares de interés religioso? *tye·ne een·for·ma·thyon so·bre los loo·ga·res de een·te·res re·lee·khyo·so*
Can we hire a guide?	¿Podemos alquilar un guía? *po·de·mos al·kee·lar oon gee·a*
Can I take photographs (of you)?	¿(Le/Te) Puedo tomar fotos? **pol/inf** *(le/te) pwe·do to·mar fo·tos*
I'll send you the photograph.	Le/Te mandaré la foto. **pol/inf** *le/te man·da·re la fo·to*
Could you take a photograph of me?	¿Me puede hacer una foto? *me pwe·de a·ther oo·na fo·to*
What's that?	¿Qué es eso? *ke es e·so*
How old is it?	¿De qué época es? *de ke e·po·ka es*

Getting In

What time does it open/ close?	¿A qué hora abren/cierran? *a ke o·ra ab·ren/thye·ran*
What's the admission charge?	¿Cuánto cuesta la entrada? *kwan·to kwes·ta la en·tra·da*

Is there a discount for ...?	¿Hay descuentos para ...?
	ai des·*kwen*·tos *pa*·ra ...

children	niños	*nee*·nyos
families	familias	fa·*mee*·lyas
groups	grupos	*groo*·pos
older people	gente mayor	*khen*·te ma·*yor*
students	estudiantes	es·too·*dyan*·tes

Galleries & Museums

When's the gallery open?	¿A qué hora abren la galería?
	a ke *o*·ra *a*·bren la ga·le·*ree*·a
When's the museum open?	¿A qué hora abren el museo?
	a ke *o*·ra *ab*·ren el moo·*se*·o
Q What's in the collection?	¿Qué hay en la colección?
	ke ai en la ko·lek·*thyon*
A It's a/an ... exhibition.	Es una exposición de ...
	es *oo*·na eks·po·see·*thyon* de ...
I like the works of ...	Me gustan las obras de ...
	me *goos*·tan las *o*·bras de ...
It reminds me of ...	Me recuerda a ...
	me re·*kwer*·da a ...
... art	arte **m** ...
	ar·te ...

graphic	gráfico	*gra*·fee·ko
impressionist	impresionista	eem·pre·syo·*nees*·ta
modernist	modernista	mo·der·*nees*·ta
Renaissance	renacentista	re·na·then·*tees*·ta

🔍 LOOK FOR

Abierto	a·*byer*·to	Open
Cerrado	the·*ra*·do	Closed
Prohibido	pro·ee·*bee*·do	Prohibited

Tours

Are there organised walking tours?	¿Organizan recorridos a pie? or·ga·*nee*·than re·ko·*ree*·dos a pye
I'd like to take cooking/ language classes.	Me gustaría ir a clases de cocina/idiomas. me goos·ta·*ree*·a eer a *kla*·ses de ko·*thee*·na/ee·*dyo*·mas

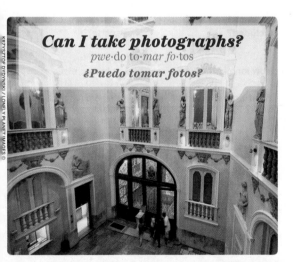

Can I take photographs?
pwe·do to·*mar* fo·tos
¿Puedo tomar fotos?

| **Can you recommend a ...?** | ¿Puede recomendar algún/alguna ...? m/f
pwe·de re·ko·men·dar al·goon/al·goo·na ... |
| **When's the next ...?** | ¿Cuándo es el/la próximo/a ...? m/f
kwan·do es el/la prok·see·mo/a ... |

boat trip	paseo m en barca	pa·se·o en bar·ka
day trip	excursión f de un día	eks·koor·syon de oon dee·a
excursion	excursión f	eks·koor·syon
tour	recorrido m	re·ko·ree·do

Do I need to take (food) with me?	¿Necesito llevar (comida)? ne·the·see·to lye·var (ko·mee·da)
Is (equipment/transport) included?	¿Incluye (equipo/transporte)? een·kloo·ye (e·kee·po/trans·por·te)
How long is the tour?	¿Cuánto dura el recorrido? kwan·to doo·ra el re·ko·ree·do
What time should I be back?	¿A qué hora tengo que volver? a ke o·ra ten·go ke vol·ver
Be back here at ...	Vuelva ... vwel·va ...
I've lost my group.	He perdido a mi grupo. e per·dee·do a mee groo·po

Senior & Disabled Travellers

KEY PHRASES

I need assistance.	Necesito asistencia.	ne·the·*see*·to a·sees·*ten*·thya
Is there wheelchair access?	¿Hay acceso para la silla de ruedas?	ai ak·*the*·so *pa*·ra la *see*·lya de *rwe*·das
Are there toilets for people with a disablity?	¿Hay aseos para minusválidos?	ai a·*se*·os *pa*·ra mee·noos·*va*·lee·dos

I have a disability.	Soy minusválido/a. **m/f** soy mee·noos·*va*·lee·do/a
I need assistance.	Necesito asistencia. ne·the·*see*·to a·sees·*ten*·thya
Are guide dogs permitted?	¿Se permite la entrada a los perros lazarillos? se per·*mee*·te la en·*tra*·da a los *pe*·ros la·tha·*ree*·lyos
Is there wheelchair access?	¿Hay acceso para la silla de ruedas? ai ak·*the*·so *pa*·ra la *see*·lya de *rwe*·das
Are there parking spaces for people with a disability?	¿Tiene aparcamiento para minusválidos? *tye*·ne a·par·ka·*myen*·to *pa*·ra mee·noos·*va*·lee·dos
Are there rails in the bathroom?	¿Hay pasamanos en el baño? ai pa·sa·*ma*·nos en el *ba*·nyo

🔍 LOOK FOR

Acceso para Sillas de Ruedas	ak·*the*·so *pa*·ra *see*·lyas de *rwe*·das	Wheelchair Entrance
Ascensor	a·then·*sor*	Elevator/Lift

Are there toilets for people with a disability?	¿Hay aseos para minusválidos? ai a·*se*·os *pa*·ra mee·noos·*va*·lee·dos
Is there somewhere I can sit down?	¿Hay algun sitio dónde me pueda sentar? ai al·*goon see*·tyo *don*·de me *pwe*·da sen·*tar*
Could you help me cross this street?	¿Me puede ayudar a cruzar la calle? me *pwe*·de a·yoo·*dar* a kroo·*thar* la *ka*·lye
Could you call me a taxi for the disabled?	¿Podría llamar a un taxi para minusválidos? po·*dree*·a lya·*mar* a oon *tak*·see *pa*·ra mee·noos·*va*·lee·dos
crutches	muletas f pl moo·*le*·tas
guide dog	perro m lazarillo *pe*·ro la·tha·*ree*·lyo
ramp	rampa f *ram*·pa
walking frame	andador m an·da·*dor*
walking stick	bastón m bas·*ton*
wheelchair	silla f de ruedas *see*·lya de *rwe*·das

Travel with Children

KEY PHRASES

Are children allowed?	¿Se admiten niños?	se ad·*mee*·ten *nee*·nyos
Is there a child discount?	¿Hay descuento para niños?	ai des·*kwen*·to *pa*·ra *nee*·nyos
Is there a baby change room?	¿Hay una sala en la que cambiar el pañal al bebé?	ai *oo*·na *sa*·la en la ke kam·*byar*·le el pa·*nyal* al be·*be*

I need a ...   Necesito ...
ne·the·*see*·to ...

baby/child seat	un asiento de seguridad para bebés/niños	oon a·*syen*·to de se·goo·ree·*da pa*·ra be·*bes*/*nee*·nyos
cot	una cuna	*oo*·na *koo*·na
potty	un orinal de niños	oon o·ree·*nal* de *nee*·nyos
stroller	un cochecito	oon ko·che·*thee*·to

Do you sell baby wipes?   ¿Vende toallitas para bebés?
ven·de to·a·*lyee*·tas *pa*·ra be·*bes*

Do you sell disposable nappies/diapers?   ¿Vende pañales de usar y tirar?
ven·de pa·*nya*·les de oo·*sar* ee tee·*rar*

Do you sell milk formula?	¿Vende leche de fórmula?	*ven·*de *le·*che de *for·*moo·la
Is there a/an ...?	¿Hay ...?	ai ...

baby change room	una sala en la que cambiarle el pañal al bebé	*oo·*na *sa·*la en la ke kam·*byar·*le el pa·*nyal* al be·*be*
child discount	descuento para niños	des·*kwen·*to *pa·*ra *nee·*nyos
child-minding service	servicio de cuidado de niños	ser·*vee·*thyo de kwee·*da·*do de *nee·*nyos
children's menu	menú infantil	me·*noo* een·fan·*teel*
family discount	descuento familiar	des·*kwen·*to fa·mee·*lyar*
highchair	trona	*tro·*na

Do you mind if I breastfeed here?	¿Le molesta que dé de pecho aquí?
	le mo·*les·*ta ke de de *pe·*cho a·*kee*
Are children allowed?	¿Se admiten niños?
	se ad·*mee·*ten *nee·*nyos
Is this suitable for (three)-year-old children?	¿Es apto para niños de (tres) años?
	es *ap·*to *pa·*ra *nee·*nyos de (tres) *a·*nyos

If your child is sick, see **health** (p158).

Social

Meeting People

KEY PHRASES

My name is ...	Me llamo ...	me *lya*·mo ...
I'm from ...	Soy de ...	soy de ...
I work in (education).	Trabajo en (enseñanza).	tra·*ba*·kho en (en·se·*nyan*·tha)
I'm ... years old.	Tengo ... años.	*ten*·go ... *a*·nyos
And you?	¿Y Usted/tú? **pol/inf**	ee oos·*te*/too

Basics

Yes.	Sí. see
No.	No. no
Please.	Por favor. por fa·*vor*
Thank you (very much).	(Muchas) Gracias. (*moo*·chas) *gra*·thyas
You're welcome.	De nada. de *na*·da
Excuse me.	Perdón/Discúlpeme. per·*don*/dees·*kool*·pe·me
Sorry.	Lo siento. lo *syen*·to

Greetings

In Spain people are often quite casual in their social interactions.
It's fine to use the following expressions in both formal and informal
situations.

Hello/Hi.	Hola. *o·la*
Good morning.	Buenos días. *bwe·nos dee·as*
Good afternoon. **(until 8pm)**	Buenas tardes. *bwe·nas tar·des*
Good evening/night.	Buenas noches. *bwe·nas no·ches*
See you later.	Hasta luego. *as·ta lwe·go*
Goodbye./Bye.	Adiós. *a·dyos*
Q How are you?	¿Qué tal? *ke tal*
A Fine, thanks. **And you?**	Bien, gracias. ¿Y Usted/tú? **pol/inf** *byen gra·thyas* *ee oos·te/too*
Q What's your name?	¿Cómo se llama Usted? **pol** *ko·mo se lya·ma oos·te* ¿Cómo te llamas? **inf** *ko·mo te lya·mas*
A My name is ...	Me llamo ... *me lya·mo ...*
I'm pleased to meet you.	Mucho gusto. *moo·cho goos·to*

SOCIAL MEETING PEOPLE

I'd like to introduce you to ...	Quisiera presentarle a ... **pol**
	kee·*sye*·ra pre·sen·*tar*·le a ...
	Quisiera presentarte a ... **inf**
	kee·*sye*·ra pre·sen·*tar*·te a ...

✄ This is ...	Ésto es...	*es*·to es ...

This is my friend.	Éste/a es mi amigo/a. **m/f**
	es·te/a es mee a·*mee*·go/a

Titles & Addressing People

Señor and *Señora* tend to be used in everyday speech. *Doña*, although rare, is used as a mark of respect towards older women, while *Don* is sometimes used to address men. An elderly neighbour, for example, might be called *Doña Lola*. For more on polite forms, see **addressing people** (p95), and **personal pronouns** (p21).

Mr	Señor
	se·*nyor*

Sir	Don
	don

Miss	Señorita
	se·nyo·*ree*·ta

Ms/Mrs	Señora
	se·*nyo*·ra

Madam	Doña
	do·nya

Making Conversation

Spain is known for its distinct regional personalities. A great conversation starter in Spain is to ask someone where they come from. Other good topics are sport, politics, history and travel.

Do you live here?	¿Vives aquí?
	vee·ves a·*kee*

LANGUAGE TIP

Addressing Friends

You may hear friends calling each other *tío* m *tee·o*, or *tía* f *tee·a*, but these words are usually used when talking about others. They're a bit crass (a little like using 'sheila' to describe a girl in Australia). Guys use *colega* ko·*le*·ga, and *hombre* om·bre, to address their workmates or male friends. In the south, people call their friends *pixas* *pee*·chas or *xoxos* *cho*·chos.

Where are you going?	¿Adónde vas?	a·*don*·de vas
What are you doing?	¿Qué haces?	ke a·thes
Q **Are you here on holidays?**	¿Estás aquí de vacaciones?	es·*tas* a·kee de va·ka·*thyo*·nes
A **I'm here for a holiday.**	Estoy aquí de vacaciones.	es·*toy* a·kee de va·ka·*thyo*·nes
A **I'm here on business.**	Estoy aquí en viaje de negocios.	es·*toy* a·kee en *vya*·khe de ne·*go*·thyos
A **I'm here to study.**	Estoy aquí estudiando.	es·*toy* a·kee es·too·*dyan*·do
That's (beautiful), isn't it?	¿Es (precioso), no?	es (pre·*thyo*·so) no
Q **How long are you here for?**	¿Cuánto tiempo te vas a quedar?	*kwan*·to *tyem*·po te vas a ke·*dar*
A **I'm here for ... weeks/days.**	Estoy aquí por ... semanas/días.	es·*toy* a·kee por ... se·*ma*·nas/*dee*·as

Nationalities

You'll find that many country names are similar to English, so even if you don't know the Spanish name, it's more than likely you'll be understood. For more countries, see the **dictionary**.

Where are you from?	¿De dónde es Usted? pol de *don*·de es oos·*te* ¿De dónde eres? inf de *don*·de e·res
I'm from (Australia).	Soy de (Australia). soy de (ow·*stra*·lya)
I'm from (Canada).	Soy de (Canadá). soy de (ka·na·*da*)

Age

How old are you?	¿Cuántos años tienes? *kwan*·tos *a*·nyos *tye*·nes
I'm ... years old.	Tengo ... años. *ten*·go ... *a*·nyos
How old is your son/ daughter?	¿Cuántos años tiene tu hijo/hija? *kwan*·tos *a*·nyos *tye*·ne too *ee*·kho/*ee*·kha
He's/She's ... years old.	Tiene ... años. *tye*·ne ... *a*·nyos
I'm younger than I look.	Soy más joven de lo que parezco. soy mas *kho*·ven de lo ke pa·*reth*·ko
Too old!	¡Demasiado viejo! de·ma·*sya*·do *vye*·kho

For your age, see **numbers & amounts** (p34).

🔊 LISTEN FOR

¡Cojonudo!	ko·kho·*noo*·do	Great!
¿De veras?	de *ve*·ras	Really?
¡Enhorabuena!	e·no·ra·*bwe*·na	Congratulations!
¡Estupendo!	es·too·*pen*·do	That's fantastic!
¡No me digas!	no me *dee*·gas	You don't say!
¡Qué guay!	ke gwai	How cool!
¿Qué hay?	ke ai	What's up?
¡Qué interesante!	ke een·te·re·*san*·te	How interesting!

Occupations & Study

Q What do you do?
¿A qué te dedicas?
a ke te de·*dee*·kas

A I work in (education/ hospitality).
Trabajo en (enseñanza/ hostelería).
tra·*ba*·kho en (en·se·*nyan*·tha/ os·te·le·*ree*·a)

A I'm a/an ...
Soy ...
soy ...

architect	arquitecto/a m/f	ar·kee·*tek*·to/a
mechanic	mecánico/a m/f	me·*ka*·nee·ko/a
student	estudiante m&f	es·too·*dyan*·te
teacher	profesor/ profesora m/f	pro·fe·*sor*/ pro·fe·*so*·ra

A I'm self-employed.
Soy trabajador/ trabajadora autónomo/a. m/f
soy tra·ba·kha·*dor*/ tra·ba·kha·*do*·ra ow·*to*·no·mo/a

A I'm retired.

Estoy jubilado/a. **m/f**
es·*toy* khoo·bee·*la*·do/a

A I'm unemployed.

Estoy en el paro.
es·*toy* en el *pa*·ro

Q What are you studying?

¿Qué estudias?
ke es·*too*·dyas

A I'm studying (languages).

Estudio (idiomas).
es·*too*·dyo (ee·*dyo*·mas)

I'm studying at ...

Estudio en ...
es·*too*·dyo en ...

For more occupations and studies, see the **dictionary**.

Family

Q Do you have (a) ...?

¿Tiene ...? **pol**
tye·ne ...
¿Tienes ...? **inf**
tye·nes ...

A I (don't) have (a) ...

(No) Tengo ...
(no) *ten*·go ...

brother	un hermano	oon er·*ma*·no
children	hijos	*ee*·khos
family	una familia	oo·na fa·*mee*·lya
partner	una pareja **m&f**	oo·na pa·*re*·kha
sister	una hermana	oo·na er·*ma*·na

Q Are you married?

¿Estás casado/a? **m/f**
es·*tas* ka·*sa*·do/a

A I'm married.

Estoy casado/a. **m/f**
es·*toy* ka·*sa*·do/a

A I'm single.

Soy soltero/a. **m/f**
soy sol·*te*·ro/a

A I live with someone.	Vivo con alguien. *vee·*vo kon *al·*gyen
A I'm separated.	Estoy separado/a. m/f es·*toy* se·pa·*ra·*do/a

Talking with Children

Do you go to school or kindergarten?	¿Vas al colegio o a la guardería? vas al ko·*le·*khyo o a la gwar·de·*ree·*a
What grade are you in?	¿En qué curso estás? en ke *koor·*so es·*tas*
Do you like school?	¿Te gusta el colegio? te *goos·*ta el ko·*le·*khyo
Do you like sport?	¿Te gusta el deporte? te *goos·*ta el de·*por·*te
Do you learn (English)?	¿Aprendes (inglés)? a·*pren·*des (een·*gles*)
I come from very far away.	Vengo de muy lejos. *ven·*go de mooy *le·*khos

Farewells

It's been great meeting you.	Me ha encantado conocerte. me a en·kan·*ta·*do ko·no·*ther·*te
Keep in touch!	¡Nos mantendremos en contacto! nos man·ten·*dre·*mos en kon·*tak·*to
Are you on Facebook?	¿Estás en Facebook? es·*tas* en *feys·*book

SOCIAL MEETING PEOPLE

LANGUAGE TIP

Spanish Idioms
Even idioms translate across languages. Here are a few golden oldies:

It's like casting pearls before swine.	Es como echar margaritas a los cerdos. (lit: it's like feeding daisies to the pigs) es *ko*·mo e·*char* mar·ga·*ree*·tas a los *ther*·dos
When it rains, it pours.	Éramos pocos y parió la abuela. (lit: there were a few of us then granny gave birth) e·ra·mos *po*·kos y pa·ree·o la a·*bwe*·la
This is like watching grass grow.	Es más largo que un día sin pan. (lit: it's longer than a day without bread) es mas *lar*·go ke oon *dee*·a seen pan

If you ever visit (South Africa), you can stay with me.	Si algún día visitas (Sudáfrica), te puedes quedar conmigo. see al·*goon* dee·a vee·*see*·tas (soo·*da*·free·ka) te *pwe*·des ke·*dar* kon·*mee*·go
Q What's your (address)?	¿Cuál es tu (dirección)? kwal es too (dee·rek·*thyon*)
A Here's my ...	Ésta es mi ... **m/f** *es*·te/*es*·ta es mee ...
A Here's my address.	Ésta es mi dirección. *es*·ta es mee dee·rek·*thyon*
A Here's my email address.	Ésta es mi dirección de email. *es*·ta es mee dee·rek·*thyon* de *ee*·mayl

For more on addresses, see **directions** (p57).

Basque

Basque (*euskara*, in Basque), is spoken at the western end of the Pyrenees and along the Bay of Biscay – from Bayonne in France to Bilbao in Spain, and inland, almost to Pamplona. Dialects are also spoken, including Bizkaian, Gipuzkoan, High Navarrese, Aezkoan, Salazarese, Lapurdian, Low Navarrese and Suberoan. No one quite knows its origin, but the most likely theory is that Basque is the lone survivor of a language family that once extended across Europe, and was wiped out by the languages of the Celts, Germanic tribes and Romans.

Speaking Spanish in the Basque-speaking towns might be expected from a foreigner, but is not as warmly received as an attempt at one of the most ancient languages of Europe.

Hi!	Kaixo! *kai*·sho
Good morning.	Egun on. e·goon *on*
Good afternoon/evening.	Arratsalde on. a·*ra*·chyal·de *on*
Goodbye.	Agur. a·*goor*
Take care.	Ondo ibili. on·do ee·*beel*·ee
How are you?	Zer moduz? ser mo·*doos*
Fine, thank you.	Ongi, eskerrik asko. on·gee e·*ske*·reek *as*·ko

🔊 **LISTEN FOR**

Euskal Herrian beti jai!	e·oos·*kal* e·*ree*·an *be*·tee yai The Basque Country's always partying!
Gora gu 'ta gutarrak!	*go*·ra goo ta *goo*·ta·rak Hurray for us!

SOCIAL MEETING PEOPLE

SOCIAL MEETING PEOPLE

Excuse me.	Barkatu. bar·*ka*·too
Please.	Mesedez. me·*se*·des
Thank you.	Eskerrik asko. es·*ke*·reek *as*·ko
You're welcome.	Ez horregatik. es o·*re*·ga·teek
Do you speak English?	Ingelesez ba al dakizu? een·*ge*·le·ses ba al da·kee·soo
I know a little Basque.	Euskara apur bat badakit. e·*oos*·ka·ra a·*poor* bat ba·da·*keet*
I don't understand.	Ez dut ulertzen. es toot oo·*ler*·tzen
Could you speak in Castillian, please?	Erdaraz egingo al didazu, mesedez? er·da·ras e·*geen*·go al dee·*da*·soo me·*se*·des
How do you say that in Basque?	Nola esaten da hori euskara? *no*·la e·*sa*·ten da o·ree e·oo·ska·*ra*

CULTURE TIP

Spanish in America

Columbus' arrival in the New World in 1492 launched the era of Spanish expansion in America, one which is also reflected in the language. *Patata*, *tomate*, *cacao* and *chocolate* are just a few examples of words that entered Spanish (and consequently English) from the indigenous American languages. Bear in mind that Spanish has evolved differently in the Americas, and it's a good idea to take Lonely Planet's *Latin American Spanish* phrasebook if that's your destination.

Catalan

Catalan (*català,* in Catalan) is spoken by up to 10 million people in the northeast of Spain, a territory that comprises Catalonia, coastal Valencia and the Balearic Islands (Majorca, Minorca and Ibiza).

Outside Spain, Catalan is also spoken in Andorra, the south of France and the town of Alguer in Sardinia. Many famous creatives have been Catalan speakers: painters like Dalí, Miró and Picasso, architects like Gaudí, and writers like Mercé Rodoreda.

Despite the fact that almost all Catalan speakers from Spain are bilingual, they appreciate it when visitors attempt to communicate, if even in the simplest way, in Catalan.

Hello!	Hola! o·la
Good morning.	Bon dia. bon *dee*·a
Good afternoon.	Bona tarda. *bo*·na *tar*·da
Good evening.	Bon vespre. bon *bes*·pra
Goodbye.	Adéu. a·*the*·oo
How are you?	Com estàs? kom as·*tas*
(Very) Well.	(Molt) Bé. (mol) be
Excuse me.	Perdoni. par·*tho*·nee
Sorry.	Ho sento. oo *sen*·to
Please.	Sisplau. sees·*pla*·oo
Thank you.	Gràcies. *gra*·see·as

🔊 LISTEN FOR

Això rai!	a·*sho* ra·ee	No problem!
Quin tip de riure!	kin tip da ri·a·oo·ra	What a laugh!

Yes./No.	Sí./No. see/no
Do you speak English?	Parla anglès? *par*·la an·*gles*
Could you speak in Castilian, please?	Pot parlar castellà sisplau? pot par·*la* kas·ta·*lya* sees·*pla*·oo
I (don't) understand.	(No) Ho entenc. (no) oo an·*teng*
How do you say ...?	Com es diu ...? kom az *dee*·oo ...

Galician

Galician (*galego,* in Galician), is an official language of the Autonomous Community of Galicias and is also widely understood in the neighbouring regions of Asturias and Castilla-Léon. It's very similar to Portuguese, as the two languages have roots in Vulgar Latin.

Galicians are likely to revert to Spanish when addressing a stranger, especially a foreigner, but making a small effort to communicate in Galician will always be welcomed.

Hello!	Ola! o·la
Good day.	Bon dia. bon *dee*·a
Good afternoon/evening.	Boa tarde. *bo*·a *tar*·de

Goodbye.	Adeus. a·*de*·oos Até logo. a·*te* lo·go
Excuse me.	Perdón. per·*don*
Please.	Por favor. por fa·*vor*
Thank you.	Grácias. *gra*·see·as
Many thanks.	Moitas grácias. *moy*·tas *gra*·see·as
That's fine.	De nada. de *na*·da
Yes./No.	Si./Non. see/non
Do you speak English?	Fala inglés? *fa*·la een·*gles*
Could you speak in Castilian, please?	Pode falar en español, por favor? *po*·de fa·*la* en e·spa·*nyol* por fa·*bor*
I (don't) understand.	(Non) Entendo. (non) en·*ten*·do
What's this called in Galician?	Como se chama iso en galego? *ko*·mo se *cha*·ma *ee*·so en ga·*le*·go

Interests

KEY PHRASES

What do you do in your spare time?	¿Qué te gusta hacer en tu tiempo libre?	ke te *goos*·ta a·*ther* en too *tyem*·po *lee*·bre
Do you like (travelling)?	¿Te gusta (viajar)?	te *goos*·ta (vya·*khar*)
I (don't) like ...	(No) Me gusta ...	(no) me *goos*·ta ...

Common Interests

What do you do in your spare time?	¿Qué te gusta hacer en tu tiempo libre? ke te *goos*·ta a·*ther* en too *tyem*·po *lee*·bre
Do you like (travelling)?	¿Te gusta (viajar)? te *goos*·ta (vya·*khar*)
I like (cooking).	Me gusta (cocinar). me *goos*·ta (ko·thee·*nar*)
I don't like (hiking).	No me gusta (el excursionismo). no me *goos*·ta (el eks·koor·syo·*nees*·mo)
I (don't) like photography.	(No) Me gusta la fotografía. (no) me *goos*·ta la fo·to·gra·*fee*·a
I (don't) like shopping.	(No) Me gusta ir de compras. (no) me *goos*·ta eer de *kom*·pras

For more activities, see **sports** (p142) and the **dictionary**.

Music

Do you like to ...? ¿Te gusta ...?
te goos·ta ...

dance	ir a bailar	eer a bai·*lar*
go to concerts	ir a concertos	eer a kon·*thyer*·tos
listen to music	escuchar música	es·koo·*char* moo·see·ka
play an instrument	tocar algún instrumento	to·kar al·*goon* eens·troo·*men*·to
sing	cantar	kan·tar

SOCIAL INTERESTS

What music do you like?
ke moo·see·ka te goos·ta
¿Qué música te gusta?

Which bands do you like?	¿Qué grupos te gustan?
	ke *groo*·pos te *goos*·tan
Which singers do you like?	¿Qué cantantes te gustan?
	ke kan·*tan*·tes te *goos*·tan
What music do you like?	¿Qué música te gusta?
	ke *moo*·see·ka te *goos*·ta
classical music	música f clásica
	moo·see·ka *kla*·see·ka
jazz	jazz m
	khath
pop	música f pop
	moo·see·ka pop
rock	música f rock
	moo·see·ka rok
world music	música f étnica
	moo·see·ka *et*·nee·ka

Cinema & Theatre

I feel like going to (a comedy).	Tengo ganas de ir a (una comedia).
	ten·go *ga*·nas de eer a (*oo*·na ko·*me*·dya)
What's showing at the cinema (tonight)?	¿Qué película dan en el cine (esta noche)?
	ke pe·*lee*·koo·la dan en el *thee*·ne (*es*·ta *no*·che)
Is it in (English)?	¿Es en (inglés)?
	es en (een·*gles*)
Is it dubbed?	¿Está doblada?
	es·*ta* dob·*la*·da
Does it have (English) subtitles?	¿Tiene subtítulos (en inglés)?
	tye·ne soob·*tee*·too·los (en een·*gles*)

Have you seen ...?	¿Has visto ...? as *vees*·to ...
Q Who's in it?	¿Quién actúa? kyen ak·*too*·a
A It stars ...	Actúa ... ak·*too*·a ...
Are those seats taken?	¿Están ocupados estos asientos? es·*tan* o·koo·pa·dos es·tos a·*syen*·tos
Q Did you like the film/ play?	¿Te gustó el cine/teatro? te goos·*to* el *thee*·ne/te·*a*·tro
A I thought it was excellent/OK.	Pienso que fue excelente/ regular. *pyen*·so ke fwe eks·the·*len*·te/ re·goo·*lar*
A I thought it was long.	Pienso que fue largo. *pyen*·so ke fwe *lar*·go
I (don't) like ...	(No) Me gusta/gustan ... sg/pl (no) me *goos*·ta/*goos*·tan ...

SOCIAL INTERESTS

animated films	películas f pl de dibujos animados	pe·*lee*·koo·las de dee·*boo*·khos a·nee·*ma*·dos
comedy	comedia f	ko·*me*·dya
documentary	documentales m pl	do·koo·men·*ta*·les
drama	drama m	*dra*·ma
(Spanish) cinema	cine m (español)	*thee*·ne (es·pa·*nyol*)
horror movies	cine m de terror	*thee*·ne de te·*ror*
sci-fi	cine m de ciencia ficción	*thee*·ne de *thyen*·thya feek·*thyon*

Off to a show? See **buying tickets** (p44) and **going out** (p130).

Books & Reading

What kind of books do you read?	¿Qué tipo de libros lees? ke *tee*·po de *lee*·bros *le*·es
On this trip I'm reading ...	En este viaje estoy leyendo ... en *es*·te *vya*·khe es·*toy* le·*yen*·do ...
Have you read ...?	¿Has leído ...? as le·*ee*·do ...
Which (Spanish) author do you recommend?	¿Qué autor (español) recomiendas? ke ow·*tor* (es·pa·*nyol*) re·ko·*myen*·das
I'd recommend ...	Recomiendo a ... re·ko·*myen*·do a ...
Where can I exchange books?	¿Dónde puedo cambiar libros? *don*·de *pwe*·do kam·*byar* *lee*·bros

For more on books and reading, see **shopping** (p80).

Volunteering

I'd like to volunteer my skills.	Me gustaría ofrecer mis conocimientos. me goos·ta·*ree*·a o·fre·*ther* mees ko·no·thee·*myen*·tos
Are there any volunteer programs available in the area?	¿Hay programas de voluntariado en la zona? ai pro·*gra*·mas de vo·loon·ta·*rya*·do en la *tho*·na

Feelings & Opinions

KEY PHRASES

Are you ...?	¿Tienes/Estás ...?	tye·nes/es·tas ...
I'm (not) ...	(No) Tengo/ Estoy ...	(no) ten·go/ es·toy ...
What did you think of it?	¿Qué pensaste de eso?	ke pen·sas·te de e·so
I thought it was ...	Pienso que fue ...	pyen·so ke fwe ...
Did you hear about ...?	¿Has oído que ...?	as o·ee·do ke ...

Feelings

Feelings are described with either nouns or adjectives: the nouns use 'have' in Spanish (eg, 'I have hunger') and the adjectives use 'be' (like in English).

Q	**Are you ...?**	¿Tienes ...? tye·nes ...
A	**I'm (not) ...**	(No) Tengo ... (no) ten·go ...

cold	frío	free·o
hot	calor	ka·lor
hungry	hambre	am·bre
in a hurry	prisa	pree·sa
thirsty	sed	se

Are you ...?	¿Estás ...? es·tas ...
I'm (not) ...	(No) Estoy ... (no) es·toy ...

annoyed	fastidiado/a m/f	fas·tee·dya·do/a
embarrassed	avergonzado/a m/f	a·ver·gon·tha·do/a
happy	feliz m&f	fe·leeth
sad	triste m&f	trees·te
tired	cansado/a m/f	kan·sa·do/a
well	bien m&f	byen

I'm a little (sad).	Estoy un poco (triste). m&f es·toy oon po·ko (trees·te)
I'm quite (disappointed).	Estoy bastante (decepcionado/a). m/f es·toy bas·tan·te (de·thep·thyo na·do/a)
I feel very (lucky).	Me siento muy (afortunado/a). m/f me syen·to mooy (a·for·too·na·do/a)

If you're not feeling well, see **health** (p158).

Opinions

Did you like it?	¿Te gustó? te goos·to
What did you think of it?	¿Qué pensaste de eso? ke pen·sas·te de e·so

A I thought it was ...

Pienso que fue ...
pyen·so ke fwe ...

A It's ...

Es ...
es ...

beautiful	bonito/a m/f	bo·*nee*·to/a
bizarre	raro/a m/f	*ra*·ro/a
entertaining	entretenido/a m/f	en·tre·te·*nee*·do/a
excellent	fantástico/a m/f	fan·*tas*·tee·ko/a
horrible	horrible m&f	o·*ree*·ble

I thought it was OK.	Pienso que estaba bien. *pyen*·so ke es·*ta*·ba byen
He's/She's the best.	Es un trozo de pan. (lit: he's/she's a piece of bread) es oon *tro*·tho de pan
I disagree!	No estoy de acuerdo! no es·*toy* de a·*kwer*·do
Yes, but ...	Sí, pero ... see *pe*·ro ...
Whatever.	Lo que sea. lo ke *se*·a

Politics & Social Issues

Q Who do you vote for?	¿A quién votas? a kyen *vo*·tas
A I support the ... party.	Apoyo al partido ... a·*po*·yo al par·*tee*·do ...
Did you hear about ...?	¿Has oído que ...? as o·*ee*·do ke ...
Are you in favour of ...?	¿Estás a favor de ...? es·*tas* a fa·*vor* de ...

SOCIAL FEELINGS & OPINIONS

🔊 LISTEN FOR

Claro.	*kla·ro*	Sure.
¡Claro que sí!	*kla·ro ke see*	Of course!
¡De ningún modo!	*de neen·goon mo·do*	No way!
Era broma.	*e·ra bro·ma*	Just joking.
Está bien.	*es·ta byen*	It's OK.
Estoy bien.	*es·toy byen*	I'm OK.
Quizás.	*kee·thas*	Maybe.
Sin problema.	*seen pro·ble·ma*	No problem.
Un momento.	*oon mo·men·to*	Just a minute.
Vale.	*va·le*	OK.
¡Ya lo creo!	*ya lo kre·o*	You bet!

How do people feel about ...?	¿Cómo se siente la gente de ...? *ko·mo se syen·te la khen·te de ...*
the economy	economía f *e·ko·no·mee·a*
health care	seguro m médico *se·goo·ro me·dee·ko*
immigration	inmigración f *een·mee·gra·thyon*
war in ...	guerra f en ... *ge·ra en ...*

The Environment

Is there an environmental problem here?	¿Aquí hay un problema con el medio ambiente? *a·kee ai oon pro·ble·ma kon el me·dyo am·byen·te*

Is this (forest) protected?	¿Está este (bosque) protegido? es·ta es·te (bos·ke) pro·te·khee·do
Where can I recycle this?	¿Dónde se puede reciclar esto? don·de se pwe·de re·thee·klar es·to
climate change	cambio m climático kam·byo klee·ma·tee·ko
pollution	contaminación f kon·ta·mee·na·thyon
recycling	reciclaje m re·thee·kla·khe

SOCIAL

FEELINGS & OPINIONS

I'm happy.
es·toy fe·leeth
Estoy feliz.

Going Out

KEY PHRASES

What's on tonight?	¿Qué hay esta noche?	ke ai es·ta no·che
Where are the clubs?	¿Dónde están las discotecas?	don·de es·tan las dees·ko·te·kas
Would you like to go for a coffee?	¿Quieres que vayamos a tomar un café?	kye·res ke va·ya·mos a to·mar oon ka·fe
What time shall we meet?	¿A qué hora quedamos?	a ke o·ra ke·da·mos
Where will we meet?	¿Dónde quedamos?	don·de ke·da·mos

Where to Go

What's there to do in the evenings?	¿Qué se puede hacer por las noches? ke se pwe·de a·ther por las no·ches
What's on ...?	¿Qué hay ...? ke ai ...

locally	en la zona	en la tho·na
this weekend	este fin de semana	es·te feen de se·ma·na
today	hoy	oy
tonight	esta noche	es·ta no·che

Where are there gay venues?	¿Dónde hay lugares gay? don·de ai loo·ga·res gai

Where are there places to eat?	¿Dónde hay lugares para comer?	*don·de ai loo·ga·res pa·ra ko·mer*
Where are the clubs?	¿Dónde están las discotecas?	*don·de es·tan las dees·ko·te·kas*
Where are there pubs?	¿Dónde hay pubs?	*don·de ai poobs*
Is there a local ... guide?	¿Hay una guía ... de la zona?	*ai oo·na gee·a ... de la tho·na*

entertainment	del ocio	del o·thyo
film	de cine	de thee·ne
gay	de lugares gay	de loo·ga·res gai
music	de música	de moo·see·ka

I feel like going to a/the ...   Tengo ganas de ir ...
ten·go ga·nas de eer ...

ballet	al ballet	al ba·le
bar	a un bar	a oon bar
cafe	a un café	a oon ka·fe
concert	a un concierto	a oon kon·thyer·to
karaoke bar	a un bar de karaoke	a oon bar de ka·ra·o·ke
movies	al cine	al thee·ne
nightclub	a una discoteca	a oo·na dees·ko·te·ka
party	a una fiesta	a oo·na fyes·ta
restaurant	a un restaurante	a oon res·tow·ran·te
theatre	al teatro	al te·a·tro

Invitations

What are you doing this evening?	¿Qué haces esta noche? ke *a*·thes es·ta *no*·che
What are you up to (right now)?	¿Qué haces (ahora)? ke *a*·thes (a·o·ra)
Would you like to go for a ...?	¿Quieres que vayamos a ...? *kye*·res ke va·*ya*·mos a ...

coffee	tomar un café	to·*mar* oon ka·*fe*
drink	tomar algo	to·*mar* al·go
meal	comer	ko·*mer*
walk	pasear	pa·se·*ar*

I feel like going dancing.	Me apetece ir a bailar. me a·pe·*te*·the eer a bai·*lar*
I feel like going out somewhere.	Me apetece salir. me a·pe·*te*·the sa·*leer*
My round.	Invito yo. een·*vee*·to yo
Do you know a good restaurant?	¿Conoces algún buen restaurante? ko·*no*·thes al·*goon* bwen res·tow·*ran*·te
Do you want to come to the (...) concert with me?	¿Quieres venir conmigo al concierto (de ...)? *kye*·res ve·*neer* kon·*mee*·go al kon·*thyer*·to (de ...)
We're having a party.	Vamos a dar una fiesta. *va*·mos a dar oo·na *fyes*·ta
Do you want to come?	¿Por qué no vienes? por ke no *vye*·nes
Are you ready?	¿Estás listo/a? **m/f** es·*tas* lees·to/a

CULTURE TIP

Movie Subtitles
Foreign movies are usually dubbed into Spanish, but in bigger cities you'll find that some
films have Spanish subtitles. Look out for *v.o.* (*version
original* ver·*syon* o·ree·khee·*nal*, 'original version') or
v.o.s. (*version original subtitulada* ver·*syon* o·ree·khee·*nal*
soob·tee·too·*la*·da, 'original version with subtitles') in
listings.

Responding to Invitations

Sure!	¡Por supuesto! por soo·*pwes*·to
Yes, I'd love to.	Me encantaría. me en·kan·ta·*ree*·a
Where will we go?	¿A dónde vamos? a *don*·de va·*mos*
That's very kind of you.	Es muy amable por tu parte. es mooy a·*ma*·ble por too *par*·te
No, I'm afraid I can't.	Lo siento pero no puedo. lo *syen*·to *pe*·ro no *pwe*·do
Sorry, I can't sing/dance.	Lo siento, no sé cantar/ bailar. lo *syen*·to no se kan·*tar*/ bai·*lar*
What about tomorrow?	¿Qué tal mañana? ke tal ma·*nya*·na

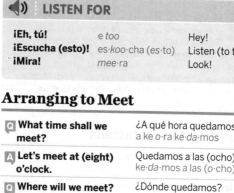

🔊 LISTEN FOR

¡Eh, tú!	e *too*	Hey!
¡Escucha (esto)!	es·*koo*·cha (es·to)	Listen (to this)!
¡Mira!	*mee*·ra	Look!

Arranging to Meet

Q What time shall we meet?	¿A qué hora quedamos? a ke o·ra ke·*da*·mos
A Let's meet at (eight) o'clock.	Quedamos a las (ocho). ke·*da*·mos a las (o·cho)
Q Where will we meet?	¿Dónde quedamos? don·de ke·*da*·mos
A Let's meet at the (entrance).	Quedamos en (la entrada). ke·*da*·mos en (la en·*tra*·da)
I'll pick you up.	Paso a recogerte. *pa*·so a re·ko·*kher*·te
I'll be coming later.	Iré más tarde. ee·*re* mas *tar*·de
Where will you be?	¿Dónde estarás? don·de es·ta·*ras*
OK!	¡Hecho! *e*·cho
I'll see you then.	Nos vemos. nos *ve*·mos
See you later/tomorrow.	Hasta luego/mañana. *as*·ta *lwe*·go/ma·*nya*·na
I'm looking forward to it.	Tengo muchas ganas de ir. *ten*·go *moo*·chas *ga*·nas de eer

Sorry I'm late.	Siento llegar tarde. *syen·to lye·gar tar·de*
Never mind.	No pasa nada. *no pa·sa na·da*

Nightclubs & Bars

Where can we go (salsa) dancing?	¿Dónde podemos ir a bailar (la salsa)? *don·de po·de·mos eer a bai·lar (la sal·sa)*
Q What type of music do you like?	¿Qué tipo de música prefieres? *ke tee·po de moo·see·ka pre·fye·res*
A I really like (reggae).	Me encanta (el reggae). *me en·kan·ta (el re·gai)*
Come on!	¡Vamos! *va·mos*
This place is great!	¡Este lugar me encanta! *es·te loo·gar me en·kan·ta*

For more on bars and drinks, see **eating out** (p177).

Drugs

I don't take drugs.	No consumo ningún tipo de drogas. *no kon·soo·mo neen·goon tee·po de dro·gas*
I take ... occasionally.	Tomo ... de vez en cuando. *to·mo ... de veth en kwan·do*
Do you want to have a smoke?	¿Nos fumamos un porro? *nos foo·ma·mos oon po·ro*
Do you have a light?	¿Tienes fuego? *tye·nes fwe·go*

See also **police** (p156).

SOCIAL GOING OUT

Romance

KEY PHRASES

Would you like to do something?	¿Quieres hacer algo?	kye·res a·ther al·go
I love you.	Te quiero.	te kye·ro
Leave me alone, please	Déjame en paz, por favor.	de·kha·me en path por fa·vor

Asking Someone Out

Don't be surprised if invitations come late in the day. Social life in Spain continues well into the night: sometimes people begin to eat dinner at 10pm and many clubs open at midnight.

Q Would you like to do something (tonight)?	¿Quieres hacer algo (esta noche)? kye·res a·ther al·go (es·ta no·che)
A Yes, I'd love to.	Me encantaría. me en·kan·ta·ree·a
A I'm busy.	Estoy ocupado/a. m/f es·toy o·koo·pa·do/a

Pick-up Lines

Would you like a drink?	¿Te apetece una copa? te a·pe·te·the oo·na ko·pa
Do you have a light?	¿Tienes fuego? tye·nes fwe·go

| You're great. | Eres estupendo/a. m/f
e·res es·too·pen·do/a |
| You mustn't come here much, because I would have noticed you sooner. | No debes venir mucho por aquí porque me habría fijado en ti antes.
no de·bes ve·neer moo·cho por a·kee por·ke me a·bree·a fee·kha·do en tee an·tes |

Rejections

I'm here with my boyfriend/girlfriend.	Estoy aquí con mi novio/a. m/f es·toy a·kee kon mee no·vyo/a
Excuse me, I have to go now.	Lo siento, pero me tengo que ir. lo syen·to pe·ro me ten·go ke eer
Leave me alone, please.	Déjame en paz, por favor. de·kha·me en path por fa·vor
Go away!	¡Vete! ve·te
Hey, I'm not interested in talking to you.	Mira tío/a, es que no me interesa hablar contigo. m/f mee·ra tee·o/a es ke no me een·te·re·sa ab·lar kon·tee·go

Getting Closer

| Can I kiss you? | ¿Te puedo besar?
te pwe·do be·sar |
| Do you want to come inside for a drink? | ¿Quieres entrar a tomar algo?
kye·res en·trar a to·mar al·go |

LANGUAGE TIP

Masculine & Feminine

In this book, masculine forms appear before the feminine forms. If you see a word ending in *-o/a*, it means the masculine form ends in *-o* and the feminine form ends in *-a* (ie you replace the *-o* ending with the *-a* ending to make it feminine), eg *hijo/a* ee·kho/a m/f (son/daughter). The same goes for the plural endings *-os/as*, eg *hijos/as* ee·khos/as m/f (sons/daughters). If you see an *(a)* between brackets at the end of a word, it means you have to add it in order to make that word feminine, eg *español(a)* es·pa·*nyol*/es·pa·*nyo*·la m/f (Spanish). In other cases we spell out the whole word, eg *actor/actriz* ak·*tor*/ak·*treeth* m/f (actor/actress). See also **gender** (p19).

Do you want a massage?	¿Quieres un masaje? *kye*·res oon ma·*sa*·khe
Let's go to bed!	¡Vámonos a la cama! *va*·mo·nos a la *ka*·ma

Sex

Kiss me!	¡Dame un beso! *da*·me oon *be*·so
I want you.	Te deseo. te de·*se*·o
I want to make love to you.	Quiero hacerte el amor. *kye*·ro a·*ther*·te el a·*mor*
Do you have a condom?	¿Tienes un condón? *tye*·nes oon kon·*don*
Q **Do you like this?**	¿Esto te gusta? *es*·to te *goos*·ta
A **I (don't) like that.**	Eso (no) me gusta. *e*·so (no) me *goos*·ta

I think we should stop now.	Pienso que deberíamos parar. *pyen*·so ke de·be·*ree*·a·mos pa·*rar*
Oh yeah!	¡Así! a·*see*
That was amazing.	Eso fue increíble. e·so fwe een·kre·*ee*·ble
Can I stay over?	¿Puedo quedarme? *pwe*·do ke·*dar*·me

Love

Q Do you love me?	¿Me quieres? me *kye*·res
A I love you.	Te quiero. te *kye*·ro
I think we're good together.	Creo que estamos muy bien juntos. *kre*·o ke es·*ta*·mos mooy byen *khoon*·tos

---

LANGUAGE TIP

Endearments

Here are a few terms of endearment you might use with the one you love.

heart	corazón m&f	ko·ra·*thon*
heaven	cielo m&f	*thye*·lo
little love	amorcito/a m/f	a·mor·*thee*·to/a
my life	mi vida m&f	mee *vee*·da
my love	mi amor m&f	mee a·*mor*
treasure	tesoro m&f	te·*so*·ro

Beliefs & Culture

KEY PHRASES

What's your religion?	¿Cuál es su/tu religión? pol/inf	kwal es soo/too re·lee·khyon
I'm ...	Soy ...	soy ...
I'm sorry, it's against my beliefs.	Lo siento, eso va en contra de mis creencias.	lo syen·to e·so va en kon·tra de mees kre·en·thyas

Religion

Q What's your religion? ¿Cuál es su/tu religión? pol/inf
kwal es soo/too re·lee·khyon

A I'm (not) ... (No) Soy ...
(no) soy ...

agnostic	agnóstico/a m/f	ag·nos·tee·ko/a
Buddhist	budista m&f	boo·dees·ta
Catholic	católico/a m/f	ka·to·lee·ko/a
Christian	cristiano/a m/f	krees·tya·no/a
Hindu	hindú m&f	een·doo
Jewish	judío/a m/f	khoo·dee·o/a
Muslim	musulmán m	moo·sool·man
	musulmana f	moo·sool·ma·na

I'm (not) religious. (No) Soy religioso/a. m/f
(no) soy re·lee·khyo·so/a

I (don't) believe in God.	(No) Creo en Dios. (no) kre·o en dyos
I (don't) believe in destiny/fate.	(No) Creo en el destino. (no) kre·o en el des·tee·no
Can I pray here?	¿Puedo rezar aquí? pwe·do re·thar a·kee

Cultural Differences

Is this a local custom?	¿Esto es una costumbre local? es·to es oo·na kos·toom·bre lo·kal
This is fun.	Esto es divertido. es·to es dee·ver·tee·do
This is (very) interesting.	Esto es (muy) interesante. es·to es (mooy) een·te·re·san·te
This is (very) different.	Esto es (muy) diferente. es·to es (mooy) dee·fe·ren·te
I'm not used to this.	No estoy acostumbrado/a a esto. m/f no es·toy a·kos·toom·bra·do/a a es·to
I'm sorry, it's against my beliefs.	Lo siento, eso va en contra de mis creencias. lo syen·to e·so va en kon·tra de mees kre·en·thyas
I'll try it.	Lo probaré. lo pro·ba·re
Sorry, I didn't mean to do/ say anything wrong.	Lo siento, lo hice/dije sin querer. lo syen·to lo ee·the/dee·khe seen ke·rer

Sports

KEY PHRASES

What sport do you play?	¿Qué deporte practicas?	ke de·*por*·te prak·*tee*·kas
What's your favourite team?	¿Cuál es tu equipo favorito?	kwal es too e·*kee*·po fa·vo·*ree*·to
What's the score?	¿Cómo van?	*ko*·mo van

Sporting Interests

Q What sport do you play?	¿Qué deporte practicas?	ke de·*por*·te prak·*tee*·kas
Q What sport do you follow?	¿A qué deporte eres aficionado/a? m/f	a ke de·*por*·te e·res a·fee·thyo·*na*·do/a
A I play/do ...	Practico ...	prak·*tee*·ko ...
A I follow ...	Soy aficionado/a al ... m/f	soy a·fee·thyo·*na*·do/a al ...

basketball	baloncesto m	ba·lon·*thes*·to
cycling	ciclismo m	thee·*klees*·mo
football (soccer)	fútbol m	*foot*·bol
tennis	tenis m	*te*·nis
volleyball	voleibol m	*vo*·ley·bol

For more sports, see the **dictionary**.

Do you like sport?	¿Te gustan los deportes? te *goos*·tan los de·*por*·tes
I like watching it.	Me gusta mirar. me *goos*·ta mee·*rar*
Who's your favourite sportsperson?	¿Quién es tu deportista favorito/a? **m/f** kyen es too de·por·*tees*·ta fa·vo·*ree*·to/a
What's your favourite team?	¿Cuál es tu equipo favorito? kwal es too e·*kee*·po fa·vo·*ree*·to

Going to a Game

Would you like to go to a (basketball) game?	¿Te gustaría ir a un partido de (baloncesto)? te goos·ta·*ree*·a eer a oon par·*tee*·do de (ba·lon·*thes*·to)
Who are you supporting?	¿Con qué equipo vas? kon ke e·*kee*·po vas
Who's playing?	¿Quién juega? kyen *khwe*·ga
Who's winning?	¿Quién gana? kyen *ga*·na
That was a (boring) game.	Ese partido fue (aburrido). e·se par·*tee*·do fwe (a·boo·*ree*·do)
That was a (great) game!	¡Ese partido fue (cojonudo)! e·se par·*tee*·do fwe (ko·kho·*noo*·do)
What's the score?	¿Cómo van? *ko*·mo van

SOCIAL SPORTS

Local Sports
If you hear the sounds of bat, ball and exertion, it may be *pelotari* (pelota players) enjoying the traditional game of *pelota vasca*, Basque handball. It's also known as *jai-alai* in Basque.

ball	pelota f	pe·*lo*·ta
striker	delantero/a m/f	de·lan·*te*·ro/a
wall	frontón m	fron·*ton*

Playing Sport

Q Do you want to play?	¿Quieres jugar? kye·res khoo·*gar*
A Yeah, that'd be great.	Sí, me encantaría. see me en·kan·ta·*ree*·a
A Not at the moment, thanks.	Ahora mismo no, gracias. a·o·ra *mees*·mo no *gra*·thyas
A I have an injury.	Tengo una lesión. *ten*·go oo·na le·*syon*
Can I join in?	¿Puedo jugar? *pwe*·do khoo·*gar*
Where's the best place to run around here?	¿Cuál es el mejor sitio para hacer footing por aquí cerca? kwal es el me·*khor see*·tyo *pa*·ra a·*ther* foo·teen por a·*kee ther*·ka
Where's the nearest gym?	¿Dónde está el gimnasio más cercano? *don*·de es·*ta* el kheem·*na*·syo mas ther·*ka*·no
Do I have to be a member to attend?	¿Hay que ser socio/a para entrar? m/f ai ke ser *so*·thyo/a *pa*·ra en·*trar*

Where's the nearest swimming pool?	¿Dónde está la piscina más cercana? *don·de es·ta la pees·thee·na mas ther·ka·na*
Where's the nearest tennis court?	¿Dónde está la pista de tenis más cercana? *don·de es·ta la pees·ta de te·nees mas ther·ka·na*
Where are the change rooms?	¿Dónde están los vestuarios? *don·de es·tan los ves·twa·ryos*
What's the charge per ...?	¿Cúanto cobran por ...? *kwan·to ko·bran por ...*

day	día	*dee·a*
game	partida	*par·tee·da*
hour	hora	*o·ra*
visit	visita	*vee·see·ta*

| Can I hire a ...? | ¿Es posible alquilar una ...? *es po·see·ble al·kee·lar oo·na ...* |

ball	pelota	*pe·lo·ta*
bicycle	bicicleta	*bee·thee·kle·ta*
court	cancha	*kan·cha*
racquet	raqueta	*ra·ke·ta*

What a goal/pass!	¡Qué gol/pase! *ke gol/pa·se*
Your/My point.	Tu/Mi punto. *too/mee poon·to*
Kick it to me!	¡Pásamelo! *pa·sa·me·lo*

SOCIAL SPORTS

◀)) LISTEN FOR

fuera de juego	*fwe*·ra de *khwe*·go	offside
penalty m	pe·*nal*·tee	penalty
portero m	por·*te*·ro	goalkeeper
saque m **de esquina**	*sa*·ke de es·*kee*·na	corner
tiro m **libre**	*tee*·ro *lee*·bre	free kick

You're a good player.	Juegas bien. *khwe*·gas byen
Thanks for the game.	Gracias por el partido. *gra*·thyas por el par·*tee*·do

Soccer/Football

Who plays for (Real Madrid)?	¿Quién juega en el (Real Madrid)? kyen *khwe*·ga en el (re·*al* ma·*dreeth*)
What a terrible team!	¡Qué equipo más espantoso! ke e·*kee*·po mas es·pan·*to*·so
He's a great player.	Es un gran jugador. es oon gran khoo·ga·*dor*
He played brilliantly in the match against (Italy).	Jugó de fenomenal en el partido contra (Italia). khoo·*go* de fe·no·me·*nal* en el par·*tee*·do *kon*·tra (ee·*ta*·lya)
Which team is at the top of the league?	¿Qué equipo está en primera posición en la liga? ke e·*kee*·po es·*ta* en pree·*me*·ra po·see·*thyon* en la *lee*·ga

Outdoors

KEY PHRASES

Do we need a guide?	¿Se necesita un guía?	se ne·the·*see*·ta oon *gee*·a
I'm lost.	Estoy perdido/a. m/f	es·*toy* per·*dee*·do/a
What's the weather like?	¿Qué tiempo hace?	ke *tyem*·po a·the

Hiking

There's plenty of walking, hiking and mountaineering to do in Spain. A recognised cross-country walking trail is known as *Gran Recorrido (GR)* gran re·ko·*ree*·do, while the shorter walking paths scattered throughout the country are called *Pequeños Recorridos (PR)* pe·*ke*·nyos re·ko·*ree*·dos.

Where can I find out about hiking trails?	¿Dónde hay información sobre caminos rurales de la zona? *don*·de ai een·for·ma·*thyon* *so*·bre ka·*mee*·nos roo·*ra*·les de la *tho*·na
Do we need a guide?	¿Se necesita un guía? se ne·the·*see*·ta oon *gee*·a
Are there guided treks?	¿Se organizan excursiones guiadas? se or·ga·*nee*·than eks·koor·*syo*·nes gee·*a*·das

Where can I ...?	**¿Dónde puedo ...?** *don·de pwe·do ...*	
buy supplies	comprar víveres	kom·*prar* vee·ver·es
find someone who knows this area	encontrar a alguien que conozca el área	en·kon·*trar* a *al*·gyen ke ko·*noth*·ka el *a*·re·a
get a map	obtener un mapa	ob·te·*ner* oon *ma*·pa
hire hiking gear	alquilar un equipo para ir de excursion	al·kee·*lar* oon e·*kee*·po *pa*·ra eer de eks·koor·*syon*

How long is the trail?	¿Cuántos kilómetros tiene el camino? *kwan*·tos kee·*lo*·me·tros *tye*·ne el ka·*mee*·no

How high is the climb?	¿A qué altura se escala? a ke al·*too*·ra se es·*ka*·la

Do we need to take bedding?	¿Se necesita llevar algo en qué dormir? se ne·the·*see*·ta lye·*var* *al*·go en ke dor·*meer*

Do we need to take food/water?	¿Se necesita llevar comida/agua? se ne·the·*see*·ta lye·*var* ko·*mee*·da/a·gwa

Is the track (well-)marked?	¿Es (bien) marcado el sendero? es (byen) mar·*ka*·do el sen·*de*·ro

Is the track open?	¿Es abierto el sendero? es a·*byer*·to el sen·*de*·ro

🔍 LOOK FOR

Por Aquí a ...	por a·*kee* a ...	This Way To ...
Prohibido Acampar	pro·ee·*bee*·do a·kam·*par*	No Camping
Terreno de Cámping	te·*re*·no de *kam*·peen	Camping Ground

Is the track scenic?	¿Es pintoresco el sendero? es peen·to·*res*·ko el sen·*de*·ro
Which is the easiest/ shortest route?	¿Cuál es el camino más fácil/corto? kwal es el ka·*mee*·no mas *fa*·theel/*kor*·to
Which is the most interesting route?	¿Cuál es el camino más interesante? kwal es el ka·*mee*·no mas een·te·re·*san*·te
Where's a/the ...?	¿Dónde hay ...? *don*·de ai ...

camping site	un cámping	oon *kam*·peen
village	un pueblo	oon *pwe*·blo
showers	duchas	*doo*·chas
toilets	servicios	ser·*vee*·thyos

Where have you come from?	¿De dónde vienes? de *don*·de *vye*·nes
How long did it take?	¿Cuánto ha tardado? *kwan*·to a tar·*da*·do
Does this path go to ...?	¿Este camino va a ...? *es*·te ka·*mee*·no va a ...
Can we go through here?	¿Se puede pasar por aquí? se *pwe*·de pa·*sar* por a·*kee*

🔍 LOOK FOR

¡Prohibido Nadar! pro·ee·*bee*·do na·*dar* No Swimming!	

Is the water OK to drink?	¿Se puede beber el agua? se *pwe*·de be·*ber* el *a*·gwa
Is it safe?	¿Es seguro? es se·*goo*·ro
Is there a hut there?	¿Hay una cabaña allí? ai *oo*·na ka·*ba*·nya a·*lyee*
When does it get dark?	¿A qué hora oscurece? a ke *o*·ra os·koo·*re*·the
I'm lost.	Estoy perdido/a. **m/f** es·*toy* per·*dee*·do/a

At the Beach

Where's the best beach?	¿Dónde está la playa mejor? *don*·de es·*ta* la *pla*·ya me·*khor*
Where's the nearest beach?	¿Dónde está la playa más cercana? *don*·de es·*ta* la *pla*·ya mas ther·*ka*·na
Is it safe to dive/swim here?	¿Es seguro bucear/nadar aquí? es se·*goo*·ro boo·the·*ar*/na·*dar* a·*kee*
What time is high/low tide?	¿A qué hora es la marea alta/baja? a ke *o*·ra es la ma·*re*·a *al*·ta/*ba*·kha
How much to rent a chair?	¿Cuánto por alquilar una silla? *kwan*·to por al·kee·*lar* *oo*·na *see*·lya

| How much to rent an umbrella? (for sun) | ¿Cuánto por alquilar un parasol?
*kwan·*to por al·kee·*lar* oon pa·ra·*sol* |

Weather

Q What's the weather like?

¿Qué tiempo hace?
ke *tyem·*po a·the

A Today it's ...

Hoy hace ...
oy a·the ...

cold	frío	*free·*o
freezing	un frío que pela	oon *free·*o ke *pe·*la
hot	mucho calor	*moo·*cho ka·*lor*
sunny	sol	sol
warm	calor	ka·*lor*
windy	viento	*vyen·*to

A (Today) It's raining.

(Hoy) Está lloviendo.
(oy) es·*ta* lyo·*vyen·*do

A (Today) It's snowing.

(Hoy) Está nevando.
(oy) es·*ta* ne·*van·*do

Q What's the weather forecast?

¿Cuál es el pronóstico del tiempo?
kwal es el pro·*nos·*tee·ko del *tyem·*po

A (Tomorrow) It will be raining.

(Mañana) Lloverá.
(ma·*nya·*na) lyo·ve·*ra*

Where can I buy a rain jacket?

¿Dónde puedo comprar un impermeable?
*don·*de *pwe·*do kom·*prar* oon eem·per·me·a·ble

SOCIAL OUTDOORS

Where can I buy sunblock?	¿Dónde puedo comprar crema solar? *don·de pwe·do kom·prar kre·ma so·lar*
Where can I buy an umbrella? (for rain)	¿Dónde puedo comprar un paraguas? *don·de pwe·do kom·prar oon pa·ra·gwas*
hail	granizo m *gra·nee·tho*
storm	tormenta f *tor·men·ta*
sun	sol m *sol*

Flora & Fauna

What ... is that?	¿Qué ... es ése/ésa? m/f *ke ... es e·se/e·sa*

animal	animal m	*a·nee·mal*
bird	pájaro m	*pa·kha·ro*
flower	flor f	*flor*
plant	planta f	*plan·ta*
tree	árbol m	*ar·bol*

Can you eat the fruit?	¿Se puede comer la fruta? *se pwe·de ko·mer la froo·ta*
Is it endangered?	¿Está en peligro de extinción? *es·ta en pe·lee·gro de eks·teen·thyon*
Is it common?	¿Es común? *es ko·moon*

For geographical and agricultural terms, and names of animals and plants, see the **dictionary**.

Safe Travel

Emergencies

KEY PHRASES

Help!	¡Socorro!	so·ko·ro
There's been an accident.	Ha habido un accidente.	a a·bee·do oon ak·thee·den·te
It's an emergency!	¡Es una emergencia!	es oo·na e·mer·khen·thee·ya

Help!	¡Socorro! so·ko·ro	
Stop!	¡Pare! pa·re	
Go away!	¡Váyase! va·ya·se	
Leave me alone!	¡Déjame en paz! de·kha·me en path	
Thief!	¡Ladrón! lad·ron	
Fire!	¡Fuego! fwe·go	
It's an emergency!	¡Es una emergencia! es oo·na e·mer·khen·thee·ya	
There's been an accident.	Ha habido un accidente. a a·bee·do oon ak·thee·den·te	
Do you have a first-aid kit?	¿Tiene un botiquín de primeros auxilios? tye·ne oon bo·tee·keen de pree·me·ros owk·see·lyos	

🔊 LISTEN FOR

¡Es peligroso!	es pe·lee·gro·so	It's dangerous!

Call the police!	¡Llame a la policía! lya·me a la po·lee·thee·a
Call a doctor!	¡Llame a un médico! lya·me a oon me·dee·ko
Call an ambulance!	¡Llame a una ambulancia! lya·me a oo·na am·boo·lan·thya
Could you help me, please?	¿Me puede ayudar, por favor? me pwe·de a·yoo·dar por fa·vor
I have to use the telephone.	Necesito usar el teléfono. ne·the·see·to oo·sar el te·le·fo·no
I'm lost.	Estoy perdido/a. m/f es·toy per·dee·do/a
Where are the toilets?	¿Dónde están los servicios? don·de es·tan los ser·vee·thyos

Police

KEY PHRASES

Where's the police station?	¿Dónde está la comisaría?	*don*·de es·*ta* la ko·mee·sa·*ree*·a
I want to contact my embassy/consulate.	Quiero ponerme en contacto con mi embajada/consulado.	*kye*·ro po·*ner*·me en kon·*tak*·to kon mee em·ba·*kha*·da/kon·soo·*la*·do
My bag was stolen.	Mi bolso fue robado.	mee *bol*·so fwe ro·*ba*·do

In an emergency, call the police. They will then put you through to other emergency services (fire brigade and ambulance). For more on making a call, see **communications** (p85).

Where's the police station?	¿Dónde está la comisaría? *don*·de es·*ta* la ko·mee·sa·*ree*·a
I want to report an offence.	Quiero denunciar un delito. *kye*·ro de·noon·*thyar* oon de·*lee*·to
I've been robbed.	Me han robado. me an ro·*ba*·do
I've been raped.	He sido violado/a. m/f e *see*·do vee·o·*la*·do/a
It was him/her.	Fue él/ella. fwe el/e·lya
My (money) was stolen.	Mi (dinero) fue robado. mee (dee·*ne*·ro) fwe ro·*ba*·do
My (bag/handbag) was stolen.	Mi (bolso) fue robado. mee (*bol*·so) fwe ro·*ba*·do

My (bags/suitcases) were stolen.	Mis (maletas) fueron robadas. mee (ma·*le*·tas) fwe·*ron* ro·*ba*·das
I've lost (my passport).	He perdido (mi pasaporte). e per·*dee*·do (mee pa·sa·*por*·te)
What am I accused of?	¿De qué me acusan? de ke me a·*ku*·san
I didn't realise I was doing anything wrong.	No sabía que estaba haciendo algo mal. no sa·*bee*·a ke es·*ta*·ba a·*thyen*·do *al*·go mal
I'm innocent.	Soy inocente. soy ee·no·*then*·te
I want to contact my embassy/consulate.	Quiero ponerme en contacto con mi embajada/ consulado. *kye*·ro po·*ner*·me en kon·*tak*·to kon mee em·ba·*kha*·da/ kon·soo·*la*·do
Can I call a lawyer?	¿Puedo llamar a un abogado? *pwe*·do lya·*mar* a oon a·bo·*ga*·do
I need a lawyer who speaks (English).	Necesito un abogado que hable (inglés). ne·the·*see*·to oon a·bo·*ga*·do ke *a*·ble (een·*gles*)
Can I have a copy, please?	¿Puede darme una copia, por favor? *pwe*·de *dar*·me *oo*·na *ko*·pya por fa·*vor*
This drug is for personal use.	Esta droga es para uso personal. es·ta *dro*·ga es *pa*·ra *oo*·so per·so·*nal*
I have a prescription for this drug.	Tengo receta para esta droga. *ten*·go re·*the*·ta *pa*·ra es·ta *dro*·ga

Health

KEY PHRASES

Where's the nearest hospital?	¿Dónde está el hospital más cercano?	*don*·de es·*ta* el os·*pee*·tal mas ther·*ka*·no
I'm sick.	Estoy enfermo/a. m/f	es·*toy* en·*fer*·mo/a
I need a doctor.	Necesito un doctor.	ne·the·*see*·to oon dok·*tor*
I'm on regular medication for ...	Estoy bajo medicación para ...	es·*toy* ba·kho me·dee·ka·*thyon* *pa*·ra ...
I'm allergic to ...	Soy alérgico/a a... m/f	soy a·*ler*·khee·ko/a a ...

Doctor

Where's the nearest ...?	¿Dónde está ... más cercano/a? m/f *don*·de es·*ta* ... mas ther·*ka*·no/a

chemist	la farmacia f	la far·*ma*·thya
dentist	el dentista m	el den·*tees*·ta
doctor	el médico m	el *me*·dee·ko
hospital	el hospital m	el os·pee·*tal*
medical centre	el consultorio m	el kon·sool·*to*·ryo
optometrist	el oculista m	el o·koo·*lees*·ta

Etiquette Tip
A polite way to respond to someone sneezing is by saying *¡Salud!* sa·*loo* (health) or *¡Jesús!* khe·*soos* (lit: 'Jesus').

I need a doctor (who speaks English).	Necesito un doctor (que hable inglés). ne·the·*see*·to oon dok·*tor* (ke a·ble een·*gles*)
Could I see a female doctor?	¿Puede examinarme una doctora? *pwe*·de ek·sa·mee·*nar*·me oo·na dok·*to*·ra
I've run out of my medication.	Se me terminaron los medicamentos. se me ter·mee·*na*·ron los me·dee·ka·*men*·tos
This is my usual medicine.	Éste es mi medicamento habitual. *es*·te es mee me·dee·ka·*men*·to a·bee·too·*al*
I don't want a blood transfusion.	No quiero que me hagan una transfusión de sangre. no *kye*·ro ke me *a*·gan oo·na trans·foo·*syon* de *san*·gre
Please use a new syringe.	Por favor, use una jeringa nueva. por fa·*vor* oo·se oo·na khe·*reen*·ga *nwe*·va
I need new contact lenses.	Necesito lentes de contacto nuevas. ne·the·*see*·to *len*·tes de kon·*tak*·to *nwe*·vas
I need new glasses.	Necesito gafas nuevas. ne·the·*see*·to *ga*·fas *nwe*·vas

I've been vaccinated for ...	Estoy vacunado/a contra ... m/f	es·*toy* va·koo·*na*·do/a *kon*·tra ...
He's/She's been vaccinated for ...	Está vacunado/a contra ... m/f	es·*ta* va·koo·*na*·do/a *kon*·tra ...

tetanus	el tétano	el *te*·ta·no
typhoid	la tifus	la *tee*·foos
hepatitis	la hepatitis	la e·pa·*tee*·tees
A/B/C	A/B/C	a/be/the
... fever	la fiebre ...	la *fye*·bre ...

For women's medical issues, see **women's health** (p162).

Symptoms & Conditions

I'm sick.	Estoy enfermo/a. m/f es·*toy* en·*fer*·mo/a
I have ...	Tengo ... *ten*·go ...
I've recently had ...	Hace poco he tenido ... a·the *po*·ko e te·*nee*·do ...
I'm on regular medication for ...	Estoy bajo medicación para ... es·*toy* ba·kho me·dee·ka·*thyon* pa·ra ...
It hurts here.	Me duele aquí. me *dwe*·le a·*kee*
I've been injured.	He sido herido/a. m/f e *see*·do e·*ree*·do/a
I've been vomiting.	He estado vomitando. e es·*ta*·do vo·mee·*tan*·do

SAFE TRAVEL HEALTH

🔊 LISTEN FOR

¿Qué le pasa?	*ke le pa·sa*	
	What's the problem?	
¿Dónde le duele?	*don·de le dwe·le*	
	Where does it hurt?	
¿Tiene fiebre?	*tye·ne fye·bre*	
	Do you have a temperature?	
¿Desde cuándo se siente así?	*des·de kwan·do se syen·te a·see*	
	How long have you been like this?	
¿Ha tenido esto antes?	*a te·nee·do es·to an·tes*	
	Have you had this before?	

I can't sleep.	No puedo dormir.
	no pwe·do dor·meer
I have a rash.	Tengo una erupción cutánea.
	ten·go oo·na e·roop·thyon koo·ta·ne·a
I have an infection.	Tengo una infección.
	ten·go oo·na in·fek·thyon
I feel ...	Me siento ...
	me syen·to ...

better	mejor m&f	*me·khor*
depressed	deprimido/a m/f	*de·pree·mee·do/a*
dizzy	mareado/a m/f	*ma·re·a·do/a*
shivery	destemplado/a m/f	*des·tem·pla·do/a*
weak	débil m&f	*de·beel*
worse	peor m&f	*pe·or*

asthma	asma m *as*·ma
diarrhoea	diarrea f dee·a·*re*·a
fever	fiebre f *fye*·bre
headache	dolor m de cabeza do·*lor* de ka·*be*·tha
sprain	torcedura f tor·the·*doo*·ra

For more symptoms & conditions, see the **dictionary**.

Women's Health

(I think) I'm pregnant.	(Creo que) Estoy embarazada. (*kre*·o ke) es·*toy* em·ba·ra·*tha*·da
I haven't had my period for ... weeks.	Hace ... semanas que no me viene la regla. *a*·the ... se·*ma*·nas ke no me *vye*·ne la *reg*·la
I'm on the Pill.	Tomo la píldora. *to*·mo la *peel*·do·ra
I've noticed a lump here.	He notado un bulto aquí. e no·*ta*·do oon *bool*·to a·*kee*
I have period pain.	Tengo dolor menstrual. *ten*·go do·*lor* mens·troo·*al*
contraception	anticonceptivos m pl an·tee·kon·thep·*tee*·vos
pregnancy test	prueba f de embarazo *prwe*·ba de em·ba·*ra*·tho
the morning-after pill	píldora f del día siguiente *peel*·do·ra del *dee*·a see·*gyen*·te

LISTEN FOR

¿Usted bebe?	oos·*te be*·be	Do you drink?
¿Usted fuma?	oos·*te foo*·ma	Do you smoke?
¿Usted toma drogas?	oos·*te to*·ma *dro*·gas	Do you take drugs?
¿Tiene Usted alergias?	*tye*·ne oos·*te* a·*ler*·khyas	Are you allergic to anything?
¿Se encuentra bajo medicación?	se en·*kwen*·tra *ba*·kho me·dee·ka·*thyon*	Are you on medication?

Allergies

I'm allergic to ...	Soy alérgico/a ... m/f soy a·*ler*·khee·ko/a ...
He/She is allergic to ...	Es alérgico/a ... m/f es a·*ler*·khee·ko/a ...

antibiotics	a los antibióticos	a los an·tee·byo·tee·kos
anti-inflammatories	a los anti-inflamatorios	a los an·tee·een·fla·ma·to·ryos
aspirin	a la aspirina	a la as·pee·ree·na
bees	a las abejas	a las a·be·khas
codeine	a la codeina	a la ko·de·ee·na
penicillin	a la penicilina	a la pe·nee·thee·lee·na
pollen	al polen	al po·len

I have a skin allergy.	Tengo una alergia en la piel. *ten*·go oo·na a·*ler*·khya en la pyel

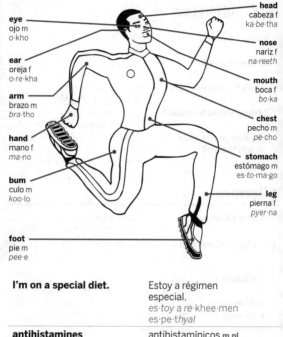

eye
ojo m
o·kho

ear
oreja f
o·re·kha

arm
brazo m
bra·tho

hand
mano f
ma·no

bum
culo m
koo·lo

foot
pie m
pee·e

head
cabeza f
ka·be·tha

nose
nariz f
na·reeth

mouth
boca f
bo·ka

chest
pecho m
pe·cho

stomach
estómago m
es·to·ma·go

leg
pierna f
pyer·na

I'm on a special diet.	Estoy a régimen especial. *es·toy a re·khee·men es·pe·thyal*
antihistamines	antihistamínicos m pl *an·tee·ees·ta·mee·nee·kos*
inhaler	inhalador m *een·a·la·dor*
sulphur-based drugs	drogas con base de azufre f pl *dro·gas kon ba·se de a·thoo·fre*

For food-related allergies, see **vegetarian & special meals** (p187).

Parts of the Body

My ... hurts.	Me duele ... me *dwe*·le ...
I can't move my ...	No puedo mover ... no *pwe*·do mo·*ver* ...
I have a cramp in my ...	Tengo calambres en ... *ten*·go ka·*lam*·bres en ...
My ... is swollen.	Mi ... está hinchado. mee ... es·*ta* een·*cha*·do

For more parts of the body, see the **dictionary**.

Chemist

I need something for ...	Necesito algo para ... ne·the·*see*·to *al*·go *pa*·ra ...
I have a prescription.	Tengo receta médica. *ten*·go re·*the*·ta *me*·dee·ka
Do I need a prescription for ...?	¿Necesito receta para ...? ne·the·*see*·to re·*the*·ta *pa*·ra ...
How many times a day?	¿Cuántas veces al día? *kwan*·tas *ve*·thes al *dee*·a

For pharmaceutical items, see the **dictionary**.

◀)) LISTEN FOR

¿Ha tomado esto antes?	a to·*ma*·do es·to *an*·tes Have you taken this before?
Dos veces al día (con la comida).	dos *ve*·thes al *dee*·a (kon la ko·*mee*·da) Twice a day (with food).

🔊 LISTEN FOR

Abra.	*a*·bra	Open wide.
No se mueva.	no se *mwe*·va	Don't move.
¡Enjuague!	en·*khwa*·ge	Rinse!

Dentist

I have a broken tooth.	Se me ha roto un diente. se me a *ro*·to oon *dyen*·te
I have a toothache.	Me duele una muela. me *dwe*·le *oo*·na *mwe*·la
I've lost a filling.	Se me ha caído un empaste. se me a ka·*ee*·do oon em·*pas*·te
My orthodontic braces broke/fell off.	Se me rompió/cayó el aparato dental. se me rom·*pyo*/ka·*yo* el a·pa·*ra*·to den·*tal*
My gums hurt.	Me duelen las encías. me *dwe*·len las en·*thee*·as
I don't want it extracted.	No quiero que me lo saquen. no *kye*·ro ke me lo *sa*·ken
I need an anaesthetic.	Necesito una anestesia. ne·the·*see*·to *oo*·ne a·nes·*te*·sya
I need a filling.	Necesito un empaste ne·the·*see*·to oon em·*pas*·te

Food

Eating Out

KEY PHRASES

Can you recommend a restaurant?	¿Puede recomendar un restaurante?	*pwe*·de re·ko·men·*dar* oon res·tow·*ran*·te
I'd like a table for two, please.	Quisiera una mesa para dos, por favor.	kee·*sye*·ra oo·na me·sa pa·ra dos por fa·*vor*
I'd like the menu, please.	Quisiera el menu, por favor.	kee·*sye*·ra el me·noo por fa·*vor*
I'd like ...	Quisiera ...	kee·*sye*·ra ...
Please bring the bill.	Por favor nos trae la cuenta.	por fa·*vor* nos *tra*·e la *kwen*·ta

Basics

The main meal in Spain, 'lunchtime' is called *la hora de comer* la o·ra de ko·*mer*. It's served between 1.30pm and 4.30pm.

breakfast	desayuno m de·sa·*yoo*·no
lunch	comida f ko·*mee*·da
dinner	cena f *the*·na
snack	tentempié m ten·tem·*pye*
eat/drink	comer/beber ko·*mer*/be·*ber*

I'd like ...	Quisiera ... kee·*sye*·ra ...
I'm starving!	¡Estoy hambriento/a! m/f es·*toy* am·*bryen*·to/a
Enjoy your meal!	¡Buen provecho! bwen pro·*ve*·cho

Finding a Place to Eat

Can you recommend a ...?	¿Puede recomendar un/una ...? m/f *pwe*·de re·ko·men·*dar* oon/*oo*·na ...

bar	bar m	bar
cafe	café m	ka·*fe*
coffee bar	cafetería f	ka·fe·te·*ree*·a
restaurant	restaurante m	res·tow·*ran*·te

Are you still serving food?	¿Siguen sirviendo comida? *see*·gen seer·*vyen*·do ko·*mee*·da
How long is the wait?	¿Cuánto hay que esperar? *kwan*·to ai ke es·pe·*rar*
Where would you go for a cheap meal?	¿Adónde se va para comer barato? a·*don*·de se va *pa*·ra ko·*mer* ba·*ra*·to
Where would you go for local specialities?	¿Adónde se va para comer comida típica? a·*don*·de se va *pa*·ra ko·*mer* ko·*mee*·da *tee*·pee·ka

FOOD EATING OUT

🔊 LISTEN FOR

Lo siento, hemos cerrado.	lo *syen*·to e·mos the·*ra*·do Sorry, we're closed.
No tenemos mesa.	no te·*ne*·mos *me*·sa We have no free tables.
Un momento.	oon mo·*men*·to One moment.

I'd like to reserve a table for (two) people.	Quisiera reservar una mesa para (dos) personas. kee·*sye*·ra re·ser·*var* oo·na *me*·sa *pa*·ra (dos) per·*so*·nas
I'd like to reserve a table for (eight) o'clock.	Quisiera reservar una mesa para las (ocho). kee·*sye*·ra re·ser·*var* oo·na *me*·sa *pa*·ra las (o·cho)

At the Restaurant

I'd like the (non)smoking section, please.	Quisiera el área de (no) fumadores, por favor. kee·*sye*·ra el *a*·re·a de (no) foo·ma·*do*·res por fa·*vor*
I'd like a table for (two), please.	Quisiera una mesa para (dos), por favor. kee·*sye*·ra oo·na *me*·sa *pa*·ra (dos) por fa·*vor*
✂ **For two, please.**	Para dos, por favor. *pa*·ra dos por fa·*vor*
I'd like the drink list, please.	Quisiera la lista de bebidas, por favor. kee·*sye*·ra la *lees*·ta de be·*bee*·das por fa·*vor*

Eating Out

Can I see the menu, please?

¿Puedo ver el menú, por favor?
pwe·do ver el me·noo por fa·vor

What would you recommend for ...?

¿Qué me recomendaría para ...?
ke me re·ko·men·da·ree·a pa·ra ...

 the main meal
el plato principal
el pla·to preen·thee·pal

dessert
postre
pos·tre

 drinks
bebidas
be·bee·das

Can you bring me some ..., please?

Por favor me trae ...
por fa·vor me tra·e ...

I'd like the bill, please.

Quisiera la cuenta, por favor.
kee·sye·ra la kwen·ta por fa·vor

I'd like the menu, please.	Quisiera el menú, por favor.	kee·sye·ra el me·noo por fa·vor

✂ **The menu, please.** | El menú, por favor. | el me·noo por fa·vor

Do you have children's meals?	¿Tienen comidas para niños?	tye·nen ko·mee·das pa·ra nee·nyos
Do you have a menu in English?	¿Tienen un menú en inglés?	tye·nen oon me·noo en een·gles
Is service included in the bill?	¿La cuenta incluye servicio?	la kwen·ta een·kloo·ye ser·vee·thyo
What would you recommend?	¿Qué recomienda?	ke re·ko·myen·da
Can you tell me which traditional foods I should try?	¿Que platos típicos debería probar?	ke pla·tos tee·pee·kos de·be·ree·a pro·bar

🔊 **LISTEN FOR**

¿Le gusta ...?	le goos·ta ... Do you like ...?
Recomiendo ...	re·ko·myen·do ... I suggest the ...
¿Cómo lo quiere preparado?	ko·mo lo kye·re pre·pa·ra·do How would you like that cooked?

I'll have what they're having.	Tomaré lo mismo que ellos. *to·ma·re lo mees·mo ke e·lyos*
Does it take long to prepare?	¿Tarda mucho en prepararse? *tar·da moo·cho en pre·pa·rar·se*
What's in that dish?	¿Que lleva ese plato? *ke lye·va e·se pla·to*
Are these complimentary?	¿Éstos son gratis? *es·tos son gra·tees*
We're just having drinks.	Sólo queremos tomar algo. *so·lo ke·re·mos to·mar al·go*

✂ **Just drinks.** | Sólo bebidas. | *so·lo be·bee·das*

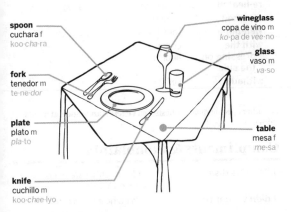

spoon
cuchara f
koo·cha·ra

wineglass
copa de vino m
ko·pa de vee·no

glass
vaso m
va·so

fork
tenedor m
te·ne·dor

plate
plato m
pla·to

table
mesa f
me·sa

knife
cuchillo m
koo·chee·lyo

Requests

Please bring a glass.	Por favor nos trae un vaso.	por fa·*vor* nos *tra*·e oon *va*·so
Please bring a serviette.	Por favor nos trae una servilleta.	por fa·*vor* nos *tra*·e *oo*·na ser·vee·*lye*·ta
I'd like it ...	Lo quiero ...	lo *kye*·ro ...
I don't want it ...	No lo quiero ...	no lo *kye*·ro ...

deep fried	frito en aceite abundante	*free*·to en a·*they*·te a·boon·*dan*·te
medium	no muy hecho	no mooy e·cho
rare	vuelta y vuelta	*vwel*·ta ee *vwel*·ta
re-heated	recalentado	re·ka·len·*ta*·do
steamed	al vapor	al va·*por*
well-done	muy hecho	mooy e·cho
with the dressing on the side	con el aliño aparte	kon el a·*lee*·nyo a·*par*·te
without ...	sin ...	seen ...

For other specific meal requests, see **vegetarian & special meals** (p187).

Compliments & Complaints

I love this dish.	Me encanta este plato. me en·*kan*·ta *es*·te *pla*·to
I didn't order this.	Yo no he pedido esto. yo no e pe·*dee*·do *es*·to

🔍 LOOK FOR

Aperitivos	a·pe·ree·*tee*·vos	Appetisers
Cervezas	ther·*ve*·thas	Beers
Caldos	*kal*·dos	Soups
De Entrada	de en·*tra*·da	Entrees
Ensaladas	en·sa·*la*·das	Salads
Postres	*pos*·tres	Desserts
Refrescos	re·*fres*·kos	Soft Drinks
Segundos Platos	se·*goon*·dos *pla*·tos	Main Courses

That was delicious!	¡Estaba buenísimo! es·*ta*·ba bwe·*nee*·see·mo
My compliments to the chef.	Mi enhorabuena al cocinero. mee en·o·ra·*bwe*·na al ko·thee·*ne*·ro
I'm full.	Estoy lleno/a. **m/f** es·*toy* *lye*·no/a
This is burnt.	Esto está quemado. es·to es·*ta* ke·*ma*·do
This is (too) cold.	Esto está (demasiado) frío. es·to es·*ta* (de·ma·*sya*·do) *free*·o
This is superb.	Esto está exquisito. es·to es·*ta* eks·kee·*see*·to
We love the local cuisine.	Nos encanta la comida típica de la zona. nos en·*kan*·ta la ko·*mee*·da *tee*·pee·ka de la *tho*·na

Paying the Bill

Please bring the bill.	Por favor nos trae la cuenta. por fa·*vor* nos *tra*·e la *kwen*·ta

✂ | **Bill, please.** | La cuenta, por favor. | la *kwen*·ta por fa·*vor* |

There's a mistake in the bill.	Hay un error en la cuenta. ai oon e·*ror* en la *kwen*·ta

For methods of payment, see **money & banking** (p91).

Nonalcoholic Drinks

I don't drink alcohol.	No bebo alcohol. no *be*·bo al·*kol*
(cup of) coffee ...	(taza de) café ... (*ta*·tha de) ka·*fe* ...
(cup of) tea ...	(taza de) té ... (*ta*·tha de) te ...
with milk	con leche kon *le*·che
without sugar	sin azúcar seen a·*thoo*·kar
soft drink	refresco m re·*fres*·ko
(boiled) water	agua (hervida) *a*·gwa (er·*vee*·da)
(sparkling) mineral water	agua mineral (con gas) *a*·gwa mee·ne·*ral* (kon gas)

FOOD EATING OUT

Alcoholic Drinks

... beer		cerveza f ... ther·*ve*·tha ...
draught	de barril	de ba·*ril*
dark	negra	*neg*·ra
light	rubia	*roo*·bee·a
nonalcoholic	sin alcohol	sin al·*kol*

small bottle of beer (250 ml)	botellín m bo·te·*lyin*
litre bottle of beer	litrona f lee·*tro*·na
bottle of beer (300 ml)	mediana f me·*dya*·na

What would you recommend?
ke re·ko·*myen*·da
¿Qué recomienda?

178

a glass/pint of beer	una caña/pinta de cerveza *oo·na ka·nya/peen·ta de ther·ve·tha*
a jug of beer	una jarra de cerveza *oo·na kha·ra de ther·ve·tha*
brandy	coñac **m** *ko·nyak*
Champagne	champán **m** *cham·pan*
cocktail	combinado **m** *kom·bee·na·do*
sangria (red-wine punch)	sangría **f** *san·gree·a*
a shot of (rum)	un chupito de (ron) *oon choo·pee·to de (ron)*
a shot of (gin)	un chupito de (ginebra) *oon choo·pee·to de (khee·ne·bra)*
a shot of (whisky)	un chupito de (güisqui) *oon choo·pee·to de (gwees·kee)*
a bottle/glass of ... wine	una botella/copa de vino ... *oo·na bo·te·lya/ko·pa de vee·no ...*

dessert	dulce	*dool·the*
red	tinto	*teen·to*
rose	rosado	*ro·sa·do*
sparkling	espumoso	*es·poo·mo·so*
white	blanco	*blan·ko*

> **CULTURE TIP**
>
> **Tapas**
>
> Tapas are scrumptious cooked bar snacks, available pretty much around the clock at bars and some clubs. You'll find they're free in some places, laid out in the bar for you to choose from. Other venues will rotate the dishes.

banderilla f/ **moruno** m/ **pinchito** m	ban·de·ree·lya/ mo·roo·no/ peen·chee·to	small tapa serving on bread or a toothpick
ración f	ra·thyon	large tapa serving
montadito m	mon·ta·dee·to	bread-topped tapa
pan tumaca m	pan too·ma·ka	tapa of toasted bread rubbed with tomatoes and garlic, served with oil
queso m **en aceite**	ke·so en a·they·te	cheese in olive oil, served as a tapa

FOOD EATING OUT

In the Bar

Excuse me!	¡Oiga! oy·ga
I'm next.	Ahora voy yo. a·o·ra voy yo
Q What would you like?	¿Qué quieres tomar? ke kye·res to·mar
A I'll have ...	Para mí ... pa·ra mee ...
Same again, please.	Otra de lo mismo. o·tra de lo mees·mo
No ice, thanks.	Sin hielo, gracias. seen ye·lo gra·thyas
I'll buy you a drink.	Te invito a una copa. te een·vee·to a oo·na ko·pa

FOOD EATING OUT

¿Dónde le gustaría sentarse?	don·de le gus·ta·ree·a sen·tar·se Where would you like to sit?
¿En qué le puedo servir?	en ke le pwe·do ser·veer What can I get for you?
¡Aquí tiene!	a·kee tye·ne Here you go!

It's my round.	Es mi ronda. es mee ron·da
You can get the next one.	La próxima la pagas tú. la prok·see·ma la pa·gas too
Do you serve meals here?	¿Sirven comidas aquí? seer·ven ko·mee·das a·kee

Drinking Up

Cheers!	¡Salud! sa·loo
Thanks, but I don't feel like it.	Lo siento, pero no me apetece. lo syen·to pe·ro no me a·pe·te·the
No thanks, I'm driving.	No gracias, tengo que conducir. no gra·thyas ten·go ke kon·doo·theer
This is hitting the spot.	Me lo estoy pasando muy bien. me lo es·toy pa·san·do mooy byen

FOOD EATING OUT

CULTURE TIP

Minis

Many Spanish bars provide massive plastic beakers of beer to cater for young revellers. It's cut with water and average tasting – but cheap and free flowing! These fountains of froth are called *minis*.

I feel fantastic!	¡Me siento fenomenal! me *syen*·to fe·no·me·*nal*
I'm feeling drunk.	Esto me está subiendo mucho. *es*·to me es·*ta* soo·*byen*·do *moo*·cho
I think I've had one too many.	Creo que he tomado demasiado. *kre*·o ke e to·*ma*·do de·ma·*sya*·do
I'm tired, I'd better go home.	Estoy cansado/a, mejor me voy a casa. **m/f** es·*toy* kan·*sa*·do/a me·*khor* me voy a *ka*·sa
I don't think you should drive.	No creo que deberías conducir. no *kre*·o ke de·be·*ree*·as kon·doo·*theer*
Can you call a taxi for me?	¿Me puedes pedir un taxi? me *pwe*·des pe·*deer* oon *tak*·see

Self-Catering

KEY PHRASES

What's the local speciality?	¿Cuál es la especialidad de la zona?	kwal es la es·pe·thya·lee·*da* de la *tho*·na
Where can I find the ... section?	¿Dónde está la sección de ...?	*don*·de es·*ta* la sek·*thyon* de ...
I'd like ...	Póngame ...	*pon*·ga·me ...

Buying Food

Where can I find the ... section?	¿Dónde está la sección de ...? *don*·de es·*ta* la sek·*thyon* de ...
dairy	productos lácteos — pro·*dook*·tos *lak*·te·os
frozen goods	productos congelados — pro·*dook*·tos kon·khe·*la*·dos
fruit and vegetable	frutas y verduras — *froo*·tas ee ver·*doo*·ras
meat	carne — *kar*·ne

Where's the health-food section/store?	¿Dónde esta la sección/ tienda de comida dietética? *don*·de es·*ta* la sek·*thyon*/ *tyen*·da de ko·*mee*·da dye·*te*·tee·ka
What's that?	¿Qué es eso? ke es *e*·so

🔊 LISTEN FOR

¿En qué le puedo servir?	en ke le *pwe*·do ser·*veer*	
	Can I help you?	
¿Qué querías?	ke ke·*ree*·as	
	What would you like?	
No tengo.	no *ten*·go	
	I don't have any.	
No queda más.	no *ke*·da mas	
	There's none left.	

Can I taste it?	¿Puedo probarlo/a? **m/f** *pwe*·do pro·*bar*·lo/a
What's the local speciality?	¿Cuál es la especialidad de la zona? kwal es la es·pe·thya·lee·*da* de la *tho*·na
How much?	¿Cuánto? *kwan*·to
How many?	¿Cuántos/as? **m/f** *kwan*·tos/as
How much is (a kilo of cheese)?	¿Cuánto vale (un kilo de queso)? *kwan*·to *va*·le (oon *kee*·lo de *ke*·so)
Do you have anything cheaper?	¿Tiene algo más barato? *tye*·ne *al*·go mas ba·*ra*·to
Do you have any other kinds?	¿Tiene otros tipos? *tye*·ne *ot*·ros *tee*·pos
Do you sell locally produced food?	¿Se venden comestibles de la zona? se *ven*·den ko·mes·*tee*·bles de la *tho*·na

Do you sell organic produce?	¿Se venden productos agrícolas biológicos? se *ven*·den pro·*dook*·tos a·*gree*·ko·las bee·o·*lo*·khee·kos
I'd like ...	Póngame ... *pon*·ga·me ...

(three) pieces	(tres) piezas	(tres) *pye*·thas
(six) slices	(seis) lonchas	(seys) *lon*·chas
(two) kilos	(dos) kilos	(dos) *kee*·los
(200) grams	(doscientos) gramos	(dos·*thyen*·tos) *gra*·mos

half a dozen	una media docena oo·na me·dya do·*the*·na
half a kilo	un medio kilo oon *me*·dyo *kee*·lo
a kilo	un kilo oon *kee*·lo
a bottle (of ...)	una botella (de ...) oo·na bo·*te*·lya (de ...)
a jar	una jarra oo·na *kha*·ra
a packet	un paquete oon pa·*ke*·te
(just) a little	(sólo) un poquito (*so*·lo) oon po·*kee*·to
many	muchos/as m/f *moo*·chos/as
(a bit) more	(un poco) más (oon *po*·ko) mas
some	algunos/as m/f al·*goo*·nos/as

🔊 LISTEN FOR

Eso es (un manchego).	e·so es (oon man·*che*·go) That's (a manchego).
Eso es (cinco euros).	e·so es (*theen*·ko e·oo·ros) That's (five euros).
¿Algo más?	*al*·go mas Anything else?

less	menos *me*·nos
that one	ése *e*·se
this	esto *es*·to
Enough!	¡Basta! *ba*·sta

For food items, see the **menu decoder** (p190) and the **dictionary**.

Cooking

cooked	cocido/a m/f ko·*thee*·do/a
dried	seco/a m/f *se*·ko/a
fresh	fresco/a m/f *fres*·ko/a
frozen	congelado/a m/f kon·khe·*la*·do/a
raw	crudo/a m/f *kroo*·do/a
smoked	ahumado/a m/f a·oo·*ma*·do/a

FOOD | **SELF-CATERING**

Could I please borrow a/an ...?	¿Me puede prestar un/una ...? m/f me pwe·de pres·tar oon/oo·na ...
Where's a/an ...?	¿Dónde hay un/una ...? m/f don·de ai oon/oo·na ...

bottle opener	abrebotellas m	a·bre·bo·te·lyas
can opener	abrelatas m	a·bre·la·tas
chopping board	tabla f para cortar	tab·la pa·ra kor·tar
corkscrew	sacacorchos m	sa·ka·kor·chos
cup	taza f	ta·tha
fork	tenedor m	te·ne·dor
frying pan	sartén f	sar·ten
glass	vaso m	va·so
knife	cuchillo m	koo·chee·lyo
plate	plato m	pla·to
saucepan	cazo m	ka·tho
spoon	cuchara f	koo·cha·ra
toaster	tostadora f	tos·ta·do·ra

For more cooking terminology, see the **dictionary**.

Vegetarian & Special Meals

KEY PHRASES

Do you have vegetarian food?	¿Tienen comida vegetariana?	tye·nen ko·mee·da ve·khe·ta·rya·na
Could you prepare a meal without ...?	¿Me puede preparar una comida sin ...?	me pwe·de pre·pa·rar oo·na ko·mee·da seen ...
I'm allergic to ...	Soy alérgico/a a ... m/f	soy a·ler·khee·ko/a a ...

Special Diets & Allergies

I'm vegetarian.	Soy vegetariano/a. m/f soy ve·khe·ta·rya·no/a
I'm on a special diet.	Estoy a régimen especial. es·toy a re·khee·men es·pe·thyal
I'm allergic to ...	Soy alérgico/a ... m/f soy a·ler·khee·ko/a ...

dairy produce	a los productos lácteos	a los pro·dook·tos lak·te·os
honey	al miel	al myel
MSG	al glutamato monosódico	al gloo·ta·ma·to mo·no·so·dee·ko
nuts	a las nueces	a las nwe·thes
seafood	a los mariscos	a los ma·rees·kos
shellfish	a los crustáceos	a los kroos·ta·thyos

Ordering Food

Is there a (vegetarian) restaurant near here?	¿Hay un restaurante (vegetariano) por aquí? ai oon res·tow·ran·te (ve·khe·ta·rya·no) por a·kee
Do you have vegetarian food?	¿Tienen comida vegetariana? tye·nen ko·mee·da ve·khe·ta·rya·na
Do you have halal food?	¿Tienen comida halal? tye·nen ko·mee·da a·lal
Do you have kosher food?	¿Tienen comida kosher? tye·nen ko·mee·da ko·sher
Do you have vegan food?	¿Tienen comida vegetariana estricta? tye·nen ko·mee·da ve·khe·ta·rya·na es·trik·ta
I don't eat red meat.	No como carne roja. no ko·mo kar·ne ro·kha
Is it cooked in/with butter?	¿Esta cocinado en/con mantequilla? es·ta ko·thee·na·do en/kon man·te·kee·lya
Could you prepare a meal without ...?	¿Me puede preparar una comida sin ...? me pwe·de pre·pa·rar oo·na ko·mee·da seen ...

eggs	huevo	we·vo
fish	pescado	pes·ka·do
meat/fish stock	caldo de carne/ pescado	kal·do de kar·ne/ pes·ka·do
pork	cerdo	ther·do
poultry	aves	a·ves

🔊 LISTEN FOR

¿Puede comer ...?	*pwe*·de ko·*mer* ...	
	Can you eat ...?	
Le preguntaré al cocinero.	le pre·goon·ta·*re* al ko·thee·*ne*·ro	
	I'll check with the cook.	
Todo lleva (carne).	*to*·do *lye*·va (*kar*·ne)	
	It all has (meat) in it.	

Is this ...?   ¿Esto es ...?
es·to es ...

free of animal produce	sin productos de animales	seen pro·*dook*·tos de a·nee·*ma*·les
free-range	de corral	de ko·ral
genetically modified	transgénico	trans·*khe*·nee·ko
gluten-free	sin gluten	seen *gloo*·ten
low in sugar	bajo en azúcar	*ba*·kho en a·*thoo*·kar
low-fat	bajo en grasas	*ba*·kho en *gra*·sas
organic	orgánico	or·*ga*·nee·ko
salt-free	sin sal	seen sal

FOOD   VEGETARIAN & SPECIAL MEALS

A

Menu
~ DECODER ~
léxico culinario

This miniguide to Spanish cuisine lists dishes and ingredients in Spanish alphabetical order (see **alphabet**, p12). Spanish nouns have their gender indicated by ⓜ or ⓕ. If it's a plural noun, you'll also see pl.

~ A ~

acebuche ⓜ a·the·*boo*·che wild olive
acedía ⓕ a·the·*dee*·a plaice/flounder
aceite ⓜ a·*they*·te oil
— de girasol de khee·ra·*sol* sunflower oil
— de oliva de o·*lee*·va olive oil
— de oliva virgen extra de o·*lee*·va *veer*·khen *eks*·tra extra virgin olive oil
aceituna ⓕ a·they·*too*·na olive
— negra *ne*·gra black olive
— verde *ver*·de green olive
ácido/a ⓜ/ⓕ a·*thee*·do/a tart (flavour)
adobo ⓜ a·*do*·bo marinade
agrios ⓜ pl a·*gryos* citrus fruits
aguacate ⓜ a·gwa·*ka*·te avocado
aguaturma ⓕ a·gwa·*toor*·ma Jerusalem artichoke
ajiaco ⓜ a·*khya*·ko spicy potato dish
ajoaceite ⓜ a·kho·a·*they*·te garlic & oil sauce • garlic mayonnaise
ajoharina ⓕ a·kho·a·*ree*·na potatoes stewed in garlic sauce
(al) ajoarriero (al) a·kho·a·*rye*·ro 'mule-driver's garlic' – anything cooked in a sauce of onions, garlic & chilli

ala ⓕ a·la (chicken) wing
alajú ⓜ a·la·*khoo* honey & almond cake
albaricoque ⓜ al·ba·ree·*ko*·ke apricot
— seco *se*·ko dried apricot
albóndigas ⓕ pl al·*bon*·dee·gas meatballs
— de pescado de pes·*ka*·do fish balls
alcachofas ⓕ pl al·ka·*cho*·fas artichokes
— guisadas a la española gee·*sa*·das a la es·pa·*nyo*·la artichokes in wine
— rellenas re·*lye*·nas stuffed artichokes
alcaparra ⓕ al·ka·*pa*·ra caper
alioli ⓜ a·lee·*o*·lee garlic mayonnaise
almejas ⓕ pl al·*me*·khas clams – superb eaten raw
— a la marinera a la ma·ree·*ne*·ra clams in white wine
— al horno al or·no baked clams
almendrado ⓜ al·men·*dra*·do almond cake or biscuit • chocolate covered ice cream bar
almendras ⓕ pl al·*men*·dras almonds
alubia ⓕ a·*loo*·bya haricot bean

anacardo ⓜ a·na·*kar*·do cashew nut

anchoas ⓕ pl an·*cho*·as anchovies – mostly eaten fresh, grilled or fried

angelote ⓜ an·khe·*lo*·te monkfish

anguila ⓕ an·*gee*·la adult eel

angulas ⓕ pl an·*goo*·las baby eels – prized as a delicacy, they resemble vermicelli

— en all i pebre en al ee *pe*·bre baby eels with pepper & garlic

apio ⓜ a·pyo celery

arándano ⓜ a·*ran*·da·no blueberry

arenque ⓜ a·*ren*·ke herring

— ahumado a·oo·*ma*·do kipper

arroz ⓜ a·*roth* rice

— a la Alcireña a la al·*thee*·re·nya baked rice dish

— abanda (de València) a·*ban*·da (de va·*len*·thya) fish paella

— con leche kon *le*·che rice pudding

— con pollo kon *po*·lyo chicken & rice

— integral een·te·*gral* brown rice

— marinera ma·ree·*ne*·ra seafood & rice

— salvaje sal·va·khe wild rice

asadillo ⓜ a·sa·dee·lyo roasted red capsicums

asados ⓜ pl a·*sa*·dos roast meats

atún ⓜ a·*toon* tuna – often served marinated & raw

— al horno al *or*·no baked tuna

avellana ⓕ a·ve·*lya*·na hazelnut

aves ⓕ pl a·ves poultry

azúcar ⓜ a·*thoo*·kar sugar

~ B ~

bacalao ⓜ ba·ka·*low* cod – usually salted & dried

— a la vizcaína a la veeth·ka·ee·na cod with chillies & capsicums

— del convento del kon·*ven*·to cod with potatoes & spinach in broth

bacón ⓜ ba·*kon* bacon

barbo ⓜ *bar*·bo red mullet

barra ⓕ *ba*·ra long stick of bread

batata ⓕ ba·*ta*·ta sweet potato

beicon ⓜ *bey*·kon streaky bacon rashers

berberechos ⓜ pl ber·be·re·chos cockles

— en vinagre en vee·*na*·gre cockles in vinegar

berenjenas ⓕ pl be·ren·*khe*·nas eggplants

— a la mallorquina a la ma·lyor·*kee*·na eggplants with garlic mayonnaise

— con setas kon se·tas eggplants with mushrooms

berza ⓕ *ber*·tha cabbage

— a la andaluza a la an·da·*loo*·tha cabbage & meat hotpot

besugo ⓜ be·*soo*·go red bream

— a la Donostiarra a la do·nos·*tya*·ra barbecued red bream with garlic & paprika

— estilo San Sebastián es·*tee*·lo san se·bas·*tyan* barbecued red bream with garlic & paprika

bienmesabe ⓜ byen·me·*sa*·be sponge cake, egg & almond confection

bisbe ⓜ *bees*·be black & white blood sausage

bistec ⓜ bees·*tek* steak

— con patatas kon pa·*ta*·tas steak with chips

bizcocha ⓕ **manchega** beeth·*ko*·cha man·*che*·ga cake soaked in milk, sugar, vanilla & cinnamon

bizcocho ⓜ beeth·*ko*·cho sponge cake

— de almendra de al·*men*·dra almond cake

— de avellana de a·ve·*lya*·na hazelnut cake

bizcochos ⓜ pl **borrachos** beeth·*ko*·chos bo·*ra*·chos cake soaked in liqueur

bocadillo ⓜ bo·ka·*dee*·lyo bread roll with a filling

C

bocas ① pl **de la isla** *bo*·kas de la *ees*·la large crab claws

bogavante ⓜ bo·ga·*van*·te lobster

bollo ⓜ *bo*·lyo crusty bread roll

bonito ⓜ bo·*nee*·to white fleshy tuna

boquerón ⓜ bo·ke·*ron* whitebait

boquerones ⓜ pl bo·ke·*ro*·nes anchovies marinated in wine vinegar

— fritos *free*·tos fried anchovies

brama ① *bra*·ma sea bream

bróculi ⓜ *bro*·ko·lee broccoli

budín ⓜ **de atún** boo·*deen* de a·*toon* baked tuna pudding

bull ⓜ **de atún** bool de a·*toon* rabbit with garlic & tuna boiled with potatoes

buñuelitos ⓜ pl boo·*nywe*·*lee*·tos small cheese or ham fritters

— de San José de san kho·*se* lemon & vanilla crepes

buñuelo ⓜ boo·*nywe*·lo fried pastry

burrida ① **de ratjada** boo·*ree*·da de rat·*kha*·da fish soup with almonds

butifarra ① **(blanca)** boo·tee·*fa*·ra (*blan*·ka) cured pork sausage

— con setas kon se·tas Catalan sausage with mushrooms

~ C ~

caballa ① ka·*ba*·lya mackerel

cabra ① *ka*·bra goat

cabracho ⓜ ka·*bra*·cho scorpion fish • mullet

cacahuete ⓜ ka·ka·*we*·te peanut

cachelos ⓜ pl ka·*che*·los potatoes with spicy sausage & pork

cádiz ⓜ *ka*·deeth fresh goats' milk cheese

calabacín ⓜ ka·la·ba·*theen* zucchini

calabaza ① ka·la·*ba*·tha pumpkin

calamares ⓜ pl ka·la·*ma*·res calamari – popular fried or stuffed

— fritos a la romana *free*·tos a la ro·*ma*·na squid rings fried in batter

— rellenos re·*lye*·nos stuffed squid

calçots ⓜ pl kal·*sots* spring onion-like vegetables chargrilled and eaten with a **romesco** dipping sauce

caldeirada ① kal·dey·*ra*·da salted cod & potatoes in a paprika sauce • fish soup

caldereta ① kal·de·*re*·ta stew

— asturiana as·too·*rya*·na fish stew

— de cordero de kor·*de*·ro lamb stew

caldillo ⓜ **de perro** kal·*dee*·lyo de pe·ro 'puppy dog soup' – stew of onions, fresh fish & orange juice

caldo ⓜ *kal*·do broth • clear soup • stock

— al estilo del Mar Menor al es·*tee*·lo del mar me·*nor* fish stew from the Mar Menor

— gallego ga·*lye*·go broth with haricot beans, ham & sausage

callos ⓜ pl *ka*·lyos tripe

camarones fritos ⓜ pl ka·ma·*ro*·nes *free*·tos deep-fried prawns

canagroc ⓜ ka·na·*grok* mushroom

cañaillas ① pl **de la Isla** ka·*nyay*·lyas de la *ees*·la boiled sea snails

canelones ⓜ pl ka·na·*lo*·nes squares of pasta for making cannellini

— con espinaca kon es·pee·*na*·ka cannelloni with spinach, anchovies & bechamel

— con pescado kon pes·*ka*·do cannelloni with cod, eggs & mushrooms

canapés ⓜ pl ka·na·*pes* de fee·*am*·bres mini hors d'oeuvres with ham, anchovies or cheese

cangrejo ⓜ kan·*gre*·kho large-clawed crab usually eaten steamed or boiled

cantalupo ⓜ kan·ta·*loo*·po cantaloupe

canutillos ⓜ pl ka·noo·*tee*·lyos cream biscuits

capones ⓜ pl **de Villalba** ka·po·nes de vee·lyal·ba Christmas dish of chicken marinated in brandy

caracoles ⓜ ka·ra·ko·les snails

caramelos ⓜ ka·ra·me·los caramels • confection

cardos ⓜ pl **fritos** kar·dos free·tos fried thistles

carne ⓕ kar·ne meat

— de membrillo de mem·bree·lyo quince 'cheese'

— molida mo·lee·da minced meat

cassolada ⓕ ka·so·la·da potato & vegetable stew with bacon & ribs

castaña ⓕ kas·ta·nya chestnut

caviar ⓜ ka·vyar caviar

caza ⓕ ka·tha game

cazón ⓜ ka·thon dogfish or shark with a sweet scallop-like flavour

cazuelitas ⓕ pl **de langostinos San Rafael** ka·thwe·lee·tas de lan·gos·tee·nos san ra·fa·el baked rice with seafood

cebolla ⓕ the·bo·lya onion

cecina ⓕ the·thee·na cured meat

cerdo ⓜ ther·do pork

cereales ⓜ pl the·re·a·les cereal

cereza ⓕ the·re·tha cherry

— silvestre seel·ves·tre wild cherry

ciervo ⓜ thyer·vo deer

cigala ⓕ thee·ga·la crayfish

ciruela ⓕ thee·rwe·la plum

— pasa pa·sa prune

civet ⓜ **de llebre** see·vet de le·bre hare stew

chalote ⓜ cha·lo·te shallot

champiñones ⓜ pl cham·pee·nyo·nes cultivated white mushrooms

chanquetes ⓜ pl chan·ke·tes whitebait • baby anchovies

(al) chilindrón (al) chee·leen·dron cooked in a tomato & red pepper sauce

chipirón ⓜ chee·pee·ron baby squid – very popular in the Basque Country

chocolate ⓜ cho·ko·la·te chocolate

— caliente ka·lee·en·te thick hot chocolate

chocos ⓜ pl cho·kos squid

chorizo ⓜ cho·ree·tho spicy red cooked sausage, similar to salami

— de Pamplona de pam·plo·na fine-textured, hard chorizo

— de Salamanca de sa·la·man·ka chunky chorizo from Salamanca

chuletas ⓕ pl choo·le·tas chops • cutlets

— al sarmiento al sar·myen·to chops prepared over wood from vines

— de buey de bwey ox chops

— de cerdo a la aragonesa de ther·do a la a·ra·go·ne·sa baked pork chops with wine & onion

churros ⓜ choo·ros fried doughnut strips bought from street-sellers or in cafes

cochifrito ⓜ **de cordero** ko·chee·free·to de kor·de·ro lamb fried with garlic & lemon

cochinillo ⓜ ko·chee·nee·lyo suckling pig

— asado a·sa·do roast suckling pig

— de pelotas de pe·lo·tas meatball stew

coco ⓜ ko·ko coconut

codornices ⓕ pl **a la plancha** ko·dor·nee·thes a la plan·cha grilled quail

codorniz ⓕ ko·dor·neeth quail

— con pimientos kon pee·myen·tos capsicums stuffed with quail

col ⓕ kol cabbage

— lombarda lom·bar·da red cabbage

coles ⓕ pl **de bruselas** ko·les de broo·se·las Brussels sprouts

coliflor ⓕ ko·lee·flor cauliflower

conejo ⓜ ko·ne·kho rabbit

— de monte de mon·te wild rabbit

coquina ⓕ ko·kee·na large clam

D

corazón ⓜ ko·ra·*thon* heart
cordero ⓜ kor·*de*·ro lamb
— al chilindrón al chee·leen·*dron* lamb in tomato & capsicum sauce
— con almendras kon al·*men*·dras lamb in almond sauce
costillas ① pl kos·*tee*·lyas ribs
crema ① *kre*·ma cream
— catalana ka·ta·*la*·na creme brulee
— de espinacas de es·pee·*na*·kas cream of spinach soup
— de naranja de na·*ran*·kha orange cream dessert
— de San José de san kho·*se* egg custard flavoured with cinnamon
— de verduras de ver·*doo*·ras cream of vegetable soup
crocante ⓜ kro·*kan*·te ice cream with chopped nuts & chocolate

~ D ~

de soja de so·kha of/with soya
despojos ⓜ pl des·*po*·khos offal
dorada ① **a la sal** do·*ra*·da a la sal salted sea bream
dulce ⓜ *dool*·the sweet
— de batata de ba·*ta*·ta sweet potato pudding from Málaga
dulces ⓜ pl *dool*·thes sweets
— de las monjas *dool*·thes de las *mon*·khas confectionery made by nuns & sold in convents or cake shops

~ E ~

embutidos ⓜ pl em·boo·*tee*·dos generic name for cured sausages
empanada ① em·pa·*na*·da savoury pie
— de carne de *kar*·ne spicy meat pie
— de espinaca de es·pee·*na*·ka spinach pie
empanadilla ① em·pa·na·*dee*·lya small pie, either sweet or savoury

empanado ⓜ em·pa·*na*·do coated in bread crumbs
emparedado ⓜ em·pa·re·*da*·do sandwich
— de jamón y espárragos de kha·*mon* ee es·*pa*·ra·gos fried ham & asparagus rolls
empiñonado ⓜ em·pee·nyo·*na*·do small marzipan-filled pastry with pinenuts
en salsa verde en *sal*·sa *ver*·de in a parsley & garlic sauce
encurtidos ⓜ pl en·koor·*tee*·dos pickles
ensaimada ① **mallorquina** en·sai·*ma*·da ma·lyor·*kee*·na spiral-shaped bun made with lard
ensalada ① en·sa·*la*·da salad
— de frutas de *froo*·tas fruit salad
— de patatas de pa·*ta*·tas potato salad
— del tiempo del *tyem*·po seasonal salad
— mixta *meeks*·ta mixed salad
escaldadillas ① pl es·kal·da·*dee*·lyas dough soaked in orange juice & fried
escalivada ① es·ka·lee·*va*·da roasted red capsicums in olive oil
escalopes ⓜ pl **de ternera rellenos** es·ka·*lo*·pes de ter·*ne*·ra re·*lye*·nos deep fried veal cutlets stuffed with egg & cheese
espaguetis ⓜ pl es·pa·*ge*·tees spaghetti
espárragos ⓜ pl es·*pa*·ra·gos asparagus
— con dos salsas kon dos *sal*·sas asparagus & tomato or paprika mayonnaise
— en vinagreta en vee·na·*gre*·ta asparagus in vinaigrette
espinacas ① pl es·pee·*na*·kas spinach
— a la catalana a la ka·ta·*la*·na spinach with pinenuts & raisins

esqueixada ① es·kee·sha·da cod dressed with olives, tomato & onion

etxeko kopa e·che·ko ko·pa ice cream dessert

~ **F** ~

fabada ① **asturiana** fa·ba·da as·too·rya·na stew made with pork, blood sausage & white beans

faisán ⓜ fai·san pheasant

faves ① pl **a la catalana** fa·ves a la ka·ta·la·na broad beans with ham

fiambres ⓜ pl fee·am·bres cold meats

— **surtidos** soor·tee·dos selection of cold meats

fideos ⓜ pl fee·de·os pasta noodles

fideua ① fee·de·wa rice or noodles with fish & shellfish

fideus ⓜ pl **a la cassola** fee·de·oos a la ka·so·la Catalan noodle dish

filete ① fee·le·te steak • any boneless slice of meat

— **a la parrilla** a la pa·ree·lya grilled beef steak

— **de ternera** de ter·ne·ra veal steak

filloas ① pl fee·lyo·as Galician pancakes filled with cream

flan ⓜ flan creme caramel

flaó ① fla·o sweet cheese flan

flor manchega ① flor man·che·ga deep-fried sweet wafers

frambuesa ① fram·bwe·sa raspberry

frangellos ⓜ pl fran·khe·lyos sweet made from cornmeal, milk & honey

fresa ① fre·sa strawberry

fricandó ⓜ **de langostinos** free·kan·do de lan·gos·tee·nos shrimp in almond sauce

frite ① free·te lamb stew, served on festive occasions

fritos ⓜ pl free·tos fritters

— **con miel** kon myel honey-roasted fritters

fritura ① free·too·ra mixed fried fish

fruta ① froo·ta fruit

— **variada** va·ree·a·da selection of fresh fruit

frutas ① pl **en almibar** froo·tas en al·mee·bar fruit in syrup

frutos ⓜ pl **secos** froo·tos se·kos nuts & dried fruit

fuet ① foo·et thin pork sausage

~ **G** ~

gachas ① pl **manchegas** ga·chas man·che·gas flavoured porridge

galleta ① ga·lye·ta biscuit

gambas ① pl gam·bas prawns

— **a la plancha** a la plan·cha grilled prawns

— **en gabardina** en ga·bar·dee·na prawns in batter

Gamonedo ⓜ ga·mo·ne·do sharp-tasting cheese, smoked & cured

garbanzos ⓜ pl gar·ban·thos chickpeas

— **con cebolla** kon the·bo·lya chickpeas in onion sauce

— **tostados** tos·ta·dos roasted chickpeas (sold as a snack)

garbure ⓜ gar·boo·re green vegetable soup • pork & ham dish

garúm ⓜ ga·room olive & anchovy dip

Gata-Hurdes ga·ta·oor·des cheese

gazpacho ⓜ gath·pa·cho cold tomato soup

— **andaluz** an·da·looz cold tomato soup with chopped salad vegetables

— **pastoril** pas·to·reel rabbit stew with tomato & garlic

gazpachos ⓜ pl **manchegos** gath·pa·chos man·che·gos game & vegetable hotpot

Gaztazarra ① gath·ta·tha·ra cheese

gitano ⓜ khee·ta·no Andalusian chickpea & tripe stew

gofio ⓜ *go*·fyo toasted cornmeal or barley

granadilla ⓕ gra·na·dee·lya passion fruit

grano ⓜ *gra*·no grain

— largo lar·go long-grain (rice)

gratinado ⓜ **de berenjenas** gra·tee·na·do de be·ren·khe·nas eggplant gratin

Grazalema ⓕ gra·tha·le·ma semi-cured sheep's milk cheese

guindilla ⓕ geen·dee·lya mild green chilli

guisado ⓜ gee·sa·do stew

— de cordero de kor·de·ro lamb ragout

— de ternera de ter·ne·ra veal ragout

guisante ⓜ gee·san·te pea

— seco se·ko split pea

— mollar mo·lyar snow pea

guisantes ⓜ pl **con jamón a la española** gee·san·tes kon kha·mon a la es·pa·nyo·la pea & ham dish

guisat ⓜ **de marisco** gee·sat de ma·rees·ko stew made with seafood

guiso ⓜ **de conejo estilo canario** gee·so de ko·ne·kho es·tee·lo ka·na·ryo rabbit stew

guiso ⓜ **de rabo de toro** gee·so de ra·bo de to·ro stewed bull's tail with potatoes

~ H ~

habas ⓕ pl *a*·bas broad beans

— a la granadina a la gra·na·dee·na broad beans with eggs & ham

— fritas free·tas fried broad beans (sold as a snack)

habichuela ⓕ a·bee·chwe·la white bean

hamburguesa ⓕ am·boor·ge·sa hamburger

harina ⓕ a·ree·na flour

— integral een·te·gral wholemeal flour

helado ⓜ e·la·do ice cream

hígado ⓜ ee·ga·do liver

higo ⓜ ee·go fig

— seco se·ko dried fig

hogaza ⓕ o·ga·tha dense, thick-crusted bread

hoja ⓕ **de parra** o·kha de pa·ra vine leaf

hojaldres ⓜ pl o·khal·dres small flaky pastries covered in sugar

hojas ⓕ pl **verdes** o·khas ver·des green vegetables

hornazo ⓜ or·na·tho bread stuffed with sausage

hortalizas ⓕ pl or·ta·lee·thas vegetables

huevo ⓜ we·vo egg

— cocido ko·thee·do boiled egg

— de chocolate de cho·ko·la·te chocolate egg

— frito free·to fried egg

huevos ⓜ pl we·vos egg dishes

— a la flamenca a la fla·men·ka baked vegetables with egg & ham

— al estilo Sóller al es·tee·lo so·lyer fried eggs served with a milk & vegetable sauce

— en salsa agria en sal·sa a·grya boiled eggs in wine & vinegar

— escalfados es·kal·fa·dos poached eggs

— revueltos re·vwel·tos scrambled eggs

~ J ~

jabalí ⓜ kha·ba·lee wild boar

— con salsa de castaños kon sal·sa de kas·ta·nyos wild boar in chestnut sauce

jamón ⓜ kha·mon ham

— cocido ko·thee·do cooked ham

— ibérico ee·ber·ik·o ham from the Iberian pig, said to be the best in Spain

— serrano se·ra·no cured mountain ham

K

jengibre ⓜ khen·gee·bre ginger

jerez (al) khe·reth (al) in a sherry sauce

judía ⓕ khoo·dee·a fresh green bean • dried kidney bean

judías ⓕ pl **del tío Lucas** khoo·dee·as del tee·o loo·kas bean stew with garlic & bacon

judías ⓕ pl **verdes a la castellana** khoo·dee·as ver·des a la kas·te·lya·na fried capsicums, garlic & green beans

judiones ⓜ pl **de la granja** kho·dee·o·nes de la gran·kha pork & bean stew

~ K ~

kiskilla kees·kee·lya shrimp (also spelled **quisquilla**)

~ L ~

langosta ⓕ lan·gos·ta lobster

— a la ibicenca a la ee·bee·then·ka lobster with stuffed squid

langostinos ⓜ pl lan·gos·tee·nos king prawns

— a la plancha a la plan·cha grilled king prawns

lavanco ⓜ la·van·ko wild duck

lechuga ⓕ le·choo·ga lettuce

legumbres ⓕ pl le·goom·bres pulses • vegetables • vegetable dishes

— secas se·kas dried pulses

leguminosas ⓕ pl le·goo·mee·no·sas legumes

lengua ⓕ len·gwa tongue

— a la aragonesa a la a·ra·go·ne·sa tongue in tomato & capsicum sauce

lenguado ⓜ len·gwa·do sole

— al chacolí con hongos al cha·ko·lee kon on·gos sole with white wine & mushrooms

lenguados ⓜ pl **al plato** len·gwa·dos al pla·to sole & mushroom casserole

lenguas ⓕ pl **con salsa de almendras** len·gwas kon sal·sa de al·men·dras tongue in almond sauce

lentejas ⓕ pl len·te·khas lentils

liebre ⓕ lye·bre hare

— con castañas kon kas·ta·nyas hare with chestnuts

— estofada es·to·fa·da stewed hare

lima ⓕ lee·ma lime

limón ⓜ lee·mon lemon

llagostí ⓜ **a l'allioli** lyan·gos·tee a la·lyee·o·lee grilled prawns in garlic mayonnaise

llenguado ⓜ **a la nyoca** lyen·gwa·do a la nyo·ka sole with pine nuts & raisins

lomo ⓜ lo·mo fillet • loin • sirloin

— curado koo·ra·do cured pork sausage

— de cerdo de ther·do loin of pork

longaniza ⓕ lon·ga·nee·tha chorizo, long & skinny sausage

lubina ⓕ loo·bee·na sea bass

— a la marinera a la ma·ree·ne·ra sea bass in parsley sauce

lucio ⓜ loo·thyo pike

~ M ~

macedonia ⓕ **de frutas** ma·the·do·nya de froo·tas fruit salad

macedonia ⓕ **de verduras** ma·the·do·nya de ver·doo·ras mixed vegetables

magdalena ⓕ ma·da·le·na small fairy cake to dunk in coffee

magras ⓕ pl ma·gras fried eggs, ham, cheese & tomato

maíz ⓜ ma·eeth maize • corn

— tierno tyer·no sweetcorn

mandarina ⓕ man·da·ree·na tangerine • mandarin

mango ⓜ man·go mango

manitas ⓕ pl **de cerdo** ma·nee·tas de ther·do pig's trotters

manitas ① pl **de cordero** ma·nee·tas de kor·de·ro leg of lamb

manteca ① man·te·ka lard

mantecado ⓜ man·te·ka·do a soft lard biscuit • dairy ice cream

mantequilla ① man·te·kee·lya butter

— sin sal seen sal unsalted butter

manzana ① man·tha·na apple

manzanas ① **asadas** man·tha·nas a·sa·das baked apples

margarina ① mar·ga·ree·na margarine

marinera (a la) ma·ree·ne·ra (a la) cooked or served in a white wine sauce

mariscos ⓜ ma·rees·kos shellfish • seafood

marmitako mar·mee·ta·ko fresh tuna & potato casserole

marrano ⓜ ma·ra·no pork

mar y cel ⓜ mar ee sel dish of sausages, rabbit, shrimp & angler fish

masa ① ma·sa pastry (dough)

mayonesa ① ma·yo·ne·sa mayonnaise

medallones ⓜ pl **de merluza** me·da·lyo·nes de mer·loo·tha hake steaks

mejillones ⓜ pl me·khee·lyo·nes mussels

— al vino blanco al vee·no blan·ko mussels in white wine

— con salsa kon sal·sa mussels with tomato sauce

mel ① **i mató** mel ee ma·to dessert of curd cheese with honey

melocotón ⓜ me·lo·ko·ton peach

melocotones ⓜ pl **al vino** me·lo·ko·to·nes al vee·no peaches in red wine

melón ⓜ me·lon melon

membrillo ⓜ mem·bree·lyo quince

menestra ① me·nes·tra mixed vegetable stew

— de pollo de po·lyo chicken & vegetable stew

merengue ⓜ me·ren·ge meringue

merluza ① mer·loo·tha hake

mermelada ① mer·me·la·da marmalade

mero ⓜ me·ro halibut • grouper • sea bass

miel ① myel honey

— de azahar de a·tha·ar orange blossom honey

— de caña de ka·nya treacle

migas ① pl mee·gas fried cubes of bread with capsicums

— a la aragonesa a la a·ra·go·ne·sa fried bread with bacon rashers in tomato sauce

— mulatas moo·la·tas cubes of bread soaked in chocolate & fried

mojarra ① mo·kha·ra type of sea bream

moje ⓜ **manchego** mo·khe man·che·go cold broth with black olives

mojete ⓜ mo·khe·te dipping sauce for bread, made from potatoes, garlic, tomatoes & paprika

— murciano moor·thya·no fish & capsicum dish

mojo ⓜ mo·kho spicy capsicum sauce

mollejas ① pl mo·lye·khas sweetbreads

mollete ⓜ mo·lye·te soft round bap roll

monas ① pl **de pascua** mo·nas de pas·kwa Easter cakes • figures made of chocolate

mongetes ① pl **seques i butifarra** mon·zhe·tes se·kes ee boo·tee·fa·ra haricot beans with roasted pork sausage

mora ① mo·ra blackberry

moraga ① **de sardina** mo·ra·ga de sar·dee·na fresh anchovies on a spit

morcilla ① mor·thee·lya black pudding, often stewed with beans & vegetables

mortadela ① mor·ta·de·la mortadella sausage

morteruelo ⓜ mor·te·rwe·lo pate dish containing offal, game & spices

mostachones ⓜ pl mos·ta·cho·nes small cakes for dipping in coffee or hot chocolate (also spelled **mostatxones**)

mostaza ① mos·ta·tha mustard
— **en grano** en gra·no mustard seed

múgil ⓜ moo·kheel grey mullet

mujol ⓜ **guisado** moo·khol gee·sa·do red mullet

mus ⓜ **de chocolate** moos de cho·ko·la·te chocolate mousse

muslo ⓜ moos·lo (chicken) leg & thigh

N

nabo ⓜ na·bo root vegetable · turnip

naranja ① na·ran·kha orange

nata ① na·ta cream
— **agria** a·grya sour cream
— **montada** mon·ta·da whipped cream

natillas ① pl na·tee·lyas creamy custard dessert
— **de chocolate** de cho·ko·la·te chocolate custard

navaja ① na·va·kha razor clam

nécora ① ne·ko·ra small crab

nueces ① pl new·thes nuts

nuez ① nweth nut
— **de América** de a·me·ree·ka pecan nut
— **de nogal** de no·gal walnut

~ Ñ ~

ñora ① nyo·ra sweet red capsicum (usually dried)

~ O ~

oca ① o·ka goose

olla ① o·lya meat & vegetable stew · cooking pot

oreja ① **de mar** o·re·kha de mar abalone

ostiones ⓜ pl **a la gaditana** os·tyo·nes a la ga·dee·ta·na Cádiz oysters with garlic, parsley & bread crumbs

ostra ① os·tra oyster

oveja ① o·ve·kha mutton

~ P ~

pá ⓜ **amb oli** pa amb o·lee toasted bread with garlic & olive oil

pacana ① pa·ka·na pecan

paella ① pa·e·lya rice dish which has many regional variations
— **marinera** ma·ree·ne·ra paella with fish & seafood
— **zamorana** tha·mo·ra·na paella with meat

palitos ⓜ pl **de queso** pa·lee·tos de ke·so cheese straws

palmera ① pal·me·ra leaf-shaped flaky pastry, often coated in chocolate

palomitas ① pl pa·lo·mee·tas popcorn

pan ⓜ pan bread
— **aceite** a·they·te flat round bread
— **árabe** a·ra·be pita bread
— **de Alá** de a·la 'Allah's Bread' – dessert
— **de boda** de bo·da sculpted bread traditionally made for weddings
— **de centeno** de then·te·no rye bread
— **duro** doo·ro stale bread, used for toasting & eating with olive oil
— **integral** een·te·gral wholemeal bread

panaché ⓜ pa·na·che mixed vegetable stew

panallets ⓜ pl pa·na·lyets marzipan sweets

panceta ① pan·the·ta salt-cured, streaky bacon

panchineta ① pan·chee·ne·ta almond tart

panecillo ⑩ pa·ne·thee·lyo small bread roll

panojas ① pl **malagueñas** pa·no·khas ma·la·ge·nyas sardine dish

papas ① pl **arrugadas** pa·pas a·roo·ga·das potatoes boiled in their jackets

pargo ⑩ par·go sea bream

parrillada ① pa·ree·lya·da grilled meat

— de mariscos de ma·rees·kos seafood grill

pastel ⑩ pas·tel cake

— de boda de bo·da wedding cake

— de chocolate de cho·ko·la·te chocolate cake

— de cierva de thyer·va meat pie

— de cumpleaños de koom·ple·a·nyos birthday cake

pastelitos ⑩ pl **de miel** pas·te·lee·tos de myel honey fritters

pataco ⑩ pa·ta·ko tuna & potato stew

patatas ① pl pa·ta·tas potatoes

— a la riojana a la ree·o·kha·na potatoes with chorizo & paprika

— alioli a·lee·o·lee potatoes in garlic mayonnaise

— bravas bra·vas potatoes in spicy tomato sauce

— con chorizo kon cho·ree·tho potatoes with chorizo

— estofadas es·to·fa·das boiled potatoes

pato ⑩ pa·to duck

— a la sevillana a la se·vee·lya·na duck with orange sauce

— alcaparrada al·ka·pa·ra·da duck with capers & almonds

pavo ⑩ pa·vo turkey

pececillos ⑩ pl pe·the·thee·lyos small fish

pechina ① pe·chee·na scallop

pecho ⑩ pe·cho breast of lamb

pechuga ① pe·choo·ga breast of poultry

pepinillo ⑩ pe·pee·nee·lyo gherkin

pepino ⑩ pe·pee·no cucumber

pepitoria ① pe·pee·to·rya sauce made with egg & almond

pepitos ⑩ pl pe·pee·tos chocolate eclair cakes filled with custard

pera ① pe·ra pear

La Peral ① la pe·ral soft cheese

perca ① per·ka perch

perdices ① pl per·dee·thes partridges

— a la manchega a la man·che·ga partridge in red wine & capsicums

— con chocolate kon cho·ko·la·te partridge with chocolate

perdiz ① per·deeth partridge

peregrina ① pe·re·gree·na scallop

pericana ① pe·ree·ka·na dish of olives, cod oil, capsicums & garlic

perrito ⑩ **caliente** pe·ree·to ka·lee·en·te hot dog

pescada ① **á galega** pes·ka·da a ga·le·ga hake fried in olive oil & served with garlic & paprika sauce

pescadilla ① pes·ka·dee·lya whiting • young hake

pescaditos ⑩ pl **rebozados** pes·ka·dee·tos re·bo·tha·dos small fish fried in batter

pescado ⑩ pes·ka·do fish

— a l'all cremat a lal kre·mat fish in burnt garlic

pescaíto ⑩ **frito** pes·ka·ee·to free·to tiny fried fish

pestiños ⑩ pl pes·tee·nyos honey-coated aniseed pastries, fried with filling

pez ① **espada** peth es·pa·da swordfish

— frito free·to fried swordfish steaks on a skewer

picada ① pee·ka·da mixture of garlic, parsley, toasted almonds & nuts, often used to thicken sauces

P

picadillo ⓜ pee·ka·dee·lyo salad consisting of diced vegetables
— **de atún** de a·toon salad made with diced tuna & capsicums
— **de ternera** de ter·ne·ra minced veal
pichón ⓜ pee·chon pigeon
pichones ⓜ pl **asados** pee·cho·nes a·sa·dos roast pigeons
pilotes ⓕ pl pee·lo·tes Catalan meatballs
pimiento ⓜ pee·myen·to capsicum
— **amarillo** a·ma·ree·lyo yellow capsicum
— **rojo** ro·kho red capsicum
— **verde** ver·de green capsicum
pimientos ⓜ pl pee·myen·tos capsicums (the ones from El Bierzo are especially good)
— **a la riojana** a la ree·o·kha·na roast red capsicum fried in oil & garlic
— **al chilindrón** al chee·leen·dron capsicum casserole
piña ⓕ pee·nya pineapple
pinchito ⓜ **moruno** peen·chee·to mo·roo·no lamb & chicken kebabs
piñón ⓜ pee·nyon pinenut
pinta ⓕ peen·ta pinto bean
pintada ⓕ peen·ta·da guinea fowl
piquillo ⓜ pee·kee·lyo sweet & spicy capsicums
pistacho ⓜ pees·ta·cho pistachio nut
pisto ⓜ **manchego** pees·to man·che·go zucchini with capsicum & tomato, fried or stewed
plátano ⓜ pla·ta·no banana
pochas ⓕ pl po·chas beans
— **a la riojana** a la ree·o·kha·na beans with chorizo in spicy paprika sauce
— **con almejas** kon al·me·khas beans with clams
pollo ⓜ po·lyo chicken
— **asado** a·sa·do roast chicken
— **con samfaina** kon sam·fai·na chicken with mixed vegetables

— **en escabeche** en es·ka·be·che marinated chicken
— **en salsa de ajo** en sal·sa de a·kho chicken in garlic sauce
— **granadina** gra·na·dee·na chicken with wine & ham
— **y langosta** ee lan·gos·ta chicken with crayfish
polvorón ⓜ pol·vo·ron almond shortbread, often eaten at Christmas
pomelo ⓜ po·me·lo grapefruit
postre ⓜ pos·tre dessert
— **de naranja** de na·ran·kha cream-filled oranges
potaje ⓜ po·ta·khe broth
— **castellano** kas·te·lya·no broth with beans & sausages
— **de garbanzos** de gar·ban·thos broth with chickpeas
— **de lentejas** de len·te·khas lentil broth
pote ⓜ **gallego** po·te ga·lye·go stew
potito ⓜ po·tee·to jar of baby food
pringada ⓕ preen·ga·da bread dipped in sauce • a marinated sandwich
productos ⓜ pl **biológicos** pro·dook·tos bee·o·lo·khee·kos organic produce
productos ⓜ pl **del mar** pro·dook·tos del mar seafood products
productos ⓜ pl **lácteos** pro·dook·tos lak·te·os dairy products
puchero ⓜ poo·che·ro casserole
pudin ⓜ poo·din pudding
puerco ⓜ pwer·ko pork
puerro ⓜ pwe·ro leek
pulpo ⓜ pool·po octopus
— ⓜ **a feira** pool·po a fey·ra spicy boiled octopus
punta ⓕ **de diamante** poon·ta de dya·man·te confection from Valencia
porrusalda ⓕ po·roo·sal·da cod & potato stew

Q

~ Q ~

queso ⓜ *ke*-so cheese
— azul *a-thool* blue cheese
— crema *kre*-ma cream cheese
quisquilla ⓕ kees-*kee*-lya shrimp
(also spelled **kiskilla**)

~ R ~

rábano ⓜ *ra*-ba-no radish
rabas ⓕ **en salsa verde** *ra*-bas en
sal-sa *ver*-de squid in green sauce
rabassola ⓕ ra-ba-*so*-la mushroom
rape ⓜ *ra*-pe monkfish
— a la gallega a la ga-*lye*-ga
monkfish with potatoes & garlic sauce
— a la Monistrol a la mo-nees-*trol*
monkfish with bechamel sauce
redondo ⓜ re-*don*-do round (of
beef)
— al horno al *or*-no roast beef
regañaos ⓜ pl re-ga-*nya*-os
pastry stuffed with sardines & red
capsicum
relleno ⓜ re-*lye*-no stuffing
remolacha ⓕ re-mo-*la*-cha
beetroot
reo ⓜ *re*-o sea trout
repollo ⓜ re-*po*-lyo cabbage
repostería ⓕ re-pos-te-*ree*-a
confectionery
requesón ⓜ re-ke-*son* cottage
cheese
riñón ⓜ ree-*nyon* kidney
róbalo ⓜ *ro*-ba-lo haddock • sea
bass
rodaballo ⓜ ro-da-*ba*-lyo turbot •
brill
romero ⓜ ro-*me*-ro rosemary
romesco ⓜ ro-*mes*-ko sweet red
capsicum, almond & garlic sauce
rosca ⓕ **de carne** *ros*-ka de *kar*-ne
meatloaf wrapped in bacon
rosco ⓜ *ros*-ko small sweet bun
rossejat ⓜ ro-se-*dyat* rice with fish
& shellfish

rovellons ⓜ pl **a la plancha**
ro-ve-*lyons* a la *plan*-cha garlic
mushrooms
ruibarbo ⓜ roo-ee-*bar*-bo rhubarb

~ S ~

salchicha ⓕ sal-*chee*-cha pork
sausage
salchichón ⓜ sal-chee-*chon* cured &
peppery white sausage
salmón ⓜ sal-*mon* salmon
— a la ribereña a la ree-be-*re*-nya
salmon in a cider sauce
— ahumado a-oo-*ma*-do smoked
salmon
salmonete ⓜ sal-mo-*ne*-te red
mullet
salmorejo ⓜ sal-mo-*re*-kho thick
gazpacho soup made from tomato,
bread, olive oil, vinegar, garlic & green
capsicum
— de Córdoba de *kor*-do-ba
gazpacho soup made with more
vinegar than usual
salpicón ⓜ sal-pee-*kon* fish or meat
salad
salsa ⓕ *sal*-sa sauce
— alioli a-lee-o-*lee* garlic & olive oil
vinaigrette • garlic mayonnaise
— de holandesa de o-lan-*de*-sa
hollandaise sauce
— de mayonesa de ma-yo-*ne*-sa
mayonnaise sauce
— de tomate de to-*ma*-te tomato
sauce
— inglesa een-*gle*-sa Worcestershire
sauce
— tártara *tar*-ta-ra tartar sauce
— verde *ver*-de parsley & garlic
sauce
samfaina ⓕ sam-*fai*-na grilled
vegetable sauce
sancocho ⓜ san-*ko*-cho fish dish
served with potatoes
sandía ⓕ san-*dee*-a watermelon

sándwich Ⓜ san·weech sandwich
— **mixto** meeks·to toasted ham & cheese sandwich
sanocho Ⓜ **canario** sa·no·cho ka·na·ryo baked monkfish with potatoes
sardinas Ⓕ sar·dee·nas sardines
— **a la parrilla** a la pa·ree·lya sardines grilled
— **en cazuela** en ka·thwe·la sardines served in a clay pot
sargo Ⓜ sar·go bream
sepia Ⓕ se·pya cuttlefish
sesos Ⓜ pl se·sos brains
setas Ⓕ pl se·tas wild mushrooms
— **a la kashera** a la ka·she·ra sauteed wild mushrooms
— **rellenas** re·lye·nas mushrooms stuffed
sofrit pagés Ⓜ so·freet pa·zhes vegetable stew
sofrito Ⓜ so·free·to fried tomato sauce
soja Ⓕ so·kha soya bean
soldaditos Ⓜ pl **de Pavía** sol·da·dee·tos de pa·vee·a cod fritters
solomillo Ⓜ so·lo·mee·lyo fillet
sopa Ⓕ so·pa soup
— **del día** del dee·a soup of the day
sopas Ⓕ pl **de leche** so·pas de le·che pieces of bread soaked in milk & cinnamon
sopas Ⓕ pl **engañadas** so·pas en·ga·nya·das soup made from capsicum, onion shoots, vinegar, figs & grapes
sorbete Ⓜ sor·be·te sorbet
sorroputún Ⓜ so·ro·poo·toon tuna casserole
suizo Ⓜ swee·tho sugared bun
sukaldi soo·kal·dee beef stew
suquet Ⓜ soo·ket clams in almond sauce
suquet de peix soo·ket de peysh fish stew

suspiros Ⓜ pl **de monja** soos·pee·ros de mon·kha 'nun's sighs' – custard sweets

~ T ~

tallarines Ⓜ pl ta·lya·ree·nes pasta noodles
tarta Ⓕ tar·ta cake • tart
— **de almendra** de al·men·dra almond tart
— **de manzana** de man·tha·na apple tart
tartaleta Ⓕ tar·ta·le·ta tartlet
tartaletas Ⓕ pl **de huevos revueltos** tar·ta·le·tas de we·vos re·vwel·tos scrambled egg tartlets
ternera Ⓕ ter·ne·ra veal
— **a la sevillana** a la se·vee·lya·na veal served with wine & olives
— **en cazuela con berenjenas** en ka·thwe·la kon be·ren·khe·nas veal & eggplant casserole
tocino Ⓜ to·thee·no salted pork • bacon
— **del cielo** del thye·lo creamy dessert made with egg yolk & sugar, with a caramel topping
tocrudo to·kroo·do 'everything raw' – salad of meat, garlic, onion & green capsicum
tomate Ⓜ to·ma·te tomatoes
— **(de) pera** (de) pe·ra plum tomato
— **frito** free·to tinned tomato sauce
tomates Ⓜ pl to·ma·tes
— **enteros y pelados** en·te·ros ee pe·la·dos tinned whole tomatoes
— **rellenos de atún** re·lye·nos de a·toon tomatoes stuffed with tuna
toro Ⓜ to·ro bull meat
torrefacto Ⓜ to·re·fak·to dark-roasted coffee beans
torrija Ⓕ to·ree·kha French toast
torta Ⓕ tor·ta pie • tart • flat bread
— **de aceite** de a·they·te sweet, flat cake or biscuit made with oil

U

— **pascualina** pas·kwa·*lee*·na spinach & egg pie, eaten at Easter
tortilla ① tor·*tee*·lya omelette
— **española** es·pa·*nyo*·la potato & onion omelette
— **francesa** fran·*the*·sa plain omelette
tortillas ① pl **de camarones** tor·*tee*·lyas de ka·ma·*ro*·nes shrimp fritters
tortita ① tor·*tee*·ta waffle
tostada ① tos·*ta*·da toasted bread
tocino ⓜ to·*thee*·no bacon
tripas ① pl *tree*·pas intestines • guts
trucha ① *troo*·cha trout
— **a la marinera** a la ma·ree·*ne*·ra trout in a white wine sauce
truchas ① pl *troo*·chas trout
— **a la navarra** a la na·*va*·ra trout with ham
— **con vino y romero** kon *vee*·no ee ro·*me*·ro trout with red wine & rosemary
trufa ① *troo*·fa truffle
— **tarta** *tar*·ta chocolate truffle cake
tumbet (de peix) ⓜ toom·*bet* (de peysh) vegetable souffle, sometimes containing fish
turrón ⓜ too·*ron* Spanish nougat

~ U ~

uva ① *oo*·va grape
— **de corinto** de ko·*reen*·to currant
— **pasa** *pa*·sa raisin
— **sultana** sool·*ta*·na sultana

~ V ~

vacuno ⓜ va·*koo*·no beef
venado ⓜ ve·*na*·do venison
verduras ① ver·*doo*·ras vegetables
vieira ① vee·*ey*·ra scallop
villagodio ⓜ vee·lya·go·*dyo* large steak
vinagre ⓜ vee·*na*·gre vinegar
visita ① vee·*see*·ta almond cake

~ Y ~

yemas ① pl *ye*·mas small round cakes • egg whites
yogur ⓜ yo·*goor* yoghurt

~ Z ~

zanahoria ① tha·na·o·*rya* carrot
zarangollo ⓜ tha·ran·go·*lyo* fried zucchini
zarzamora ① thar·tha·*mo*·ra blackberry
zarzuela ① **de mariscos** thar·*thwe*·la de ma·*rees*·kos spicy shellfish stew
zarzuela ① **de pescado** thar·*thwe*·la de pes·*ka*·do fish in almond sauce
zurrukutano ⓜ thoo·roo·koo·*ta*·no cod & green capsicum soup

Dictionary
ENGLISH *to* SPANISH
inglés–español

A

Nouns in the dictionary have their gender indicated by ⓜ or ⓕ. If it's a plural noun, you'll also see pl. Where a word that could be either a noun or a verb has no gender indicated, it's a verb.

A

(to be) able poder po·*der*

aboard a bordo a *bor*·do

abortion aborto ⓜ a·*bor*·to

about sobre so·bre

above arriba a·*ree*·ba

abroad en el extranjero en el eks·tran·*khe*·ro

accept aceptar a·thep·*tar*

accident accidente ⓜ ak·thee·*den*·te

accommodation alojamiento ⓜ ·lo·kha·*myen*·to

across a través a tra·*ves*

activist activista ⓜ&ⓕ ak·tee·*vees*·ta

acupuncture acupuntura ⓕ ·koo·poon·*too*·ra

adaptor adaptador ⓜ a·dap·ta·*dor*

address dirección ⓕ dee·rek·*thyon*

administration administración ⓕ d·mee·nees·tra·*thyon*

admission price precio ⓜ de entrada ·re·thyo de en·*tra*·da

admit admitir ad·mee·*teer*

adult adulto ⓜ a·*dool*·to

advertisement anuncio ⓜ ·*noon*·thyo

advice consejo ⓜ kon·*se*·kho

aerobics aeróbic ⓜ ai·ro·beek

Africa África ⓕ a·*free*·ka

after después de des·*pwes* de

aftershave bálsamo de aftershave bal·sa·mo de ahf·ter·sha·eev

again otra vez o·tra veth

age edad ⓕ e·*da*

aggressive agresivo/a ⓜ/ⓕ a·gre·see·vo/a

agree estar de acuerdo es·*tar* de a·*kwer*·do

agriculture agricultura ⓕ a·gree·kul·*too*·ra

AIDS SIDA ⓜ *see*·da

air aire ⓜ ai·re

air mail por vía aérea por vee·a a·e·re·a

air-conditioned con aire acondicionado kon ai·re a·kon·dee·thyo·na·do

air-conditioning aire ⓜ acondicionado ai·re a·kon·dee·thyo·na·do

airline aerolínea ⓕ ai·ro·lee·nya

airport aeropuerto ⓜ ai·ro·pwer·to

airport tax tasa ⓕ del aeropuerto ta·sa del ai·ro·pwer·to

alarm clock despertador ⓜ des·per·ta·*dor*

alcohol alcohol ⓜ al·*kol*

all todo *to*·do

allergy alergia ⓕ a·*ler*·khya

B

allow permitir per·mee·teer
almonds almendras ① pl al·men·dras
almost casi ka·see
alone solo/a ⓜ/① so·lo/a
already ya ya
also también tam·byen
altar altar ⓜ al·tar
altitude altura ① al·too·ra
always siempre syem·pre
amateur amateur ⓜ&① a·ma·ter
ambassador embajador/embajadora
ⓜ/① em·ba·kha·dor/em·ba·kha·do·ra
among entre en·tre
anarchist anarquista ⓜ&①
a·nar·kees·ta
ancient antiguo/a ⓜ/① an·tee·gwo/a
and y ee
angry enfadado/a ⓜ/① en·fa·da·do/a
animal animal ⓜ a·nee·mal
ankle tobillo ⓜ to·bee·lyo
answer respuesta ① res·pwes·ta
answering machine contestador ⓜ automático kon·tes·ta·dor
ow·to·ma·tee·ko
ant hormiga ① or·mee·ga
anthology antología ①
an·to·lo·khee·a
antibiotics antibióticos ⓜ pl
an·tee·byo·tee·kos
antinuclear antinuclear
an·tee·noo·kle·ar
antique antigüedad ① an·tee·gwe·da
antiseptic antiséptico ⓜ
an·tee·sep·tee·ko
any alguno/a ⓜ/① al·goo·no/a
appendix apéndice ⓜ a·pen·dee·the
apple manzana ① man·tha·na
appointment cita ① thee·ta
apricot albaricoque ⓜ al·ba·ree·ko·ke
archaeological arqueológico/a ⓜ/①
ar·keo·lo·khee·ko/a
architect arquitecto/a ⓜ/①
ar·kee·tek·to/a
architecture arquitectura ①
ar·kee·tek·too·ra
argue discutir dees·koo·teer

arm brazo ⓜ bra·tho
army ejército ⓜ e·kher·thee·to
arrest detener de·te·ner
arrivals llegadas ① pl lye·ga·das
arrive llegar lye·gar
art arte ⓜ ar·te
art gallery museo ⓜ de arte
moo·se·o de ar·te
artichoke alcachofa ① al·ka·cho·fa
artist artista ⓜ&① ar·tees·ta
ashtray cenicero ⓜ the·nee·the·ro
Asia Asia ① a·sya
ask (a question) preguntar
pre·goon·tar
ask (for something) pedir pe·deer
aspirin aspirina ① as·pee·ree·na
assault asalto ⓜ a·sal·to
asthma asma ⓜ as·ma
athletics atletismo ⓜ at·le·tees·mo
atmosphere atmósfera ①
at·mos·fe·ra
aubergine berenjena ① be·ren·khe·na
aunt tía ① tee·a
Australia Australia ① ow·stra·lya
Australian Rules football fútbol ⓜ
australiano foot·bol ow·stra·lya·no
automatic teller machine cajero ⓜ
automático ka·khe·ro ow·to·ma·tee·ko
autumn otoño ⓜ o·to·nyo
avenue avenida ① a·ve·nee·da
avocado aguacate ⓜ a·gwa·ka·te

B

B&W (film) blanco y negro blan·ko
ee ne·gro
baby bebé ⓜ be·be
baby food comida ① de bebé
ko·mee·da de be·be
baby powder talco ⓜ tal·ko
babysitter canguro ⓜ kan·goo·ro
back (of body) espalda ① es·pal·da
back (of chair) respaldo ⓜ res·pal·do
backpack mochila ① mo·chee·la
bacon tocino ⓜ to·thee·no
bad malo/a ⓜ/① ma·lo/a
bag bolso ⓜ bol·so

baggage equipaje ⓜ e·kee·pa·khe

baggage allowance ⓜ límite de equi-
aje lee·mee·te de e·kee·pa·khe

baggage claim recogida ⓕ de equi-
ajes re·ko·khee·da de e·kee·pa·khes

bakery panadería ⓕ pa·na·de·ree·a

balance (account) saldo ⓜ sal·do

balcony balcón ⓜ bal·kon

ball pelota ⓕ pe·lo·ta

ballet ballet ⓜ ba·le

banana plátano ⓜ pla·ta·no

band grupo ⓜ groo·po

bandage vendaje ⓜ ven·da·khe

band-aids tiritas ⓕ pl tee·ree·tas

bank banco ⓜ ban·ko

bank account cuenta ⓕ bancaria
kwen·ta ban·ka·rya

banknotes billetes ⓜ pl (de banco)
bee·lye·tes (de ban·ko)

baptism bautizo ⓜ bow·tee·tho

bar bar ⓜ bar

bar (with music) pub ⓜ poob

bar work trabajo ⓜ de camarero/a
ⓜ/ⓕ tra·ba·kho de ka·ma·re·ro/a

basket canasta ⓕ ka·nas·ta

basketball baloncesto ⓜ
ba·lon·thes·to

bath bañera ⓕ ba·nye·ra

bathing suit bañador ⓜ ba·nya·dor

bathroom baño ⓜ ba·nyo

battery (car) batería ⓕ ba·te·ree·a

battery (small) pila ⓕ pee·la

be ser ser · estar es·tar

beach playa ⓕ pla·ya

bean sprouts brotes ⓜ pl de soja
bro·tes de so·kha

beans judías khoo·dee·as

beautiful hermoso/a ⓜ/ⓕ
er·mo·so/a

beauty salon salón ⓜ de belleza
sa·lon de be·lye·tha

because porque por·ke

bed cama ⓕ ka·ma

bedding ropa ⓕ de cama ro·pa de
ka·ma

bedroom habitación ⓕ a·bee·ta·thyon

bee abeja ⓕ a·be·kha

beef carne ⓕ de vaca kar·ne de va·ka

beer cerveza ⓕ ther·ve·tha

beetroot remolacha ⓕ re·mo·la·cha

before antes an·tes

beggar mendigo/a ⓜ/ⓕ
men·dee·go/a

begin comenzar ko·men·thar

behind detrás de de·tras de

Belgium Bélgica ⓕ bel·khee·ka

below abajo a·ba·kho

best lo mejor lo me·khor

bet apuesta ⓕ a·pwes·ta

better mejor me·khor

between entre en·tre

bible biblia ⓕ bee·blya

bicycle bicicleta ⓕ bee·thee·kle·ta

big grande gran·de

bike bici ⓕ bee·thee

bike chain cadena ⓕ de bici ka·de·na
de bee·thee

bike path camino ⓜ de bici
ka·mee·no de bee·thee

bill cuenta ⓕ kwen·ta

biodegradable biodegradable
bee·o·de·gra·da·ble

biography biografía ⓕ bee·o·gra·fee·a

bird pájaro ⓜ pa·kha·ro

birth certificate partida ⓕ de
nacimiento par·tee·da de
na·thee·myen·to

birthday cumpleaños ⓜ
koom·ple·a·nyos

birthday cake pastel ⓜ
de cumpleaños pas·tel de
koom·ple·a·nyos

biscuit ⓕ galleta ga·lye·ta

bite (dog) mordedura ⓕ
mor·de·doo·ra

bite (food) bocado ⓜ bo·ka·do

bite (insect) picadura ⓕ
pee·ka·doo·ra

black negro/a ⓜ/ⓕ ne·gro/a

blanket manta ⓕ man·ta

bleed sangrar san·grar

blind ciego/a ⓜ/ⓕ thye·go/a

B

blister ampolla ⓕ am·po·lya

blocked atascado/a ⓜ/ⓕ a·tas·ka·do/a

blood sangre ⓕ san·gre

blood group grupo ⓜ sanguíneo groo·po san·gee·neo

blood pressure presión ⓕ arterial pre·syon ar·te·ryal

blood test análisis ⓜ de sangre a·na·lee·sees de san·gre

blue azul a·thool

board (ship, etc) embarcarse em·bar·kar·se

boarding house pensión ⓕ pen·syon

boarding pass tarjeta ⓕ de embarque tar·khe·ta de em·bar·ke

bone hueso ⓜ we·so

book libro ⓜ lee·bro

book (make a reservation) reservar re·ser·var

booked out lleno/a ⓜ/ⓕ lye·no/a

bookshop librería ⓕ lee·bre·ree·a

boots botas ⓕ pl bo·tas

border frontera ⓕ fron·te·ra

boring aburrido/a ⓜ/ⓕ a·boo·ree·do/a

borrow tomar prestado to·mar pres·ta·do

botanic garden jardín ⓜ botánico khar·deen bo·ta·nee·ko

both ambos/as ⓜ/ⓕ pl am·bos/bas

bottle botella ⓕ bo·te·lya

bottle opener abrebotellas ⓜ a·bre·bo·te·lyas

bowl bol ⓜ bol

box caja ⓕ ka·kha

boxer shorts calzones ⓜ pl kal·tho·nes

boxing boxeo ⓜ bo·se·o

boy chico ⓜ chee·ko

boyfriend novio ⓜ no·vyo

bra sujetador ⓜ soo·khe·ta·dor

brakes frenos ⓜ pl fre·nos

branch (office) sucursal ⓕ soo·koor·sal

brandy coñac ⓜ ko·nyak

brave valiente va·lyen·te

bread pan ⓜ pan

bread (brown) pan moreno pan mo·re·no

bread rolls bollos bo·lyos

bread (rye) pan de centeno pan de then·te·no

bread (sourdough) pan de masa fermentada pan de ma·sa fer·men·ta·da

bread (white) pan blanco pan blan·ko

bread (wholemeal) pan integral pan een·te·gral

break romper rom·per

break down descomponerse des·kom·po·ner·se

breakfast desayuno ⓜ des·a·yoo·no

breasts senos ⓜ pl se·nos

breathe respirar res·pee·rar

brewery fábrica ⓕ de cerveza fab·ree·ka de ther·ve·tha

bribe soborno ⓜ so·bor·no

bribe sobornar so·bor·nar

bridge puente ⓜ pwen·te

briefcase maletín ⓜ ma·le·teen

brilliant cojonudo/a ⓜ/ⓕ ko·kho·noo·do/a

bring traer tra·er

brochure folleto ⓜ fo·lye·to

broken roto/a ⓜ/ⓕ ro·to/a

bronchitis bronquitis ⓜ bron·kee·tees

brother hermano ⓜ er·ma·no

brown marrón ma·ron

bruise cardenal ⓜ kar·de·nal

brussels sprouts coles ⓕ pl de Bruselas ko·les de broo·se·las

bucket cubo ⓜ koo·bo

Buddhist budista ⓜ&ⓕ boo·dees·ta

buffet buffet ⓜ boo·fe

bug bicho ⓜ bee·cho

build construir kons·troo·eer

building edificio ⓜ e·dee·fee·thyo

bull toro ⓜ to·ro

bullfight corrida ⓕ ko·ree·da

bullring plaza ⓕ de toros pla·tha de to·ros

bum (of body) culo ⓜ koo·lo

burn quemadura ⓕ ke·ma·*doo*·ra
bus autobús ⓜ ow·to·*boos*
bus (intercity) autocar ⓜ ow·to·*kar*
bus station estación de auto-
buses/autocares ⓕ es·ta·*thyon* de
ow·to·*boo*·ses/ow·to·*ka*·res
bus stop parada ⓕ de autobús
pa·*ra*·da de ow·to·*boos*
business negocios ⓜ pl ne·*go*·thyos
business class clase ⓕ preferente
kla·se pre·fe·*ren*·te
business person comerciante ⓜ&ⓕ
ko·mer·*thyan*·te
busker artista callejero/a ⓜ/ⓕ
ar·*tees*·ta ka·lye·*khe*·ro/a
busy ocupado/a ⓜ/ⓕ o·koo·*pa*·do/a
but pero *pe*·ro
butcher's shop carnicería ⓕ
kar·nee·the·*ree*·a
butter mantequilla ⓕ man·te·*kee*·lya
butterfly mariposa ⓕ ma·ree·*po*·sa
buttons botones ⓜ pl bo·*to*·nes
buy comprar kom·*prar*

C

cabbage col kol
cable cable ⓜ *ka*·ble
cable car teleférico ⓜ te·le·*fe*·ree·ko
cafe café ⓜ ka·*fe*
cake pastel ⓜ pas·*tel*
cake shop pastelería ⓕ
pas·te·le·*ree*·a
calculator calculadora ⓕ
kal·koo·la·*do*·ra
calendar calendario ⓜ ka·len·*da*·ryo
calf ternero ⓜ ter·*ne*·ro
camera cámara ⓕ (fotográfica)
ka·ma·ra (fo·to·*gra*·fee·ka)
camera shop tienda ⓕ de fotografía
tyen·da de fo·to·gra·*fee*·a
camp acampar a·kam·*par*
camping store tienda ⓕ de cámping
tyen·da de *kam*·peen
campsite cámping ⓜ *kam*·peen
can lata ⓕ *la*·ta
can (be able) poder po·*der*

can opener abrelatas ⓜ a·bre·*la*·tas
Canada Canadá ⓕ ka·na·*da*
cancel cancelar kan·the·*lar*
cancer cáncer ⓜ *kan*·ther
candle vela ⓕ *ve*·la
cantaloupe cantalupo ⓜ
kan·ta·*loo*·po
capsicum (red/green) pimiento ⓜ
rojo/verde pee·*myen*·to ro·kho/*ver*·de
car coche ⓜ *ko*·che
car hire alquiler ⓜ de coche al·kee·*ler*
de *ko*·che
car owner's title papeles ⓜ pl del
coche pa·*pe*·les del *ko*·che
car registration matrícula ⓕ
ma·*tree*·koo·la
caravan caravana ⓕ ka·ra·*va*·na
cards cartas ⓕ pl *kar*·tas
care (about something) preocuparse
por pre·o·koo·*par*·se por
care (for someone) cuidar de
kwee·*dar* de
caring bondadoso/a ⓜ/ⓕ
bon·da·*do*·so/a
carpark aparcamiento ⓜ
a·par·ka·*myen*·to
carpenter carpintero/a ⓜ/ⓕ
kar·peen·*te*·ro/a
carrot zanahoria ⓕ tha·na·*o*·rya
carry llevar lye·*var*
carton cartón ⓜ kar·*ton*
cash dinero ⓜ en efectivo dee·*ne*·ro
en e·fek·*tee*·vo
cash (a cheque) cambiar (un
cheque) kam·*byar* (oon *che*·ke)
cash register caja ⓕ registradora
ka·kha re·khees·tra·*do*·ra
cashew nut anacardo ⓜ a·na·*kar*·do
cashier caja ⓕ *ka*·kha
casino casino ⓜ ka·*see*·no
cassette casete ⓜ ka·*se*·te
castle castillo ⓜ kas·*tee*·lyo
casual work trabajo ⓜ eventual
tra·*ba*·kho e·ven·*twal*
cat gato/a ⓜ/ⓕ *ga*·to/a
cathedral catedral ⓕ ka·te·*dral*

C

Catholic católico/a ⓜ/ⓕ ka·to·lee·ko/a
cauliflower coliflor ⓕ ko·lee·*flor*
caves cuevas ⓕ pl *kwe*·vas
CD cómpact ⓜ *kom*·pakt
celebrate (an event) celebrar
the·le·*brar*
celebration celebración ⓕ
the·le·bra·*thyon*
cemetery cementerio ⓜ
the·men·*te*·ryo
cent centavo ⓜ then·*ta*·vo
centimetre centímetro ⓜ
then·*tee*·me·tro
central heating calefacción ⓕ
central ka·le·fak·*thyon* then·*tral*
centre centro ⓜ *then*·tro
ceramic cerámica ⓕ the·*ra*·mee·ka
cereal cereales ⓜ pl the·re·*a*·les
certificate certificado ⓜ
ther·tee·fee·*ka*·do
chair silla ⓕ *see*·lya
champagne champán ⓜ cham·*pan*
chance oportunidad ⓕ
o·por·too·nee·*da*
change (money) cambio ⓜ *kam*·byo
change cambiar kam·*byar*
changing rooms vestuarios ⓜ pl
ves·*twa*·ryos
charming encantador/encantadora
ⓜ/ⓕ en·kan·ta·*dor*/en·kan·ta·*do*·ra
chat up ligar lee·*gar*
cheap barato/a ⓜ/ⓕ ba·*ra*·to/a
cheat tramposo/a ⓜ/ⓕ tram·*po*·so/a
check revisar re·vee·*sar*
check (bank) cheque ⓜ *che*·ke
check-in facturación ⓕ de equipajes
fak·too·ra·*thyon* de e·kee·pa·khes
checkpoint control ⓜ kon·*trol*
cheese queso ⓜ *ke*·so
chef cocinero ⓜ ko·thee·*ne*·ro
chemist (person) farmacéutico/a
ⓜ/ⓕ far·ma·the·oo·ti·ko/a
chemist (shop) farmacia ⓕ
far·*ma*·thya
chess ajedrez ⓜ a·khe·*dreth*
chess board tablero ⓜ de ajedrez
ta·*ble*·ro de a·khe·*dreth*

chest pecho ⓜ *pe*·cho
chewing gum chicle ⓜ *chee*·kle
chicken pollo ⓜ *po*·lyo
chicken breast pechuga ⓕ
pe·*choo*·ga
chickpeas garbanzos ⓜ pl
gar·*ban*·thos
child niño/a ⓜ/ⓕ *nee*·nyo/a
child seat asiento ⓜ de seguridad
para bebés a·*syen*·to de se·goo·ree·*da*
pa·ra be·*bes*
childminding service guardería ⓕ
gwar·de·*ree*·a
children hijos ⓜ pl ee·khos
chilli guindilla ⓕ geen·*dee*·lya
chilli sauce salsa ⓕ de guindilla
sal·sa de geen·dee·lya
chocolate chocolate ⓜ cho·ko·*la*·te
choose escoger es·ko·*kher*
Christian cristiano/a ⓜ/ⓕ
krees·*tya*·no/a
Christian name nombre ⓜ de pila
nom·bre de *pee*·la
Christmas Navidad ⓕ na·vee·*da*
Christmas Eve Nochebuena ⓕ
no·che·*bwe*·na
church iglesia ⓕ ee·*gle*·sya
cider sidra ⓕ *see*·dra
cigar cigarro ⓜ thee·*ga*·ro
cigarette cigarrillo ⓜ thee·ga·*ree*·lyo
cigarette lighter mechero ⓜ
me·*che*·ro
cigarette machine máquina ⓕ de
tabaco *ma*·kee·na de ta·*ba*·ko
cigarette paper papel ⓜ de fumar
pa·*pel* de foo·*mar*
cinema cine ⓜ *thee*·ne
circus circo ⓜ *theer*·ko
citizenship ciudadanía ⓕ
thyu·da·da·*nee*·a
city ciudad ⓕ thyu·*da*
city centre centro ⓜ de la ciudad
then·tro de la thyu·*da*
city walls murallas ⓕ pl moo·*ra*·lyas
civil rights derechos civiles ⓜ pl
de·*re*·chos thee·*vee*·les
classical clásico/a ⓜ/ⓕ *kla*·see·ko/a

C

clean limpio/a ⓜ/ⓕ *leem*·pyo/a

cleaning limpieza ⓕ leem·*pye*·tha

client cliente/a ⓜ/ⓕ klee·*en*·te/a

cliff acantilado ⓜ a·kan·tee·*la*·do

climb subir soo·*beer*

cloak capote ⓜ ka·po·te

cloakroom guarrdaropa ⓜ gwar·da·ro·pa

clock reloj ⓜ re·*lokh*

close cerrar the·*rar*

closed cerrado/a ⓜ/ⓕ the·*ra*·do/a

clothes line cuerda ⓕ para tender la ropa *kwer*·da pa·ra ten·*der* la *ro*·pa

clothing ropa ⓕ *ro*·pa

clothing store tienda ⓕ de ropa *tyen*·da de *ro*·pa

cloud nube ⓕ *noo*·be

cloudy nublado noo·*bla*·do

clove (garlic) diente ⓜ (de ajo) *dyen*·te (de a·kho)

cloves clavos ⓜ pl *kla*·vos

clutch embrague ⓕ em·*bra*·ge

coach entrenador/entrenadora ⓜ/ⓕ en·tre·na·*dor*/en·tre·na·*do*·ra

coast costa ⓕ *kos*·ta

cocaine cocaína ⓕ ko·ka·ee·na

cockroach cucaracha ⓕ koo·ka·*ra*·cha

cocoa cacao ⓜ ka·*kow*

coconut coco ⓜ *ko*·ko

codeine codeína ⓕ ko·de·ee·na

coffee café ⓜ ka·*fe*

coins monedas ⓕ pl mo·*ne*·das

cold frío/a ⓜ/ⓕ *free*·o/a

cold (illness) resfriado ⓜ res·*free*·a·do

colleague colega ⓜ&ⓕ ko·*le*·ga

collect call llamada ⓕ a cobro revertido lya·*ma*·da a *ko*·bro re·ver·*tee*·do

college residencia ⓕ de estudiantes re·see·*den*·thya de es·too·*dyan*·tes

colour color ⓜ ko·*lor*

colour (film) película ⓕ en color pe·*lee*·koo·la en ko·*lor*

comb peine ⓜ *pey*·ne

come venir ve·*neer*

come (arrive) llegar lye·*gar*

comedy comedia ⓕ ko·*me*·dya

comfortable cómodo/a ⓜ/ⓕ *ko*·mo·do/a

communion comunión ⓕ ko·moo·*nyon*

communist comunista ⓜ&ⓕ ko·moo·*nees*·ta

companion compañero/a ⓜ/ⓕ kom·pa·*nye*·ro/a

company compañía ⓕ kom·pa·*nyee*·a

compass brújula ⓕ *broo*·khoo·la

complain quejarse ke·*khar*·se

computer ordenador ⓜ or·de·na·*dor*

computer game juegos ⓜ pl de ordenador *khwe*·gos de or·de·na·*dor*

concert concierto ⓜ kon·*thyer*·to

conditioner acondicionador ⓜ a·kon·dee·thyo·na·*dor*

condoms condones ⓜ pl kon·*do*·nes

confession confesión ⓕ kon·fe·*syon*

confirm confirmar kon·feer·*mar*

connection conexión ⓕ ko·ne·*ksyon*

conservative conservador/conservadora ⓜ/ⓕ kon·ser·va·*dor*/kon·ser·va·*do*·ra

constipation estreñimiento ⓜ es·tre·nyee·*myen*·to

consulate consulado ⓜ kon·soo·*la*·do

contact lenses lentes ⓜ pl de contacto *len*·tes de kon·*tak*·to

contraceptives anticonceptivos ⓜ pl an·tee·kon·thep·*tee*·vos

contract contrato ⓜ kon·*tra*·to

convenience store negocio ⓜ de artículos básicos ne·*go*·thyo de ar·*tee*·koo·los *ba*·see·kos

convent convento ⓜ kon·*ven*·to

cook cocinero ⓜ ko·thee·*ne*·ro

cook cocinar ko·thee·*nar*

cookie galleta ⓕ ga·*lye*·ta

corn maíz ⓜ ma·*eeth*

corn flakes copos ⓜ pl de maíz *ko*·pos de ma·*eeth*

corner esquina ⓕ es·*kee*·na

corrupt corrupto/a ⓜ/ⓕ ko·*roop*·to/a

cost costar kos·*tar*

cottage cheese requesón ⓜ re·ke·*son*
cotton algodón ⓜ al·go·*don*
cotton balls bolas ① pl de algodón
bo·las de al·go·*don*
cough tos ① tos
cough medicine jarabe ⓜ kha·ra·be
count contar kon·*tar*
counter mostrador ⓜ mos·tra·*dor*
country país ⓜ pa·*ees*
countryside campo ⓜ *kam*·po
coupon cupón ⓜ koo·*pon*
courgette calabacín ⓜ ka·la·ba·*theen*
court (tennis) pista ① *pees*·ta
cous cous cus cus ⓜ koos koos
cover charge precio ⓜ del cubierto
pre·thyo del koo·*byer*·to
cow vaca ① *va*·ka
crab cangrejo ⓜ kan·*gre*·kho
crackers galletas ① pl saladas
ga·*lye*·tas sa·*la*·das
crafts artesanía ① ar·te·sa·*nee*·a
crash choque ⓜ *cho*·ke
crazy loco/a ⓜ/① *lo*·ko/a
cream (food) crema *kre*·ma
cream (moisturising) crema ①
hidratante *kre*·ma ee·dra·*tan*·te
cream cheese queso ⓜ crema *ke*·so
kre·ma
creche guardería ① gwar·de·*ree*·a
credit card tarjeta ① de crédito
tar·*khe*·ta de *kre*·dee·to
cricket críquet ⓜ *kree*·ket
crop cosecha ① ko·*se*·cha
crowded abarrotado/a ⓜ/①
a·ba·ro·*ta*·do/a
cucumber pepino ⓜ pe·*pee*·no
cuddle abrazo ⓜ a·*bra*·tho
cup taza ① *ta*·tha
cupboard armario ⓜ ar·*ma*·ryo
currency exchange cambio ⓜ (de
dinero) *kam*·byo (de dee·*ne*·ro)
current (electricity) corriente ①
ko·*ryen*·te
current affairs informativo ⓜ
een·for·ma·*tee*·vo
curry curry ⓜ *koo*·ree

curry powder curry ⓜ en polvo
koo·ree en *pol*·vo
customs aduana ① a·*dwa*·na
cut cortar kor·*tar*
cutlery cubiertos ⓜ pl koo·*byer*·tos
CV historial ⓜ profesional ees·to·*ryal*
pro·fe·syo·*nal*
cycle andar en bicicleta an·*dar* en
bee·thee·*kle*·ta
cycling ciclismo ⓜ thee·*klees*·mo
cyclist ciclista ⓜ&① thee·*klees*·ta
cystitis cistitis ① thees·*tee*·tees

D

dad papá ⓜ pa·*pa*
daily diariamente dya·rya·*men*·te
dance bailar bai·*lar*
dancing bailar ⓜ bai·*lar*
dangerous peligroso/a ⓜ/①
pe·lee·*gro*·so/a
dark oscuro/a ⓜ/① os·*koo*·ro/a
date citarse thee·*tar*·se
date (a person) salir con sa·*leer* kon
date (time) fecha ① *fe*·cha
date of birth fecha ① de nacimiento
fe·cha de na·thee·*myen*·to
daughter hija ① *ee*·kha
dawn alba ① *al*·ba
day día ⓜ *dee*·a
day after tomorrow pasado mañana
pa·*sa*·do ma·*nya*·na
day before yesterday anteayer
an·te·a·*yer*
dead muerto/a ⓜ/① *mwer*·to/a
deaf sordo/a ⓜ/① *sor*·do/a
deal (cards) repartir re·par·*teer*
decide decidir de·thee·*deer*
deep profundo/a ⓜ/① pro·*foon*·do/a
deforestation deforestación ①
de·fo·res·ta·*thyon*
degree título ⓜ *tee*·too·lo
delay demora ① de·*mo*·ra
delirious delirante de·lee·*ran*·te
deliver entregar en·tre·*gar*
democracy democracia ①
de·mo·*kra*·thya

demonstration manifestación ①
ma·nee·fes·ta·*thyon*

Denmark Dinamarca ①
dee·na·*mar*·ka

dental floss hilo ⓜ dental ee·lo
den·*tal*

dentist dentista ⓜ&① den·*tees*·ta

deny negar ne·*gar*

deodorant desodorante ⓜ
de·so·do·*ran*·te

depart salir de sa·*leer* de

department store grande almacen
ⓜ *gran*·de al·ma·*then*

departure salida ① sa·*lee*·da

deposit depósito ⓜ de·*po*·see·to

descendant descendiente ⓜ
des·then·*dyen*·te

desert desierto ⓜ de·*syer*·to

design diseño ⓜ dee·se·nyo

destination destino ⓜ des·*tee*·no

destroy destruir des·troo·*eer*

detail detalle ⓜ de·*ta*·lye

diabetes diabetes ① dee·a·be·tes

diaper pañal ⓜ pa·*nyal*

diaphragm diafragma ⓜ
dee·a·*frag*·ma

diarrhoea diarrea ① dee·a·*re*·a

diary agenda ① a·*khen*·da

dice (die) dados ⓜ pl *da*·dos

dictionary diccionario ⓜ
deek·thyo·*na*·ryo

die morir mo·*reer*

diet régimen ⓜ *re*·khee·men

different diferente ⓜ/① dee·fe·*ren*·te

difficult difícil ⓜ/① dee·*fee*·theel

dining car vagón ⓜ restaurante
va·*gon* res·tow·*ran*·te

dinner cena ① *the*·na

direct directo/a ⓜ/① dee·*rek*·to/a

direct-dial marcar directo mar·*kar*
dee·*rek*·to

director director/directora ⓜ/①
dee·rek·*tor*/dee·rek·*to*·ra

dirty sucio/a ⓜ/① *soo*·thyo/a

disabled minusválido/a ⓜ/①
mee·noos·va·*lee*·do/a

disco discoteca ① dees·ko·*te*·ka

discount descuento ⓜ des·*kwen*·to

discover descubrir des·koo·*breer*

discrimination discriminación ①
dees·kree·mee·na·*thyon*

disease enfermedad ① en·fer·me·*da*

disk disco ⓜ *dees*·ko

dive bucear boo·the·*ar*

diving submarinismo
soob·ma·ree·*nees*·mo

diving equipment equipo ⓜ de
inmersión ① e·*kee*·po de een·mer·*syon*

dizzy mareado/a ⓜ/① ma·re·a·do/a

do hacer a·*ther*

doctor doctor/doctora ⓜ/① dok·*tor*/
dok·*to*·ra

documentary documental ⓜ
do·koo·men·*tal*

dog perro/a ⓜ/① *pe*·ro/a

dole paro ⓜ *pa*·ro

doll muñeca ① moo·*nye*·ka

domestic flight vuelo ⓜ doméstico
vwe·lo do·*mes*·tee·ko

donkey burro ⓜ *boo*·ro

door puerta ① *pwer*·ta

dope droga ① *dro*·ga

double doble ⓜ/① *do*·ble

double bed cama ① de matrimonio
ka·ma de ma·tree·mo·nyo

double room habitación ① doble
a·bee·ta·*thyon* do·ble

down abajo a·*ba*·kho

downhill cuesta abajo *kwes*·ta a·*ba*·kho

dozen docena ① do·*the*·na

draw dibujar dee·boo·*khar*

dream soñar so·*nyar*

dress vestido ⓜ ves·*tee*·do

dried fruit fruto ⓜ seco *froo*·to se·ko

drink bebida ① be·*bee*·da

drink beber be·*ber*

drive conducir kon·doo·*theer*

drivers licence carnet ⓜ de conducir
kar·*ne* de kon·doo·*theer*

drug droga ① *dro*·ga

drug addiction drogadicción ①
dro·ga·deek·*thyon*

E

drug dealer traficante ⓜ de drogas tra·fee·*kan*·te de *dro*·gas

drums batería ⓕ ba·te·ree·a

drumstick (chicken) muslo *moos*·lo

drunk borracho/a ⓜ/ⓕ bo·*ra*·cho/a

dry secar se·*kar*

duck pato ⓜ *pa*·to

dummy (pacifier) chupete ⓜ choo·*pe*·te

E

each cada *ka*·da

ear oreja ⓕ o·*re*·kha

early temprano tem·*pra*·no

earn ganar ga·*nar*

earplugs tapones ⓜ pl para los oídos ta·*po*·nes *pa*·ra los o·*ee*·dos

earrings pendientes ⓜ pl pen·*dyen*·tes

Earth Tierra ⓕ *tye*·ra

earthquake terremoto ⓜ te·re·*mo*·to

east este *es*·te

Easter Pascua ⓕ *pas*·kwa

Easter Week Semana ⓕ Santa se·*ma*·na *san*·ta

easy fácil *fa*·theel

eat comer ko·*mer*

economy class clase ⓕ turística *kla*·se too·*rees*·tee·ka

eczema eczema ⓕ ek·*the*·ma

editor editor/editora ⓜ/ⓕ e·dee·*tor*/ e·dee·*to*·ra

education educación ⓕ e·doo·ka·*thyon*

eggplant berenjenas ⓕ pl be·ren·*khe*·nas

egg huevo ⓜ *we*·vo

elections elecciones ⓕ pl e·lek·*thyo*·nes

electrical store tienda ⓕ de productos eléctricos *tyen*·da de pro·*dook*·tos e·*lek*·tree·kos

electricity electricidad ⓕ e·lek·tree·thee·*da*

elevator ascensor ⓜ as·then·*sor*

embarrassed avergonzado/a ⓜ/ⓕ a·ver·gon·*tha*·do/a

embassy embajada ⓕ em·ba·*kha*·da

emergency emergencia ⓕ e·mer·*khen*·thya

emotional emocional e·mo·thyo·*nal*

employee empleado/a ⓜ/ⓕ em·ple·a·do/a

employer jefe/a ⓜ/ⓕ *khe*·fe/a

empty vacío/a ⓜ/ⓕ va·*thee*·o/a

end fin ⓜ feen

end acabar a·ka·*bar*

endangered species especies ⓕ pl en peligro de extinción es·*pe*·thyes en pe·*lee*·gro de eks·teen·*thyon*

engagement compromiso ⓜ kom·pro·*mee*·so

engine motor ⓜ mo·*tor*

engineer ingeniero/a ⓜ/ⓕ een·khe·*nye*·ro/a

engineering ingeniería ⓕ een·khe·nye·*ree*·a

England Inglaterra ⓕ een·gla·*te*·ra

English inglés ⓜ een·*gles*

enjoy (oneself) divertirse dee·ver·*teer*·se

enough suficiente ⓜ/ⓕ soo·fee·*thyen*·te

enter entrar en·*trar*

entertainment guide guía ⓕ del ocio *gee*·a del o·*thyo*

envelope sobre ⓜ *so*·bre

environment medio ⓜ ambiente *me*·dyo am·*byen*·te

epilepsy epilepsia ⓕ e·pee·*lep*·sya

equal opportunity igualdad ⓕ de oportunidades ee·gwal·*da* de o·por·too·nee·*da*·des

equality igualdad ⓕ ee·gwal·*da*

equipment equipo ⓜ e·*kee*·po

escalator escaleras ⓕ pl mecánicas es·ka·*le*·ras me·*ka*·nee·kas

euro euro ⓜ e·*oo*·ro

Europe Europa ⓕ e·oo·*ro*·pa

euthanasia eutanasia ⓕ e·oo·ta·*na*·sya

evening noche ⓕ *no*·che

everything todo *to*·do

example ejemplo ⓜ e·*khem*·plo
excellent excelente ⓜ/ⓕ
eks·the·*len*·te
exchange cambio ⓜ *kam*·byo
exchange (money) cambiar kam·*byar*
exchange rate tipo ⓜ de cambio
tee·po de *kam*·byo
exchange (give gifts) regalar
re·ga·*lar*
excluded no incluido no
een·kloo·*ee*·do
exhaust tubo ⓜ de escape *too*·bo de
es·*ka*·pe
exhibit exponer eks·po·*ner*
exhibition exposición ⓕ
eks·po·see·*thyon*
exit salida ⓕ sa·*lee*·da
expensive caro/a ⓜ/ⓕ *ka*·ro/a
experience experiencia ⓕ
eks·pe·*ryen*·thya
express expreso/a ⓜ/ⓕ eks·*pre*·so/a
express mail correo ⓜ urgente
ko·*re*·o oor·*khen*·te
extension (visa) prolongación ⓕ
pro·lon·ga·*thyon*
eye ojo ⓜ o·kho
eye drops gotas ⓕ pl para los ojos
go·tas *pa*·ra los o·khos

F

fabric tela ⓕ *te*·la
face cara ⓕ *ka*·ra
face cloth toallita ⓕ to·a·*lyee*·ta
factory fábrica ⓕ *fa*·bree·ka
factory worker obrero/a ⓜ/ⓕ
o·*bre*·ro/a
fall caída ⓕ ka·*ee*·da
family familia ⓕ fa·*mee*·lya
family name apellido ⓜ a·pe·*lyee*·do
famous famoso/a ⓜ/ⓕ fa·*mo*·so/a
fan (hand held) abanico ⓜ
a·ba·*nee*·ko
fan (electric) ventilador ⓜ
ven·tee·la·*dor*
fanbelt correa ⓕ del ventilador
ko·*re*·a del ven·tee·la·*dor*

far lejos *le*·khos
farm granja ⓕ *gran*·kha
farmer agricultor/agricultora ⓜ/ⓕ
a·gree·kool·*tor*/a·gree·kool·*to*·ra
fast rápido/a ⓜ/ⓕ *ra*·pee·do/a
fat gordo/a ⓜ/ⓕ *gor*·do/a
father padre ⓜ *pa*·dre
father-in-law suegro ⓜ *swe*·gro
fault falta ⓕ *fal*·ta
faulty defectuoso/a ⓜ/ⓕ
de·fek·*two*·so/a
feed dar de comer dar de ko·*mer*
feel sentir sen·*teer*
feelings sentimientos ⓜ pl
sen·tee·*myen*·tos
fence cerca ⓕ *ther*·ka
fencing esgrima ⓕ es·*gree*·ma
festival festival ⓜ fes·tee·*val*
fever fiebre ⓕ *fye*·bre
few pocos/as ⓜ/ⓕ *po*·kos/as
fiance prometido ⓜ pro·me·*tee*·do
fiancee prometida ⓕ pro·me·*tee*·da
fiction ficción ⓕ feek·*thyon*
field campo ⓜ *kam*·po
fig higo ⓜ *ee*·go
fight pelea ⓕ pe·*le*·a
fight luchar loo·*char*
fill llenar lye·*nar*
fillet filete ⓜ fee·*le*·te
film película ⓕ pe·*lee*·koo·la
film speed sensibilidad ⓕ
sen·see·bee·lee·*da*
filtered con filtro kon *feel*·tro
find encontrar en·kon·*trar*
fine multa ⓕ *mool*·ta
finger dedo ⓜ *de*·do
finish terminar ter·mee·*nar*
fire fuego ⓜ *fwe*·go
firewood leña ⓕ *le*·nya
first primero/a ⓜ/ⓕ pree·*me*·ro/a
first class primera clase pree·*me*·ra
kla·se
first-aid kit maletín ⓜ de primeros
auxilios ma·le·*teen* de pree·*me*·ros
ow·*ksee*·lyos
fish pez ⓜ peth

G

fish (as food) pescado ⓜ pes·ka·do
fish shop pescadería ⓕ
pes·ka·de·ree·a
fishing pesca ⓕ pes·ka
flag bandera ⓕ ban·de·ra
flannel franela ⓕ fra·ne·la
flashlight linterna ⓕ leen·ter·na
flat llano/a ⓜ/ⓕ lya·no/a
flea pulga ⓕ pool·ga
flooding inundación ⓕ
ee·noon·da·thyon
floor suelo ⓜ swe·lo
florist florista ⓜ&ⓕ flo·rees·ta
flour harina ⓕ a·ree·na
flower flor ⓕ flor
flower seller vendedor/vend-
edora ⓜ/ⓕ de flores ven·de·dor/
ven·de·do·ra de flo·res
fly volar vo·lar
foggy brumoso/a ⓜ/ⓕ broo·mo·so
follow seguir se·geer
food comida ⓕ ko·mee·da
food supplies víveres ⓜ pl vee·ve·res
foot pie ⓜ pye
football fútbol ⓜ foot·bol
footpath acera ⓕ a·the·ra
foreign extranjero/a ⓜ/ⓕ
eks·tran·khe·ro/a
forest bosque ⓜ bos·ke
forever para siempre pa·ra syem·pre
forget olvidar ol·vee·dar
forgive perdonar per·do·nar
fork tenedor ⓜ te·ne·dor
fortnight quincena ⓕ keen·the·na
foul sucio/a ⓜ/ⓕ soo·thyo/a
foyer vestíbulo ⓜ ves·tee·boo·lo
fragile frágil fra·kheel
France Francia ⓕ fran·thya
free (not bound) libre lee·bre
free (of charge) gratis gra·tees
freeze helarse e·lar·se
friend amigo/a ⓜ/ⓕ a·mee·go/a
frost escarcha ⓕ es·kar·cha
frozen foods productos congelados
ⓜ pl pro·dook·tos kon·khe·la·dos
fruit fruta ⓕ froo·ta

fruit picking recolección ⓕ de fruta
re·ko·lek·thyon de froo·ta
fry freír fre·eer
frying pan sartén ⓕ sar·ten
full lleno/a ⓜ/ⓕ lye·no/a
full-time a tiempo completo a
tyem·po kom·ple·to
fun diversión ⓕ dee·ver·syon
funeral funeral ⓜ foo·ne·ral
funny gracioso/a ⓜ/ⓕ gra·thyo·so/a
furniture muebles ⓜ pl mwe·bles
future futuro ⓜ foo·too·ro

G

gay gay gai
general general khe·ne·ral
Germany Alemania ⓕ a·le·ma·nya
gift regalo ⓜ re·ga·lo
gig bolo ⓜ bo·lo
gin ginebra ⓕ khee·ne·bra
ginger jengibre ⓜ khen·khee·bre
girl chica ⓕ chee·ka
girlfriend novia ⓕ no·vya
give dar dar
glandular fever fiebre ⓕ glandular
fye·bre glan·doo·lar
glass (material) vidrio ⓜ vee·dryo
glass (drinking) vaso ⓜ va·so
glasses gafas ⓕ pl ga·fas
gloves guantes ⓜ pl gwan·tes
go ir eer
go out with salir con sa·leer kon
go shopping ir de compras eer de
kom·pras
goal gol ⓜ gol
goalkeeper portero/a ⓜ/ⓕ por·te·ro/a
goat cabra ⓕ ka·bra
goat's cheese queso ⓜ de cabra
ke·so de ka·bra
god Dios ⓜ dyos
goggles gafas ⓕ pl de submarinismo
ga·fas de soob·ma·ree·nees·mo
golf ball pelota ⓕ de golf pe·lo·ta
de golf
golf course campo ⓜ de golf kam·po
de golf

good bueno/a ⓜ/ⓕ *bwe·*no/a
government gobierno ⓜ
go·*byer·*no
gram gramo ⓜ *gra·*mo
grandchild nieto/a ⓜ/ⓕ *nye·*to/a
grandfather abuelo ⓜ a·*bwe·*lo
grandmother abuela ⓕ a·*bwe·*la
grapefruit pomelo ⓜ po·*me·*lo
grapes uvas ⓕ pl *oo·*vas
graphic art arte ⓜ gráfico *ar·*te
*gra·*fee·ko
grass hierba ⓕ *yer·*ba
grave tumba ⓕ *toom·*ba
gray gris grees
great fantástico/a ⓜ/ⓕ
fan·*tas·*tee·ko/a
green verde *ver·*de
greengrocery (shop) verdulería ⓕ
ver·doo·le·*ree·*a
grocer (shopkeeper) verdulero/a
ⓜ/ⓕ ver·doo·le·ro/a
grey gris grees
grocery tienda ⓕ de comestibles
*tyen·*da de ko·mes·*tee·*bles
grow crecer kre·*ther*
g-string tanga ⓕ *tan·*ga
guess adivinar a·dee·vee·*nar*
guide (audio) guía ⓕ audio *gee·*a
*ow·*dyo
guide (person) guía ⓜ&ⓕ *gee·*a
guide dog perro lazarillo ⓜ *pe·*ro
la·tha·*ree·*lyo
guidebook guía ⓕ *gee·*a
guided tour recorrido ⓜ guiado
re·ko·*ree·*do gee·*a·*do
guilty culpable kool·*pa·*ble
guitar guitarra ⓕ gee·*ta·*ra
gum chicle ⓜ *chee·*kle
gymnastics gimnasia ⓕ rítmica
kheem·*na·*sya reet·mee·ka
gynaecologist ginecólogo ⓜ
khee·ne·ko·lo·go

hair pelo ⓜ *pe·*lo
hairbrush cepillo ⓜ the·*pee·*lyo

hairdresser peluquero/a ⓜ/ⓕ
pe·loo·*ke·*ro/a
halal halal a·*lal*
half medio/a ⓜ/ⓕ *me·*dyo/a
half a litre medio litro ⓜ *me·*dyo
*lee·*tro
hallucinate alucinar a·loo·thee·*nar*
ham jamón ⓜ kha·*mon*
hammer martillo ⓜ mar·*tee·*lyo
hammock hamaca ⓕ a·*ma·*ka
hand mano ⓕ *ma·*no
handbag bolso ⓜ *bol·*so
handicrafts artesanía ⓕ
ar·te·sa·*nee·*a
handlebar manillar ⓜ ma·nee·*lyar*
handmade hecho a mano *e·*cho a
*ma·*no
handsome hermoso ⓜ er·*mo·*so
happy feliz fe·*leeth*
harassment acoso ⓜ a·*ko·*so
harbour puerto ⓜ *pwer·*to
hard duro/a ⓜ/ⓕ *doo·*ro/a
hardware store ferretería ⓕ
fe·re·te·*ree·*a
hash hachís ⓜ a·*chees*
hat sombrero ⓜ som·*bre·*ro
have tener te·*ner*
have a cold estar constipado/a ⓜ/ⓕ
es·*tar* kons·tee·*pa·*do/a
have fun divertirse dee·ver·*teer·*se
hay fever alergia ⓕ al polen a·*ler·*khya
al *po·*len
he él el
head cabeza ⓕ ka·*be·*tha
headache dolor ⓜ de cabeza do·*lor*
de ka·*be·*tha
headlights faros ⓜ pl *fa·*ros
health salud ⓕ sa·*loo*
hear oír o·*eer*
hearing aid audífono ⓜ ow·*dee·*fo·no
heart corazón ⓜ ko·ra·*thon*
heart condition condición ⓕ
cardíaca kon·dee·*thyon* kar·*dee·*a·ka
heat calor ⓜ ka·*lor*
heater estufa ⓕ es·*too·*fa
heavy pesado/a ⓜ/ⓕ pe·*sa·*do/a

I

helmet casco ⓜ *kas*·ko
help ayudar a·yoo·*dar*
hepatitis hepatitis ⓕ e·pa·tee·*tees*
her su soo
herbalist herbolario/a ⓜ/ⓕ
er·bo·la·*ree*·o/a
herbs hierbas ⓕ pl *yer*·bas
here aquí a·*kee*
heroin heroína ⓕ e·ro·ee·na
herring arenque ⓜ a·*ren*·ke
high alto/a ⓜ/ⓕ *al*·to/a
high school instituto ⓜ
eens·tee·*too*·to
hike ir de excursión eer de
eks·koor·*syon*
hiking excursionismo ⓜ
eks·koor·syo·*nees*·mo
hiking boots botas ⓕ pl de montaña
bo·tas de mon·*ta*·nya
hiking routes caminos ⓜ pl rurales
ka·*mee*·nos roo·*ra*·les
hill colina ⓕ ko·*lee*·na
Hindu hindú ⓜ&ⓕ een·*doo*
hire alquilar al·kee·*lar*
his su soo
historical histórico/a ⓜ/ⓕ
ees·*to*·ree·ko/a
hitchhike hacer dedo a·*ther* de·do
HIV positive seropositivo/a ⓜ/ⓕ
se·ro·po·see·*tee*·vo/a
hockey hockey ⓜ *kho*·kee
holiday día festivo ⓜ *dee*·a fes·*tee*·vo
holidays vacaciones ⓕ pl
va·ka·*thyo*·nes
homeless sin hogar seen o·*gar*
homemaker ama ⓕ de casa a·ma
de *ka*·sa
homosexual homosexual ⓜ&ⓕ
o·mo·sek·*swal*
honey miel ⓕ myel
honeymoon luna ⓕ de miel *loo*·na
de myel
horoscope horóscopo ⓜ
o·*ros*·ko·po
horse caballo ⓜ ka·*ba*·lyo
horse riding equitación ⓕ
e·kee·ta·*thyon*

horseradish rábano ⓜ picante
ra·ba·no pee·*kan*·te
hospital hospital ⓜ os·pee·*tal*
hospitality hostelería ⓕ os·te·le·*ree*·a
hot caliente ka·*lyen*·te
hot water agua caliente ⓕ *a*·gwa
ka·*lyen*·te
hotel hotel ⓜ o·*tel*
house casa ⓕ *ka*·sa
housework trabajo ⓜ de casa
tra·*ba*·kho de *ka*·sa
how cómo *ko*·mo
how much cuánto *kwan*·to
hug abrazo ⓜ a·*bra*·tho
huge enorme e·*nor*·me
human rights derechos ⓜ pl humanos de·*re*·chos oo·*ma*·nos
humanities humanidades ⓕ pl
oo·ma·nee·*da*·des
hungry hambriento/a ⓜ/ⓕ
am·*bryen*·to/a
hungry tener hambre te·*ner* am·bre
hunting caza ⓕ *ka*·tha
hurt dañar da·*nyar*
husband marido ⓜ ma·*ree*·do

I

I yo yo
ice hielo ⓜ *ye*·lo
ice axe piolet ⓜ pyo·*le*
ice cream helado ⓜ e·*la*·do
ice cream parlour heladería ⓕ
e·la·de·*ree*·a
ice hockey hockey ⓜ sobre hielo
kho·kee so·bre *ye*·lo
identification identificación ⓕ
ee·den·tee·fee·ka·*thyon*
identification card carnet ⓜ de
identidad kar·*net* de ee·den·tee·*da*
idiot idiota ⓜ&ⓕ ee·*dyo*·ta
if si see
ill enfermo/a ⓜ/ⓕ en·*fer*·mo/a
immigration inmigración ⓕ
een·mee·gra·*thyon*
important importante eem·por·*tan*·te
in a hurry de prisa de *pree*·sa

in front of enfrente de en·*fren*·te de
included incluido een·kloo·ee·do
income tax impuesto ⓜ sobre la renta eem·*pwes*·to so·bre la *ren*·ta
India India ⓕ *een*·dya
indicator indicador ⓜ een·dee·ka·*dor*
indigestion indigestión ⓕ een·dee·khes·*tyon*
industry industria ⓕ een·*doos*·trya
infection infección ⓕ een·fek·*thyon*
inflammation inflamación ⓕ een·fla·ma·*thyon*
influenza gripe ⓕ *gree*·pe
ingredient ingrediente ⓜ een·gre·*dyen*·te
inject inyectarse een·yek·*tar*·se
injection inyección ⓕ een·yek·*thyon*
injury herida ⓕ e·*ree*·da
innocent inocente ee·no·*then*·te
inside adentro a·*den*·tro
instructor profesor/profesora ⓜ/ⓕ pro·fe·*sor*/pro·fe·*so*·ra
insurance seguro ⓜ se·*goo*·ro
interesting interesante een·te·re·*san*·te
intermission descanso ⓜ des·*kan*·so
international internacional een·ter·na·thyo·*nal*
internet internet *een*·ter·net
internet cafe cibercafé thee·ber·ka·*fe*
interpreter intérprete ⓜ&ⓕ een·*ter*·pre·te
intersection cruce ⓜ *croo*·the
interview entrevista ⓕ en·tre·*vees*·ta
invite invitar een·vee·*tar*
Ireland Irlanda ⓕ eer·*lan*·da
iron plancha ⓕ *plan*·cha
island isla ⓕ *ees*·la
IT informática ⓕ een·for·*ma*·tee·ka
Italy Italia ⓕ ee·*ta*·lya
itch picazón ⓕ pee·ka·*thon*
itemised detallado/a ⓜ/ⓕ de·ta·*lya*·do/a
itinerary itinerario ⓜ ee·tee·ne·*ra*·ryo
IUD DIU ⓜ de·ee·oo

J

jacket chaqueta ⓕ cha·*ke*·ta
jail cárcel ⓕ *kar*·thel
jam mermelada ⓕ mer·me·*la*·da
Japan Japón ⓜ kha·*pon*
jar jarra ⓕ *kha*·ra
jaw mandíbula ⓕ man·*dee*·boo·la
jealous celoso/a ⓜ/ⓕ the·*lo*·so/a
jeans vaqueros ⓜ pl va·*ke*·ros
jeep yip ⓜ yeep
jet lag jet lag ⓜ dyet lag
jewellery shop joyería ⓕ kho·ye·*ree*·a
Jewish judío/a ⓜ/ⓕ khoo·*dee*·o/a
job trabajo ⓜ tra·*ba*·kho
jockey jockey ⓜ *dyo*·kee
jogging footing ⓜ *foo*·teen
joke broma ⓕ *bro*·ma
joke bromear bro·me·*ar*
journalist periodista ⓜ&ⓕ pe·ryo·*dees*·ta
judge juez ⓜ&ⓕ khweth
juice jugo ⓜ *khoo*·go • zumo ⓜ *thoo*·mo
jump saltar sal·*tar*
jumper (sweater) jersey ⓜ kher·*say*
jumper leads cables ⓜ pl de arranque *ka*·bles de a·*ran*·ke

K

ketchup salsa ⓕ de tomate *sal*·sa de to·*ma*·te
key llave ⓕ *lya*·ve
keyboard teclado ⓜ te·*kla*·do
kick dar una patada dar oo·na pa·*ta*·da
kick (a goal) meter (un gol) me·*ter* (oon gol)
kill matar ma·*tar*
kilogram kilogramo ⓜ kee·lo·*gra*·mo
kilometre kilómetro ⓜ kee·*lo*·me·tro
kind amable a·*ma*·ble
kindergarten escuela ⓕ de párvulos es·*kwe*·la de *par*·voo·los
king rey ⓜ rey
kiss beso ⓜ *be*·so
kiss besar be·*sar*

L

kitchen cocina ① ko·*thee*·na
kitten gatito/a ⑩/① ga·*tee*·to/a
kiwifruit kiwi ⑩ *kee*·wee
knapsack mochila ① mo·*chee*·la
knee rodilla ① ro·*dee*·lya
knife cuchillo ⑩ koo·*chee*·lyo
know (someone) conocer ko·no·*ther*
know (something) saber sa·*ber*
kosher kosher *ko*·sher

L

labourer obrero/a ⑩/① o·*bre*·ro/a
lace encaje ⑩ en·*ka*·khe
lager cerveza ① rubia ther·*ve*·tha *roo*·bya
lake lago ⑩ *la*·go
lamb cordero ⑩ kor·*de*·ro
land tierra ① *tye*·ra
landlady propietaria ① pro·pye·*ta*·rya
landlord propietario ⑩ pro·pye·*ta*·ryo
languages idiomas ⑩ pl ee·*dyo*·mas
laptop ordenador ⑩ portátil or·de·na·*dor* por·*ta*·teel
lard manteca ① man·*te*·ka
large grande *gran*·de
late tarde *tar*·de
laugh reírse re·*eer*·se
laundrette lavandería ① la·van·de·*ree*·a
laundry lavadero ⑩ la·va·*de*·ro
law ley ① ley
lawyer abogado/a ⑩/① a·bo·*ga*·do/a
leader líder ⑩&① *lee*·der
leaf hoja ① *o*·kha
learn aprender a·pren·*der*
leather cuero ⑩ *kwe*·ro
leave dejar de·*khar*
leave (behind/over) quedar ke·*dar*
lecturer profesor/profesora ⑩/① pro·fe·*sor*/pro·fe·*so*·ra
ledge saliente ① sa·*lyen*·te
leek puerro ⑩ *pwe*·ro
left izquierda ① eeth·*kyer*·da
left luggage consigna ① kon·*seeg*·na
left-wing de izquierdas de eeth·*kyer*·das

leg pierna ① *pyer*·na
legal legal le·*gal*
legislation legislación ① le·khees·la·*thyon*
lemon limón ⑩ lee·*mon*
lemonade limonada ① lee·mo·*na*·da
lens objetivo ⑩ ob·khe·*tee*·vo
Lent Cuaresma ① kwa·*res*·ma
lentils lentejas ① pl len·*te*·khas
lesbian lesbiana ① les·bee·*a*·na
less menos *me*·nos
letter carta ① *kar*·ta
lettuce lechuga ① le·*choo*·ga
liar mentiroso/a ⑩/① men·tee·*ro*·so/a
library biblioteca ① bee·blyo·*te*·ka
lice piojos ⑩ pl *pyo*·khos
license plate number matrícula ① ma·*tree*·koo·la
lie (not stand) tumbarse toom·*bar*·se
life vida ① *vee*·da
lifejacket chaleco ⑩ salvavidas cha·*le*·ko sal·va·*vee*·das
lift ascensor ⑩ as·then·*sor*
light (weight) leve *le*·ve
light luz ① looth
light bulb bombilla ① bom·*bee*·lya
light meter fotómetro ⑩ fo·*to*·me·tro
lighter encendedor ⑩ en·then·de·*dor*
like gustar(le) goos·*tar*(le)
lime lima ① *lee*·ma
line línea ① *lee*·ne·a
lip balm bálsamo ⑩ de labios *bal*·sa·mo de *la*·byos
lips labios ⑩ pl *la*·byos
lipstick pintalabios ⑩ peen·ta·*la*·byos
liquor store bodega ① bo·*de*·ga
listen escuchar es·koo·*char*
live (life) vivir vee·*veer*
live (somewhere) ocupar o·koo·*par*
liver hígado ⑩ *ee*·ga·do
lizard lagartija ① la·gar·*tee*·kha
local de cercanías de ther·ka·*nee*·as
lock cerradura ① the·ra·*doo*·ra
lock cerrar the·*rar*
locked cerrado/a ⑩/① con llave the·*ra*·do/a kon *lya*·ve

M

lollies caramelos ⓜ pl ka·ra·me·los
long largo/a ⓜ/ⓕ lar·go/a
long-distance a larga distancia a lar·ga dees·tan·thya
look mirar mee·rar
look after cuidar kwee·dar
look for buscar boos·kar
lookout mirador ⓜ mee·ra·dor
lose perder per·der
lost perdido/a ⓜ/ⓕ per·dee·do/a
lost property office oficina ⓕ de objetos perdidos o·fee·thee·na de ob·khe·tos per·dee·dos
loud ruidoso/a ⓜ/ⓕ rwee·do·so/a
love querer ke·rer
lover amante ⓜ&ⓕ a·man·te
low bajo/a ⓜ/ⓕ ba·kho/a
lubricant lubricante ⓜ loo·bree·kan·te
luck suerte ⓕ swer·te
lucky afortunado/a ⓜ/ⓕ a·for·too·na·do/a
luggage equipaje ⓜ e·kee·pa·khe
luggage lockers consigna ⓕ automática kon·seeg·na ow·to·ma·tee·ka
luggage tag etiqueta ⓕ de equipaje e·tee·ke·ta de e·kee·pa·khe
lump bulto ⓜ bool·to
lunch almuerzo ⓜ al·mwer·tho
lungs pulmones ⓜ pl pool·mo·nes
luxury lujo ⓜ loo·kho

M

machine máquina ⓕ ma·kee·na
made of (cotton) hecho a de (algodón) e·cho a de (al·go·don)
magazine revista ⓕ re·vees·ta
magician mago/a ⓜ/ⓕ ma·go/a
mail correo ⓜ ko·re·o
mailbox buzón ⓜ boo·thon
main principal preen·thee·pal
make hacer a·ther
make fun of burlarse de boor·lar·se de
make-up maquillaje ⓜ ma·kee·lya·khe
mammogram mamograma ⓜ ma·mo·gra·ma

man hombre ⓜ om·bre
manager gerente ⓜ&ⓕ khe·ren·te
mandarin mandarina ⓕ man·da·ree·na
mango mango ⓜ man·go
manual worker obrero/a ⓜ/ⓕ o·bre·ro/a
many muchos/as ⓜ/ⓕ pl moo·chos/as
map mapa ⓜ ma·pa
margarine margarina ⓕ mar·ga·ree·na
marijuana marihuana ⓕ ma·ree·wa·na
marital status estado ⓜ civil es·ta·do thee·veel
market mercado ⓜ mer·ka·do
marmalade mermelada ⓕ mer·me·la·da
marriage matrimonio ⓜ ma·tree·mo·nyo
marry casarse ka·sar·se
martial arts artes ⓜ pl marciales ar·tes mar·thya·les
mass misa ⓕ mee·sa
massage masaje ⓜ ma·sa·khe
masseur/masseuse masajista ⓜ&ⓕ ma·sa·khees·ta
mat esterilla ⓕ es·te·ree·lya
match partido ⓜ par·tee·do
matches cerillas ⓕ pl the·ree·lyas
mattress colchón ⓜ kol·chon
maybe quizás kee·thas
mayonnaise mayonesa ⓕ ma·yo·ne·sa
mayor alcalde ⓜ&ⓕ al·kal·de
measles sarampión ⓜ sa·ram·pyon
meat carne ⓕ kar·ne
mechanic mecánico/a ⓜ/ⓕ me·ka·nee·ko
media medios ⓜ pl de comunicación me·dyos de ko·moo·nee·ka·thyon
medicine medicina ⓕ me·dee·thee·na
meditation meditación ⓕ me·dee·ta·thyon
meet encontrar en·kon·trar

melon melón Ⓜ me·*lon*

member miembro Ⓜ *myem*·bro

menstruation menstruación Ⓕ mens·trwa·*thyon*

menu menú Ⓜ me·*noo*

message mensaje Ⓜ men·*sa*·khe

metal metal Ⓜ me·*tal*

metre metro Ⓜ *me*·tro

metro station estación Ⓕ de metro es·ta·*thyon* de *me*·tro

microwave microondas Ⓜ mee·kro·*on*·das

midnight medianoche Ⓕ me·dya·*no*·che

migraine migraña Ⓕ mee·*gra*·nya

military service servicio Ⓜ militar ser·*vee*·thyo mee·lee·*tar*

milk leche Ⓕ *le*·che

millimetre milímetro Ⓜ mee·*lee*·me·tro

million millón Ⓜ mee·*lyon*

mince (meat) carne Ⓕ molida *kar*·ne mo·*lee*·da

mind (object) cuidar kwee·*dar*

mineral water agua Ⓜ mineral *a*·gwa mee·ne·*ral*

mints pastillas Ⓕ pl de menta pas·*tee*·lyas de *men*·ta

minute minuto Ⓜ mee·*noo*·to

mirror espejo Ⓜ es·*pe*·kho

miscarriage aborto Ⓜ natural a·*bor*·to na·too·*ral*

miss (feel sad) echar de menos e·*char* de *me*·nos

mistake error Ⓜ e·*ror*

mix mezclar meth·*klar*

mobile phone teléfono Ⓜ móvil te·*le*·fo·no *mo*·veel

modem módem Ⓜ *mo*·dem

moisturiser crema Ⓕ hidratante *kre*·ma ee·dra·*tan*·te

monastery monasterio Ⓜ mo·nas·*te*·ryo

money dinero Ⓜ dee·*ne*·ro

month mes Ⓜ mes

monument monumento Ⓜ mo·noo·*men*·to

(full) moon luna Ⓕ (llena) *loo*·na (*lye*·na)

morning (6am–1pm) mañana Ⓕ ma·*nya*·na

morning sickness náuseas Ⓕ pl del embarazo *now*·se·as del em·ba·*ra*·tho

mosque mezquita Ⓕ meth·*kee*·ta

mosquito mosquito Ⓜ mos·*kee*·to

mosquito coil rollo Ⓜ repelente contra mosquitos *ro*·lyo re·pe·*len*·te *kon*·tra mos·*kee*·tos

mosquito net mosquitera Ⓕ mos·kee·*te*·ra

mother madre Ⓕ *ma*·dre

mother-in-law suegra Ⓕ *swe*·gra

motorboat motora Ⓕ mo·*to*·ra

motorcycle motocicleta Ⓕ mo·to·thee·*kle*·ta

motorway autovía Ⓕ ow·to·*vee*·a

mountain montaña Ⓕ mon·*ta*·nya

mountain bike bicicleta Ⓕ de montaña bee·thee·*kle*·ta de mon·*ta*·nya

mountain path sendero Ⓜ sen·*de*·ro

mountain range cordillera Ⓕ kor·dee·*lye*·ra

mountaineering alpinismo Ⓜ al·pee·*nees*·mo

mouse ratón Ⓜ ra·*ton*

mouth boca Ⓕ *bo*·ka

movie película Ⓕ pe·*lee*·koo·la

mud lodo Ⓜ *lo*·do

muesli muesli Ⓜ *mwes*·lee

mum mamá Ⓕ ma·*ma*

muscle músculo Ⓜ *moos*·koo·lo

museum museo Ⓜ moo·*se*·o

mushroom champiñón Ⓜ cham·pee·*nyon*

music música Ⓕ *moo*·see·ka

musician músico/a Ⓜ/Ⓕ *moo*·see·ko/a

Muslim musulmán/musulmana Ⓜ/Ⓕ moo·sool·*man*/moo·sool·*ma*·na

mussels mejillones Ⓜ pl me·khee·*lyo*·nes

mustard mostaza Ⓕ mos·*ta*·tha

mute mudo/a ⓜ/ⓕ *moo·do/a*
my mi *mee*

N

nail clippers cortauñas ⓜ pl *kor·ta·oo·nyas*
name nombre ⓜ *nom·bre*
napkin servilleta ⓕ *ser·vee·lye·ta*
nappy pañal ⓜ *pa·nyal*
nappy rash irritación ⓕ de pañal *ee·ree·ta·thyon de pa·nyal*
national park parque ⓜ nacional *par·ke na·thyo·nal*
nationality nacionalidad ⓕ *na·thyo·na·lee·da*
nature naturaleza ⓕ *na·too·ra·le·tha*
naturopathy naturopatia ⓕ *na·too·ro·pa·tya*
nausea náusea ⓕ *now·se·a*
near cerca *ther·ka*
nearby cerca *ther·ka*
nearest más cercano/a ⓜ/ⓕ *mas ther·ka·no/a*
necessary necesario/a ⓜ/ⓕ *ne·the·sa·ryo/a*
neck cuello ⓜ *kwe·lyo*
necklace collar ⓜ *ko·lyar*
need necesitar *ne·the·see·tar*
needle (sewing) aguja ⓕ *a·goo·kha*
needle (syringe) jeringa ⓕ *khe·reen·ga*
neither tampoco *tam·po·ko*
net red ⓜ *red*
Netherlands Holanda ⓕ *o·lan·da*
never nunca *noon·ka*
new nuevo/a ⓜ/ⓕ *nwe·vo/a*
New Year Año Nuevo ⓜ *a·nyo nwe·vo*
New Year's Eve Nochevieja ⓕ *no·che·vye·kha*
New Zealand Nueva Zelanda ⓕ *nwe·va the·lan·da*
news noticias ⓕ pl *no·tee·thyas*
news stand quiosco ⓜ *kyos·ko*
newsagency quiosco ⓜ *kyos·ko*
newspaper periódico ⓜ *pe·ryo·dee·ko*

next (month) el próximo (mes) el *prok·see·mo (mes)*
next to al lado de al *la·do de*
nice simpático/a ⓜ/ⓕ *seem·pa·tee·ko/a*
nickname apodo ⓜ *a·po·do*
night noche ⓕ *no·che*
no no *no*
noisy ruidoso/a ⓜ/ⓕ *rwee·do·so/a*
none nada *na·da*
nonsmoking no fumadores no *foo·ma·do·res*
noodles fideos ⓜ pl *fee·de·os*
noon mediodía ⓜ *me·dyo·dee·a*
north norte ⓜ *nor·te*
nose nariz ⓕ *na·reeth*
notebook cuaderno ⓜ *kwa·der·no*
nothing nada *na·da*
now ahora *a·o·ra*
nuclear energy energía ⓕ nuclear *e·ner·khee·a noo·kle·ar*
nuclear testing pruebas ⓕ pl nucleares *prwe·bas noo·kle·a·res*
nuclear waste desperdicios ⓜ pl nucleares *des·per·dee·thyos noo·kle·a·res*
number número ⓜ *noo·me·ro*
nun monja ⓕ *mon·kha*
nurse enfermero/a ⓜ/ⓕ *en·fer·me·ro/a*
nuts nueces ⓕ pl *nwe·thes*
nuts (raw) nueces ⓕ pl (crudas) *nwe·thes (kroo·das)*
nuts (roasted) nueces ⓕ pl (tostadas) *nwe·thes (tos·ta·das)*

O

oats avena ⓕ *a·ve·na*
ocean océano ⓜ *o·the·a·no*
off (food) pasado/a ⓜ/ⓕ *pa·sa·do/a*
office oficina ⓕ *o·fee·thee·na*
office worker oficinista ⓜ&ⓕ *o·fee·thee·nees·ta*
offside fuera de juego *fwe·ra de khwe·go*
often a menudo a *me·noo·do*
oil aceite ⓜ *a·they·te*

old viejo/a ⓜ/ⓕ *vye·*kho/a

olive oil aceite ⓜ de oliva a·*they*·te de o·*lee*·va

Olympic Games Juegos ⓜ pl Olímpicos *khwe*·gos o·*leem*·pee·kos

on en en

once vez ⓕ veth

one-way ticket billete ⓜ sencillo bee·*lye*·te sen·*thee*·lyo

onion ⓕ cebolla the·*bo*·lya

only sólo *so*·lo

open abierto/a ⓜ/ⓕ a·*byer*·to/a

open abrir a·*breer*

opening hours horas ⓕ pl de abrir o·ras de a·*breer*

opera ópera ⓕ o·pe·ra

opera house teatro ⓜ de la ópera te·*a*·tro de la o·pe·ra

operation operación ⓕ o·pe·ra·*thyon*

operator operador/operadora ⓜ/ⓕ o·pe·ra·*dor*/o·pe·ra·*do*·ra

opinion opinión ⓕ o·pee·*nyon*

opposite frente a *fren*·te a

or o o

orange (fruit) naranja ⓕ na·*ran*·kha

orange (colour) naranja na·*ran*·kha

orange juice zumo ⓜ de naranja *thoo*·mo de na·*ran*·kha

orchestra orquesta ⓕ or·*kes*·ta

order orden ⓜ *or*·den

order ordenar or·de·*nar*

ordinary corriente ko·*ryen*·te

orgasm orgasmo ⓜ or·*gas*·mo

original original o·ree·khee·*nal*

other otro/a ⓜ/ⓕ o·tro/a

our nuestro/a ⓜ/ⓕ *nwes*·tro/a

outside exterior ⓜ eks·te·*ryor*

ovarian cyst quiste ⓜ ovárico *kees*·te o·*va*·ree·ko

oven horno ⓜ *or*·no

overcoat abrigo ⓜ a·*bree*·go

overdose sobredosis ⓕ so·bre·do·sees

owe deber de·*ber*

owner dueño/a ⓜ/ⓕ *dwe*·nyo/a

oxygen oxígeno ⓜ ok·*see*·khe·no

oyster ⓕ ostra *os*·tra

ozone layer capa ⓕ de ozono *ka*·pa de o·*tho*·no

pacemaker marcapasos ⓜ mar·ka·pa·sos

pacifier chupete ⓜ choo·pe·te

package paquete ⓜ pa·ke·te

packet paquete ⓜ pa·ke·te

padlock candado ⓜ kan·da·do

page página ⓕ *pa*·khee·na

pain dolor ⓜ do·*lor*

painful doloroso/a ⓜ/ⓕ do·lo·ro·so/a

painkillers analgésicos ⓜ pl a·nal·*khe*·see·kos

paint pintar peen·*tar*

painter pintor/pintora ⓜ/ⓕ peen·*tor*/peen·*to*·ra

painting pintura ⓕ peen·*too*·ra

pair (couple) pareja ⓕ pa·*re*·kha

palace palacio ⓜ pa·*la*·thyo

pan cazuela ⓕ ka·*thwe*·la

pants pantalones ⓜ pl pan·ta·*lo*·nes

panty liners salvaeslips ⓜ pl sal·va·e·*sleeps*

pantyhose medias ⓕ pl *me*·dyas

pap smear citología ⓕ thee·to·lo·*khee*·a

paper papel ⓜ pa·*pel*

paperwork trabajo ⓜ administrativo tra·*ba*·kho ad·mee·nees·tra·*tee*·vo

paraplegic parapléjico/a ⓜ/ⓕ pa·ra·*ple*·khee·ko/a

parasailing esquí ⓜ acuático con paracaídas es·*kee* a·*kwa*·tee·ko kon pa·ra·ka·*ee*·das

parcel paquete ⓜ pa·ke·te

parents padres ⓜ pl *pa*·dres

park parque ⓜ *par*·ke

park (car) estacionar es·ta·thyo·*nar*

parliament parlamento ⓜ par·la·*men*·to

parsley perejil ⓜ pe·re·*kheel*

part parte ⓕ *par*·te

part-time a tiempo parcial a *tyem*·po par·*thyal*

party fiesta ① *fyes*·ta
party (political) partido ⑩ par·*tee*·do
pass pase ⑩ *pa*·se
passenger pasajero/a ⑩/①
pa·sa·*khe*·ro
passport pasaporte ⑩ pa·sa·*por*·te
passport number número ⑩ de
pasaporte *noo*·me·ro de pa·sa·*por*·te
past pasado ⑩ pa·*sa*·do
pasta pasta ① *pas*·ta
pâté (food) paté ⑩ pa·*te*
path sendero ⑩ sen·*de*·ro
pay pagar pa·*gar*
payment pago ⑩ *pa*·go
peace paz ① *path*
peach melocotón ⑩ me·lo·ko·*ton*
peanuts cacahuetes ⑩ pl
ka·ka·*we*·tes
pear pera ① *pe*·ra
peas guisantes ⑩ pl gee·*san*·tes
pedal pedal ⑩ pe·*dal*
pedestrian peatón ⑩&① pe·a·*ton*
pedestrian crossing paso ⑩ de
cebra pa·so de *the*·bra
pen bolígrafo ⑩ bo·*lee*·gra·fo
pencil lápiz ⑩ *la*·peeth
penis pene ⑩ *pe*·ne
penknife navaja ① na·*va*·kha
pensioner pensionista ⑩&①
pen·syo·*nees*·ta
people gente ① *khen*·te
pepper (vegetable) pimiento ⑩
pee·*myen*·to
pepper (spice) pimienta ①
pee·*myen*·ta
per (day) por (dia) por (*dee*·a)
percent por ciento por *thyen*·to
performance actuación ①
ak·twa·*thyon*
perfume perfume ⑩ per·*foo*·me
period pain dolor ⑩ menstrual do·*lor*
mens·*trwal*
permission permiso ⑩ per·*mee*·so
permit permiso ⑩ per·*mee*·so
permit permitir per·mee·*teer*

person persona ① per·*so*·na
perspire sudar soo·*dar*
petition petición ① pe·tee·*thyon*
petrol gasolina ① ga·so·*lee*·na
pharmacy farmacia ① far·*ma*·thya
phone book guía ① telefónica gee·a
te·le·fo·*nee*·ka
phone box cabina ① telefónica
ka·*bee*·ka te·le·fo·*nee*·ka
phone card tarjeta ① de teléfono
tar·*khe*·ta de te·*le*·fo·no
photo foto ① *fo*·to
photographer fotógrafo/a ⑩/①
fo·*to*·gra·fo/a
photography fotografía ①
fo·to·gra·*fee*·a
phrasebook libro ⑩ de frases *lee*·bro
de *fra*·ses
pick up ligar lee·*gar*
pickaxe piqueta ① pee·*ke*·ta
pickles encurtidos ⑩ pl
en·koor·*tee*·dos
picnic comida ① en el campo
ko·*mee*·da en el *kam*·po
pie pastel ⑩ pas·*tel*
piece pedazo ⑩ pe·*da*·tho
pig cerdo ⑩ *ther*·do
pill pastilla ① pas·*tee*·lya
pill, the (contraceptive) píldora ①
peel·do·ra
pillow almohada ① al·*mwa*·da
pillowcase funda ① de almohada
foon·da de al·*mwa*·da
pineapple piña ① *pee*·nya
pink rosa *ro*·sa
pistachio pistacho ⑩ pees·*ta*·cho
place lugar ⑩ loo·*gar*
place of birth lugar ⑩ de nacimiento
loo·*gar* de na·thee·*myen*·to
plane avión ⑩ a·*vyon*
planet planeta ⑩ pla·*ne*·ta
plant planta ① *plan*·ta
plant sembrar sem·*brar*
plastic plástico ⑩ *plas*·tee·ko
plate plato ⑩ *pla*·to
plateau meseta ① me·*se*·ta

platform plataforma ① pla·ta·*for*·ma

play obra ① o·bra

play (musical instrument) tocar to·*kar*

play (sport/games) jugar khoo·*gar*

plug tapar ta·*par*

plum ciruela thee·*rwe*·la

pocket bolsillo ⑩ bol·*see*·lyo

poetry poesía ① po·e·*see*·a

point apuntar a·poon·*tar*

point (tip) punto ⑩ *poon*·to

poisonous venenoso/a ⑩/①
ve·ne·*no*·so/a

poker póquer ⑩ *po*·ker

police policía ① po·lee·*thee*·a

police station comisaría ①
ko·mee·sa·*ree*·a

policy política ① po·*lee*·tee·ka

policy (insurance) póliza ①
po·lee·tha

politician político ⑩ po·*lee*·tee·ko

politics política ① po·*lee*·tee·ka

pollen polen ⑩ *po*·len

polls sondeos ⑩ pl son·*de*·os

pollution contaminación ①
kon·ta·mee·na·*thyon*

poor pobre *po*·bre

popular popular po·poo·*lar*

pork cerdo ⑩ *ther*·do

pork sausage chorizo ⑩ cho·*ree*·tho

port puerto ⑩ *pwer*·to

port (wine) oporto ⑩ o·*por*·to

possible posible po·*see*·ble

post code código postal ⑩ *ko*·dee·go
pos·*tal*

post office correos ⑩ ko·*re*·os

postage franqueo ⑩ fran·*ke*·o

postcard postal ① pos·*tal*

poster póster ⑩ *pos*·ter

pot (kitchen) cazuela ① ka·*thwe*·la

pot (plant) tiesto ⑩ *tyes*·to

potato patata ① pa·*ta*·ta

pottery alfarería ① al·fa·re·*ree*·a

pound (money) libra ① *lee*·bra

poverty pobreza ① po·*bre*·tha

power poder ⑩ po·*der*

prawns gambas ① pl *gam*·bas

prayer oración ① o·ra·*thyon*

prayer book devocionario ⑩
de·vo·thyo·*na*·ryo

prefer preferir pre·fe·*reer*

pregnancy test prueba ① del
embarazo *prwe*·ba del em·ba·*ra*·tho

pregnant embarazada ①
em·ba·ra·*tha*·da

premenstrual tension tensión ①
premenstrual ten·*syon* pre·mens·*trwa*

prepare preparar pre·pa·*rar*

president presidente/a ⑩/①
pre·see·*den*·te/a

pressure presión ① pre·*syon*

pretty bonito/a ⑩/① bo·*nee*·to/a

prevent prevenir pre·ve·*neer*

price precio ⑩ *pre*·thyo

priest sacerdote ⑩ sa·ther·*do*·te

prime minister primer ministro/
primera ministra ⑩/① pre·*mer*
mee·*nees*·tro/pree·*me*·ra
mee·*nees*·tra

prison cárcel ① *kar*·thel

prisoner prisionero/a ⑩/①
pree·syon·*ne*·ro/a

private privado/a ⑩/① pree·va·do/a

private hospital clínica ① *klee*·nee·k

produce producir pro·doo·*theer*

profit beneficio ⑩ be·ne·*fee*·thyo

programme programa ⑩ pro·*gra*·ma

projector proyector ⑩ pro·yek·*tor*

promise promesa ① pro·*me*·sa

protect proteger pro·te·*kher*

protected (species) protegido/a
⑩/① pro·te·*khee*·do/a

protest protesta ① pro·*tes*·ta

protest protestar pro·tes·*tar*

provisions provisiones ① pl
pro·vee·*syo*·nes

prune ciruela ① pasa thee·*rwe*·la pa·s

pub pub ⑩ poob

public telephone teléfono ⑩ públic
te·*le*·fo·no poo·blee·ko

public toilet servicios ⓜ pl
er·vee·thyos
pull tirar tee·*rar*
pump bomba ⓕ *bom*·ba
pumpkin calabaza ⓕ ka·la·*ba*·tha
puncture pinchar peen·*char*
punish castigar kas·tee·*gar*
puppy cachorro ⓜ ka·*cho*·ro
pure puro/a ⓜ/ⓕ *poo*·ro/a
purple lila *lee*·la
push empujar em·poo·*khar*
put poner po·*ner*

Q

qualifications cualificaciones ⓕ pl
·wa·lee·fee·ka·*thyo*·nes
quality calidad ⓕ ka·lee·*da*
quarantine cuarentena ⓕ
·wa·ren·*te*·na
quarrel pelea ⓕ pe·*le*·a
quarter cuarto ⓜ *kwar*·to
queen reina ⓕ *rey*·na
question pregunta ⓕ pre·*goon*·ta
question cuestionar kwes·tyo·*nar*
queue cola ⓕ *ko*·la
quick rápido/a ⓜ/ⓕ *ra*·pee·do/a
quiet tranquilo/a ⓜ/ⓕ tran·*kee*·lo/a
quiet tranquilidad ⓕ tran·kee·lee·*da*
quit dejar de·*khar*

R

rabbit conejo ⓜ ko·*ne*·kho
race (people) raza ⓕ *ra*·tha
race (sport) carrera ⓕ ka·*re*·ra
racetrack (bicycles) velódromo ⓜ
·*e*·lo·dro·mo
racetrack (cars) circuito ⓜ de
carreras theer·*kwee*·to de ka·*re*·ras
racetrack (horses) hipódromo ⓜ
·e·po·dro·mo
racetrack (runners) pista ⓕ *pees*·ta
racing bike bicicleta ⓕ de carreras
ee·thee·*kle*·ta de ka·*re*·ras
racquet raqueta ⓕ ra·*ke*·ta
radiator radiador ⓜ ra·dya·*dor*
radish rábano ⓜ *ra*·ba·no

railway station estación ⓕ de tren
es·ta·*thyon* de tren
rain lluvia ⓕ *lyoo*·vya
raincoat impermeable ⓜ
eem·per·me·a·ble
raisin uva ⓕ pasa oo·va *pa*·sa
rally concentración ⓕ
kon·then·tra·*thyon*
rape violar vyo·*lar*
rare raro/a ⓜ/ⓕ *ra*·ro/a
rash irritación ⓕ ee·ree·ta·*thyon*
raspberry frambuesa ⓕ fram·*bwe*·sa
rat rata ⓕ *ra*·ta
rate of pay salario ⓜ sa·*la*·ryo
raw crudo/a ⓜ/ⓕ *kroo*·do/a
razor afeitadora ⓕ a·fey·ta·*do*·ra
razor blades cuchillas ⓕ pl de afeitar
koo·*chee*·lyas de a·fey·*tar*
read leer le·*er*
ready listo/a ⓜ/ⓕ *lees*·to/a
real estate agent agente inmobiliario
ⓜ a·*khen*·te een·mo·bee·*lya*·ryo
realise darse cuenta de *dar*·se
kwen·ta de
realistic realista re·a·*lees*·ta
reason razón ⓕ ra·*thon*
receipt recibo ⓜ re·*thee*·bo
receive recibir re·thee·*beer*
recently recientemente
re·thyen·te·*men*·te
recognise reconocer re·ko·no·*ther*
recommend recomendar
re·ko·men·*dar*
recording grabación ⓕ gra·ba·*thyon*
recyclable reciclable re·thee·*kla*·ble
recycle reciclar re·thee·*klar*
red rojo/a ⓜ/ⓕ *ro*·kho/a
referee árbitro ⓜ *ar*·bee·tro
reference referencias ⓕ pl
re·fe·*ren*·thyas
refrigerator nevera ⓕ ne·*ve*·ra •
frigerífico ⓜ free·ge·ree·fee·ko
refugee refugiado/a ⓜ/ⓕ
re·foo·*khya*·do/a
refund reembolso ⓜ re·em·*bol*·so
refund reembolsar re·em·bol·*sar*
refuse negar ne·*gar*

registered mail correo Ⓜ certificado ko·re·o ther·tee·fee·ka·do
regret lamentar la·men·tar
relationship relación Ⓕ re·la·thyon
relax relajarse re·la·khar·se
relic reliquia Ⓕ re·lee·kya
religion religión Ⓕ re·lee·khyon
religious religioso/a Ⓜ/Ⓕ re·lee·khyo·so/a
remember recordar re·kor·dar
remote remoto/a Ⓜ/Ⓕ re·mo·to/a
remote control mando Ⓜ a distancia man·do a dees·tan·thya
rent alquiler Ⓜ al·kee·ler
rent alquilar al·kee·lar
repair reparar re·pa·rar
repeat repetir re·pe·teer
republic república Ⓕ re·poo·blee·ka
reservation reserva Ⓕ re·ser·va
reserve reservar re·ser·var
rest descansar des·kan·sar
restaurant restaurante Ⓜ res·tow·ran·te
retired jubilado/a Ⓜ/Ⓕ khoo·bee·la·do/a
return volver vol·ver
return ticket billete Ⓜ de ida y vuelta bee·lye·te de ee·da ee vwel·ta
review crítica Ⓕ kree·tee·ka
rhythm ritmo Ⓜ reet·mo
rice arroz Ⓜ a·roth
rich rico/a Ⓜ/Ⓕ ree·ko/a
ride paseo Ⓜ pa·se·o
ride montar mon·tar
right (correct) correcto/a Ⓜ/Ⓕ ko·rek·to/a
right (not left) derecha de·re·cha
right-wing derechista de·re·chees·ta
ring (phone) llamada Ⓕ lya·ma·da
ring llamar por telefono lya·mar por te·le·fo·no
rip-off estafa Ⓕ es·ta·fa
risk riesgo Ⓜ ryes·go
river río Ⓜ ree·o
road carretera Ⓕ ka·re·te·ra
rob robar ro·bar
rock (stone) roca Ⓕ ro·ka

rock (music) rock Ⓜ rok
rock climbing escalada Ⓕ es·ka·la·da
rock group grupo Ⓜ de rock groo·po de rok
rollerblading patinar pa·tee·nar
romantic romántico/a Ⓜ/Ⓕ ro·man·tee·ko/a
room habitación Ⓕ a·bee·ta·thyon
room number número Ⓜ de la habitación noo·me·ro de la a·bee·ta·thyon
rope cuerda Ⓕ kwer·da
round redondo/a Ⓜ/Ⓕ re·don·do/a
roundabout glorieta Ⓕ glo·rye·ta
route ruta Ⓕ roo·ta
rowing remo Ⓜ re·mo
rubbish basura Ⓕ ba·soo·ra
rug alfombra Ⓕ al·fom·bra
rugby rugby Ⓜ roog·bee
ruins ruinas Ⓕ pl rwee·nas
rules reglas Ⓕ pl re·glas
rum ron ron
run correr ko·rer
run out of quedarse sin ke·dar·se seen

S

sad triste trees·te
saddle sillín Ⓜ see·lyeen
safe seguro/a Ⓜ/Ⓕ se·goo·ro/a
safe caja Ⓕ fuerte ka·kha fwer·te
safe sex sexo Ⓜ seguro sek·so se·goo·ro
saint santo/a Ⓜ/Ⓕ san·to/a
salad ensalada Ⓕ en·sa·la·da
salami (Spanish sausage) chorizo cho·ree·tho
salary salario Ⓜ sa·la·ryo
sales tax IVA Ⓜ ee·va
salmon salmón Ⓜ sal·mon
salt sal Ⓕ sal
same igual ee·gwal
sand arena Ⓕ a·re·na
sandals sandalias Ⓕ pl san·da·lyas
sanitary napkins compresas Ⓕ pl kom·pre·sas

auna sauna ① *sow*·na

ausage salchicha ① sal·*chee*·cha

ave salvar sal·*var*

ay decir de·*theer*

cale/climb trepar tre·*par*

carf bufanda ① boo·*fan*·da

chool escuela ① es·*kwe*·la

cience ciencias ① pl *thyen*·thyas

cientist científico/a ⓜ/①
hyen·tee·fee·ko·a

cissors tijeras ① pl tee·*khe*·ras

core marcar mar·*kar*

coreboard marcador ⓜ mar·ka·*dor*

cotland Escocia ① es·ko·thya

creen pantalla ① pan·*ta*·lya

cript guión ⓜ gee·*on*

culpture escultura ① es·kool·*too*·ra

ea mar ⓜ *mar*

easick mareado/a ⓜ/①
na·re·a·do·a

easide costa ① *kos*·ta

eason estación ① es·ta·*thyon*

eason (in sport) temporada ①
em·po·*ra*·da

eat asiento ⓜ a·*syen*·to

eatbelt cinturón ⓜ de seguridad
heen·too·ron de se·goo·ree·da

second (place) segundo/a ⓜ/①
e·goon·do·a

second (time) segundo ⓜ se·*goon*·do

secondhand de segunda mano de
e·goon·da ma·no

secretary secretario/a ⓜ/①
se·kre·*ta*·ryo·a

see ver ver

selfish egoísta e·go·*ees*·ta

self-service autoservicio ⓜ
ow·to·ser·vee·thyo

sell vender ven·*der*

send enviar en·vee·*ar*

sensible prudente proo·*den*·te

sensual sensual sen·*swal*

separate separado/a ⓜ/①
se·pa·*ra·do*·a

separate separar se·pa·*rar*

series serie ① *se*·rye

serious serio/a ⓜ/① *se*·ryo·a

service station gasolinera ①
ga·so·lee·*ne*·ra

service charge carga ① *kar*·ga

several varias/os ⓜ/① *va*·ryas/os

sew coser ko·*ser*

sex sexo ⓜ *sek*·so

sexism machismo ⓜ ma·*chees*·mo

sexy sexy *sek*·see

shadow sombra ① *som*·bra

shampoo champú ⓜ cham·*poo*

shape forma ① *for*·ma

share (a dorm) compartir (un
dormitorio) kom·par·*teer* (oon
dor·mee·*to*·ryo)

share (with) compartir kom·par·*teer*

shave afeitarse a·fey·*tar*·se

shaving cream espuma ① de afeitar
es·*poo*·ma de a·fey·*tar*

she ella ① *e*·lya

sheep oveja ① o·*ve*·kha

sheet (bed) sábana ① *sa*·ba·na

sheet (of paper) hoja ① *o*·kha

shelf estante ⓜ es·*tan*·te

ship barco ⓜ *bar*·ko

ship enviar en·vee·*ar*

shirt camisa ① ka·*mee*·sa

shoe shop zapatería ①
tha·pa·te·*ree*·a

shoes zapatos ⓜ pl tha·*pa*·tos

shoot disparar dees·pa·*rar*

shop tienda ① *tyen*·da

shoplifting ratería ① ra·te·*ree*·a

shopping centre centro ⓜ comercial
then·tro ko·mer·*thyal*

short (height) bajo/a ⓜ/① *ba*·kho/a

short (length) corto/a ⓜ/① *kor*·to/a

shortage escasez ① es·ka·*seth*

shorts pantalones ⓜ pl cortos
kor·tos pan·ta·*lo*·nes

shoulders hombros ⓜ pl *om*·bros

shout gritar gree·*tar*

show espectáculo ⓜ es·pek·*ta*·koo·lo

show mostrar mos·*trar*

show enseñar en·se·*nyar*

shower ducha ① *doo*·cha

S

shrine capilla ① ka·pee·lya

shut cerrado/a ⓜ/① the·ra·do/a

shut cerrar the·rar

shy tímido/a ⓜ/① tee·mee·do/a

sick enfermo/a ⓜ/① en·fer·mo/a

side lado ⓜ la·do

sign señal ① se·nyal

sign firmar feer·mar

signature firma ① feer·ma

silk seda ① se·da

silver plateado/a ⓜ/① pla·te·a·do/a

silver plata ① pla·ta

similar similar see·mee·lar

simple sencillo/a ⓜ/① sen·thee·lyo/a

since desde (mayo) des·de (ma·yo)

sing cantar kan·tar

Singapore Singapur ⓜ seen·ga·poor

singer cantante ⓜ&① kan·tan·te

single soltero/a ⓜ/① sol·te·ro/a

single room habitación ① individual a·bee·ta·thyon een·dee·vee·dwal

singlet camiseta ① ka·mee·se·ta

sister hermana ① er·ma·na

sit sentarse sen·tar·se

size (clothes) talla ① ta·lya

skateboarding monopatinaje ⓜ mo·no·pa·tee·na·khe

ski esquiar es·kee·ar

skiing esquí ⓜ es·kee

skimmed milk leche ① desnatada le·che des·na·ta·da

skin piel ① pyel

skirt falda ① fal·da

sky cielo ⓜ thye·lo

skydiving paracaidismo ⓜ pa·ra·kai·dees·mo

sleep dormir dor·meer

sleeping bag saco ⓜ de dormir sa·ko de dor·meer

sleeping car coche cama ⓜ ko·che ka·ma

sleeping pills pastillas ① pl para dormir pas·tee·lyas pa·ra dor·meer

(to be) sleepy tener sueño te·ner swe·nyo

slide diapositiva ① dya·po·see·tee·va

slow lento/a ⓜ/① len·to/a

slowly despacio des·pa·thyo

small pequeño/a ⓜ/① pe·ke·nyo/a

smell olor ⓜ o·lor

smell oler o·ler

smile sonreír son·re·eer

smoke fumar foo·mar

snack tentempié ⓜ ten·tem·pye

snail caracol ⓜ ka·ra·kol

snake serpiente ① ser·pyen·te

snorkel tubos ⓜ pl respiratorios too·bos res·pee·to·ryos

snorkel buceo ⓜ boo·the·o

snow nieve ① nye·ve

snowboarding surf ⓜ sobre la nieve soorf so·bre la nye·ve

soap jabón ⓜ kha·bon

soap opera telenovela ① te·le·no·ve·la

soccer fútbol ⓜ foot·bol

social welfare estado ⓜ del bienestar es·ta·do del byen·es·tar

socialist socialista ⓜ&① so·thya·lees·ta

socks calcetines ⓜ pl kal·the·tee·nes

soft drink refresco ⓜ re·fres·ko

soldier soldado ⓜ sol·da·do

some alguno/a ⓜ/① al·goon/al·goo·na

someone alguien al·gyen

something algo al·go

sometimes de vez en cuando de veth en kwan·do

son hijo ⓜ ee·kho

song canción ① kan·thyon

soon pronto pron·to

sore dolorido/a ⓜ/① do·lo·ree·do/a

soup sopa ① so·pa

sour cream nata ① agria na·ta a·grya

south sur ⓜ soor

souvenir recuerdo ⓜ re·kwer·do

souvenir shop tienda ① de recuerdos tyen·da de re·kwer·dos

soy milk leche ① de soja le·che de so·kha

soy sauce salsa ① de soja sal·sa de so·kha

pace espacio ⓜ es·*pa*·thyo
pain España ⓕ es·*pa*·nya
parkling espumoso/a ⓜ/ⓕ
s·poo·*mo*·so
peak hablar a·*blar*
pecial especial es·pe·*thyal*
pecialist especialista ⓜ&ⓕ
s·pe·thya·*lees*·ta
peed velocidad ⓕ ve·lo·thee·*da*
peeding exceso ⓜ de velocidad
ks·*the*·so de ve·lo·thee·*da*
peedometer velocímetro ⓜ
e·lo·*thee*·me·tro
pider araña ⓕ a·*ra*·nya
pinach espinacas ⓕ pl
s·pee·*na*·kas
poon cuchara ⓕ koo·*cha*·ra
port deportes ⓜ pl de·*por*·tes
ports store tienda ⓕ deportiva
yen·da de·por·*tee*·va
portsperson deportista ⓜ&ⓕ
e·por·*tees*·ta
prain torcedura ⓕ tor·the·*doo*·ra
pring (wire) muelle ⓜ *mwe*·lye
pring (season) primavera ⓕ
ree·ma·ve·ra
quare (shape) cuadrado ⓜ
wa·dra·do
(main) square plaza ⓕ (mayor)
la·tha (ma·*yor*)
tadium estadio ⓜ es·*ta*·dyo
tage escenario ⓜ es·the·*na*·ryo
tairway escalera ⓕ es·ka·*le*·ra
tamp sello ⓜ *se*·lyo
tandby ticket billete ⓜ de lista de
spera bee·*lye*·te de *lees*·ta de es·*pe*·ra
tars estrellas ⓕ pl es·*tre*·lyas
tart comenzar ko·men·*thar*
tation estación ⓕ es·ta·*thyon*
tatue estatua ⓕ es·*ta*·twa
tay (remain) quedarse ke·*dar*·se
tay (somewhere) alojarse
·lo·*khar*·se
teak (beef) bistec ⓜ bees·*tek*
teal robar ro·*bar*
teep escarpado/a ⓜ/ⓕ
·s·kar·*pa*·do/a

step paso ⓜ *pa*·so
stereo equipo ⓜ de música e·*kee*·po
de *moo*·see·ka
stingy tacaño/a ⓜ/ⓕ ta·*ka*·nyo/a
stock caldo ⓜ *kal*·do
stockings medias ⓕ pl *me*·dyas
stomach estómago ⓜ es·*to*·ma·go
stomachache dolor ⓜ de estómago
do·*lor* de es·*to*·ma·go
stone piedra ⓕ *pye*·dra
stoned colocado/a ⓜ/ⓕ ko·lo·*ka*·do/a
stop parada ⓕ pa·*ra*·da
stop parar pa·*rar*
storm tormenta ⓕ tor·*men*·ta
story cuento ⓜ *kwen*·to
stove cocina ⓕ ko·*thee*·na
straight recto/a ⓜ/ⓕ *rek*·to/a
strange extraño/a ⓜ/ⓕ ek·*stra*·nyo/a
stranger desconocido/a ⓜ/ⓕ
des·ko·no·*thee*·do/a
strawberry fresa ⓕ *fre*·sa
stream arroyo ⓜ a·*ro*·yo
street calle ⓕ *ka*·lye
string cuerda ⓕ *kwer*·da
strong fuerte *fwer*·te
stubborn testarudo/a ⓜ/ⓕ
tes·ta·*roo*·do/a
student estudiante ⓜ&ⓕ
es·too·*dyan*·te
studio estudio ⓜ es·*too*·dyo
stupid estúpido/a ⓜ/ⓕ
es·*too*·pee·do/a
style estilo ⓜ es·*tee*·lo
subtitles subtítulos ⓜ pl
soob·*tee*·too·los
suburb barrio ⓜ *ba*·ryo
subway parada ⓕ de metro pa·*ra*·da
de *me*·tro
suffer sufrir soo·*freer*
sugar azúcar ⓜ a·*thoo*·kar
suitcase maleta ⓕ ma·*le*·ta
summer verano ⓜ ve·*ra*·no
sun sol ⓜ sol
sunblock crema ⓕ solar *kre*·ma so·*lar*
sunburn quemadura ⓕ de sol
ke·ma·*doo*·ra de sol

sun-dried tomato tomate ⓜ secado al sol to·ma·te se·ka·do al sol
sunflower oil aceite ⓜ de girasol a·they·te de khee·ra·sol
sunglasses gafas ⓕ pl de sol ga·fas de sol
(to be) sunny hace sol a·the sol
sunrise amanecer ⓜ a·ma·ne·ther
sunset puesta ⓕ del sol pwes·ta del sol
supermarket supermercado ⓜ soo·per·mer·ka·do
superstition superstición ⓕ soo·pers·tee·thyon
supporters hinchas ⓜ&ⓕ pl een·chas
surf hacer surf a·ther soorf
surface mail por vía terrestre por vee·a te·res·tre
surfboard tabla de surf ⓕ ta·bla de soorf
surname apellido ⓜ a·pe·lyee·do
surprise sorpresa ⓕ sor·pre·sa
survive sobrevivir so·bre·vee·veer
sweater jersey ⓜ kher·sey
Sweden Suecia ⓕ swe·thya
sweet dulce dool·the
sweets (candy) dulces ⓜ pl dool·thes
swim nadar na·dar
swimming pool piscina ⓕ pees·thee·na
swimsuit bañador ⓜ ba·nya·dor
Switzerland Suiza ⓕ swee·tha
synagogue sinagoga ⓕ see·na·go·ga
synthetic sintético/a ⓜ/ⓕ seen·te·tee·ko/a
syringe jeringa ⓕ khe·reen·ga

table mesa ⓕ me·sa
table tennis ping pong ⓜ peeng pong
tablecloth mantel ⓜ man·tel
tail rabo ⓜ ra·bo
tailor sastre ⓜ sas·tre
take (away) llevar lye·var

take (the train) tomar to·mar
take (photo) sacar sa·kar
take photographs sacar fotos sa·kar fo·tos
talk hablar a·blar
tall alto/a ⓜ/ⓕ al·to/a
tampons tampones ⓜ pl tam·po·nes
tanning lotion bronceador ⓜ bron·the·a·dor
tap grifo ⓜ gree·fo
tasty sabroso/a ⓜ/ⓕ sa·bro·so/a
taxes impuestos ⓜ pl eem·pwes·tos
taxi taxi ⓜ tak·see
taxi stand parada ⓕ de taxis pa·ra·da de tak·sees
tea té ⓜ te
teacher profesor/profesora ⓜ/ⓕ pro·fe·sor/pro·fe·so·ra
team equipo ⓜ e·kee·po
teaspoon cucharita ⓕ koo·cha·ree·ta
technique técnica ⓕ tek·nee·ka
teeth dientes ⓜ pl dyen·tes
telegram telegrama ⓜ te·le·gra·ma
telephone teléfono ⓜ te·le·fo·no
telephone llamar (por teléfono) lya·mar (por te·le·fo·no)
telephone centre central ⓕ telefónica then·tral te·le·fo·nee·ka
telescope telescopio ⓜ te·les·ko·pyo
television televisión ⓕ te·le·vee·syon
tell decir de·theer
temperature (fever) fiebre ⓕ fye·bre
temperature (weather) temperatura ⓕ tem·pe·ra·too·ra
temple templo ⓜ tem·plo
tennis tenis ⓜ te·nees
tennis court pista ⓕ de tenis pees·ta de te·nees
tent tienda ⓕ (de campaña) tyen·da (de kam·pa·nya)
tent pegs piquetas ⓕ pl pee·ke·tas
terrible terrible te·ree·ble
test prueba ⓕ prwe·ba
thank dar gracias dar gra·thyas
theatre teatro ⓜ te·a·tro
their su soo

T

they ellos/ellas ⓜ/ⓕ e·lyos/e·lyas
thief ladrón/ladrona ⓜ/ⓕ la·dron/la·dro·na
thin delgado/a ⓜ/ⓕ del·ga·do/a
think pensar pen·sar
third tercio ⓜ ter·thyo
thirst sed ⓕ se
this éste/a ⓜ/ⓕ es·te/a
this month este mes es·te mes
thread hilo ⓜ ee·lo
throat garganta ⓕ gar·gan·ta
ticket billete ⓜ bee·lye·te
ticket collector revisor/revisora ⓜ/ⓕ re·vee·sor/re·vee·so·ra
ticket machine máquina ⓕ de billetes ma·kee·na de bee·lye·tes
ticket office taquilla ⓕ ta·kee·lya
tide marea ⓕ ma·re·a
tight apretado/a ⓜ/ⓕ a·pre·ta·do/a
time (watch) hora ⓕ o·ra
time (passing) tiempo ⓜ tyem·po
time difference diferencia ⓕ de horas dee·fe·ren·thya de o·ras
timetable horario ⓜ o·ra·ryo
tin hojalata ⓕ o·kha·la·ta
tin opener abrelatas ⓜ a·bre·la·tas
tiny pequeñito/a ⓜ/ⓕ pe·ke·nyee·to/a
tip propina ⓕ pro·pee·na
tired cansado/a ⓜ/ⓕ kan·sa·do/a
tissues pañuelos ⓜ pl de papel pa·nywe·los de pa·pel
toast tostada ⓕ tos·ta·da
toaster tostadora ⓕ tos·ta·do·ra
tobacco tabaco ⓜ ta·ba·ko
tobacconist estanquero ⓜ es·tan·ke·ro
tobogganing ir en tobogán eer en to·bo·gan
today hoy oy
toe dedo ⓜ del pie de·do del pye
tofu tofú ⓜ to·foo
together juntos/as ⓜ/ⓕ khoon·tos/as
toilet servicio ⓜ ser·vee·thyo
toilet paper papel ⓜ higiénico pa·pel ee·khye·nee·ko

tomato tomate ⓜ to·ma·te
tomato sauce salsa ⓕ de tomate sal·sa de to·ma·te
tomorrow mañana ma·nya·na
tomorrow afternoon mañana por la tarde ma·nya·na por la tar·de
tomorrow evening mañana por la noche ma·nya·na por la no·che
tomorrow morning mañana por la mañana ma·nya·na por la ma·nya·na
tone tono ⓜ to·no
tonight esta noche es·ta no·che
too (expensive) demasiado (caro/a) ⓜ/ⓕ de·ma·sya·do (ka·ro/a)
tooth diente ⓜ dyen·te
tooth (back) muela ⓕ mwe·la
toothache dolor ⓜ de muelas do·lor de mwe·las
toothbrush cepillo ⓜ de dientes the·pee·lyo de dyen·tes
toothpaste pasta ⓕ dentífrica pas·ta den·tee·free·ka
toothpick palillo ⓜ pa·lee·lyo
torch linterna ⓕ leen·ter·na
touch tocar to·kar
tour excursión ⓕ eks·koor·syon
tourist turista ⓜ&ⓕ too·rees·ta
tourist (slang) guiri ⓜ gee·ree
tourist office oficina ⓕ de turismo o·fee·thee·na de too·rees·mo
towards hacia a·thya
towel toalla ⓕ to·a·lya
tower torre ⓕ to·re
toxic waste residuos ⓜ pl tóxicos re·see·dwos tok·see·kos
toyshop juguetería ⓕ khoo·ge·te·ree·a
track (car racing) autódromo ⓜ ow·to·dro·mo
track (footprints) rastro ⓜ ras·tro
trade comercio ⓜ ko·mer·thyo
traffic tráfico ⓜ tra·fee·ko
traffic lights semáforos ⓜ pl se·ma·fo·ros
trail camino ⓜ ka·mee·no
train tren ⓜ tren
train station estación ⓕ de tren es·ta·thyon de tren

U

tram tranvía ⓜ tran·vee·a

transit lounge sala ① de tránsito sa·la de tran·see·to

translate traducir tra·doo·theer

transport medios ⓜ pl de transporte me·dyos de trans·por·te

travel viajar vya·khar

travel agency agencia ① de viajes a·khen·thya de vya·khes

travel books libros ⓜ pl de viajes lee·bros de vya·khes

travel sickness mareo ⓜ ma·re·o

travellers cheque cheque ⓜ de viajero che·ke de vya·khe·ro

tree árbol ⓜ ar·bol

trip viaje ⓜ vya·khe

trousers pantalones ⓜ pl pan·ta·lo·nes

truck camión ⓜ ka·myon

trust confianza ① kon·fee·an·tha

trust confiar kon·fee·ar

try probar pro·bar

try (to do something) intentar (hacer algo) een·ten·tar (a·ther al·go)

T-shirt camiseta ① ka·mee·se·ta

tube (tyre) cámara ① de aire ka·ma·ra de ai·re

tuna atún ⓜ a·toon

tune melodía ① me·lo·dee·a

turkey pavo ⓜ pa·vo

turn doblar do·blar

TV tele ① te·le

TV series serie ① se·rye

tweezers pinzas ① pl peen·thas

twice dos veces dos ve·thes

twin beds dos camas ① pl dos ka·mas

twins gemelos ⓜ pl khe·me·los

type tipo ⓜ tee·po

type escribir a máquina es·kree·beer a ma·kee·na

typical típico/a ⓜ/① tee·pee·ko/a

tyre neumático ⓜ ne·oo·ma·tee·ko

U

ultrasound ecografía ① e·ko·gra·fee·a

umbrella (rain) paraguas ⓜ pa·ra·gwas

umbrella (sun) parasol ⓜ pa·ra·sol

umpire árbitro ⓜ ar·bee·tro

uncomfortable incómodo/a ⓜ/① een·ko·mo·do/a

underpants (men) calzoncillos ⓜ pl kal·thon·thee·lyos

underpants (women) bragas ① pl bra·gas

understand comprender kom·pren·der

underwear ropa interior ① ro·pa een·te·ryor

unemployed en el paro en el pa·ro

unfair injusto een·khoos·to

uniform uniforme ⓜ oo·nee·for·me

universe universo ⓜ oo·nee·ver·so

university universidad ① oo·nee·ver·see·da

unleaded sin plomo seen plo·mo

unsafe inseguro/a ⓜ/① een·se·goo·ro/a

until (June) hasta (junio) as·ta (khoo·nyo)

unusual extraño/a ⓜ/① eks·tra·nyo/a

up arriba a·ree·ba

uphill cuesta arriba kwes·ta a·ree·ba

urgent urgente oor·khen·te

USA Estados ⓜ pl Unidos es·ta·dos oo·nee·dos

useful útil oo·teel

V

vacant vacante va·kan·te

vacation vacaciones ① pl va·ka·thyo·nes

vaccination vacuna ① va·koo·na

vagina vagina ① va·khee·na

validate validar va·lee·dar

valley valle ⓜ va·lye

valuable valioso/a ⓜ/① va·lyo·so/a

value valor ⓜ va·lor

van caravana ① ka·ra·va·na

veal ternera ① ter·ne·ra

vegetable verdura ① ver·doo·ra

vegetables verduras ① pl ver·doo·ras

vegetarian vegetariano/a ⓜ/ⓕ
ve·khe·ta·*rya*·no·a
venereal disease enfermedad ⓕ
venérea en·fer·me·*da* ve·ne·re·a
venue local ⓜ lo·*kal*
very muy mooy
video tape cinta ⓕ de vídeo *theen*·ta
de vee·de·o
view vista ⓕ vees·ta
village pueblo ⓜ *pwe*·blo
vinegar vinagre ⓜ vee·*na*·gre
vineyard viñedo ⓜ vee·*nye*·do
virus virus ⓜ *vee*·roos
visa visado ⓜ vee·*sa*·do
visit visitar vee·see·*tar*
vitamins vitaminas ⓕ pl
vee·ta·*mee*·nas
vodka vodka ⓕ *vod*·ka
voice voz ⓕ voth
volume volumen ⓜ vo·*loo*·men
vote votar vo·*tar*

W

wage sueldo ⓜ *swel*·do
wait esperar es·pe·*rar*
waiter camarero/a ⓜ/ⓕ ka·ma·re·ro/a
waiting room sala ⓕ de espera *sa*·la
de es·pe·ra
walk caminar ka·mee·*nar*
wall (inside) pared ⓕ pa·re
wallet cartera ⓕ kar·*te*·ra
want querer ke·*rer*
war guerra ⓕ *ge*·ra
wardrobe vestuario ⓜ ves·*twa*·ryo
warm templado/a ⓜ/ⓕ tem·*pla*·do/a
warn advertir ad·ver·*teer*
wash (oneself) lavarse la·*var*·se
wash (something) lavar la·*var*
wash cloth toallita ⓕ to·a·*lyee*·ta
washing machine lavadora ⓕ
a·va·*do*·ra
watch reloj ⓜ de pulsera re·*lokh* de
pool·*se*·ra
watch mirar mee·*rar*

water agua ⓕ *a*·gwa
— tap del grifo del *gree*·fo
— bottle cantimplora ⓕ
kan·teem·*plo*·ra
waterfall cascada ⓕ kas·*ka*·da
watermelon ⓕ sandía san·*dee*·a
waterproof impermeable
eem·per·me·*a*·ble
waterskiing esquí ⓜ acuático es·*kee*
a·*kwa*·tee·ko
wave ola ⓕ o·la
way camino ⓜ ka·*mee*·no
we nosotros/nosotras ⓜ/ⓕ
no·so·tros/no·so·tras
weak débil ⓜ&ⓕ *de*·beel
wealthy rico/a ⓜ/ⓕ *ree*·ko/a
wear llevar lye·*var*
weather tiempo ⓜ *tyem*·po
wedding boda ⓕ *bo*·da
wedding cake tarta ⓕ nupcial *tar*·ta
noop·*thyal*
wedding present regalo ⓜ de bodas
re·*ga*·lo de *bo*·das
weekend fin de semana ⓜ feen de
se·*ma*·na
weigh pesar pe·*sar*
weight peso ⓜ *pe*·so
weights pesas ⓕ pl *pe*·sas
welcome bienvenida ⓕ
byen·ve·*nee*·da
welcome dar la bienvenida dar la
byen·ve·*nee*·da
welfare bienestar ⓜ byen·es·*tar*
well bien byen
well pozo ⓜ *po*·tho
west oeste ⓜ o·es·te
wet mojado/a ⓜ/ⓕ mo·*kha*·do/a
what lo que lo ke
wheel rueda ⓕ *rwe*·da
wheelchair silla ⓕ de ruedas *see*·lya
de *rwe*·das
when cuando *kwan*·do
where donde *don*·de
whiskey güisqui ⓜ *gwees*·kee
white blanco/a ⓜ/ⓕ *blan*·ko/a
white-water rafting rafting ⓜ
rahf·teen

Y

who quien kyen
why por qué por ke
wide ancho/a ⓜ/ⓕ *an*·cho/a
wife esposa ⓕ es·*po*·sa
win ganar ga·*nar*
wind viento ⓜ *vyen*·to
window ventana ⓕ ven·*ta*·na
window-shopping mirar los escaparates mee·*rar* los es·ka·pa·*ra*·tes
windscreen parabrisas ⓜ pa·ra·*bree*·sas
windsurfing hacer windsurf a·*ther ween*·soorf
wine vino ⓜ *vee*·no
wineglass copa ⓕ de vino *ko*·pa de *vee*·no
winery bodega ⓕ bo·*de*·ga
wings alas ⓕ pl *a*·las
winner ganador/ganadora ⓜ/ⓕ ga·na·*dor*/ga·na·*do*·ra
winter invierno ⓜ een·*vyer*·no
wire alambre ⓜ a·*lam*·bre
wish desear de·se·*ar*
with con kon
within (an hour) dentro de (una hora) *den*·tro de (oo·na o·ra)
without sin seen
woman mujer ⓕ moo·*kher*
wonderful maravilloso/a ⓜ/ⓕ ma·ra·vee·*lyo*·so/a
wood madera ⓕ ma·*de*·ra
wool lana ⓕ *la*·na
word palabra ⓕ pa·*la*·bra
work trabajo ⓜ tra·*ba*·kho
work trabajar tra·ba·*khar*
work experience experiencia ⓕ laboral eks·pe·*ryen*·thya la·bo·*ral*
work permit permiso ⓜ de trabajo per·*mee*·so de tra·*ba*·kho
workout entreno ⓜ en·*tre*·no
workshop taller ⓜ ta·*lyer*
world mundo ⓜ *moon*·do
World Cup Copa ⓕ Mundial *ko*·pa moon·*dyal*

worms lombrices ⓕ pl lom·*bree*·thes
worried preocupado/a ⓜ/ⓕ pre·o·koo·*pa*·do/a
worship adoración ⓕ a·do·ra·*thyon*
wrist muñeca ⓕ moo·*nye*·ka
write escribir es·kree·*beer*
writer escritor/escritora ⓜ/ⓕ es·kree·*tor*/es·kree·*to*·ra
wrong equivocado/a ⓜ/ⓕ e·kee·vo·*ka*·do/a

Y

yellow amarillo/a ⓜ/ⓕ a·ma·*ree*·lyo/a
yes sí see
(not) yet todavía (no) to·da·*vee*·a (no)
yesterday ayer a·*yer*
yoga yoga ⓜ *yo*·ga
yogurt yogur ⓜ yo·*goor*
you inf sg tú too
you ⓜ/ⓕ inf pl vosotros/as vo·*so*·tros/as
you pol pl Ustedes oo·*ste*·des
you pol sg Usted oo·*ste*
young joven *kho*·ven
your pol sg su soo
your inf sg tu too
youth hostel albergue ⓜ juvenil al·*ber*·ge khoo·ve·*neel*

Z

zodiac zodíaco ⓜ tho·*dee*·a·ko
zoo zoológico ⓜ zo·o·*lo*·khee·ko

A

Dictionary

SPANISH *to* ENGLISH

español–inglés

Nouns in the dictionary have their gender indicated by Ⓜ or Ⓕ. If it's a plural noun, you'll also see pl. Where a word that could be either a noun or a verb has no gender indicated, it's a verb.

A

abajo a·ba·kho below

abanico Ⓜ a·ba·nee·ko fan (hand held)

abarrotado a·ba·ro·ta·do crowded

abeja Ⓕ a·be·kha bee

abierto/a Ⓜ/Ⓕ a·byer·to/a open

abogado/a Ⓜ/Ⓕ a·bo·ga·do/a lawyer

aborto Ⓜ a·bor·to abortion

abrazo Ⓜ a·bra·tho hug

abrebotellas Ⓜ a·bre·bo·te·lyas bottle opener

abrelatas Ⓜ a·bre·la·tas can opener • tin opener

abrigo Ⓜ a·bree·go overcoat

abrir a·breer open

abuela Ⓕ a·bwe·la grandmother

abuelo Ⓜ a·bwe·lo grandfather

aburrido/a Ⓜ/Ⓕ a·boo·ree·do/a bored • boring

acabar a·ka·bar end

acampar a·kam·par camp

acantilado Ⓜ a·kan·tee·la·do cliff

accidente Ⓜ ak·thee·den·te accident

aceite Ⓜ a·they·te oil

aceptar a·thep·tar accept

acera Ⓕ a·the·ra footpath

acondicionador Ⓜ a·kon·dee·thyo·na·dor conditioner

acoso Ⓜ a·ko·so harassment

activista Ⓜ&Ⓕ ak·tee·vees·ta activist

actuación Ⓕ ak·twa·thyon performance

acupuntura Ⓕ a·koo·poon·too·ra acupuncture

adaptador Ⓜ a·dap·ta·dor adaptor

adentro a·den·tro inside

adivinar a·dee·vee·nar guess

administración Ⓕ ad·mee·nees·tra·thyon administration

admitir ad·mee·teer admit

adoración Ⓕ a·do·ra·thyon worship

aduana Ⓕ a·dwa·na customs

adulto/a Ⓜ/Ⓕ a·dool·to/a adult

aeróbic Ⓜ ai·ro·beek aerobics

aerolínea Ⓕ ai·ro·lee·nya airline

aeropuerto Ⓜ ai·ro·pwer·to airport

afeitadora Ⓕ a·fey·ta·do·ra razor

afeitarse a·fey·tar·se shave

afortunado/a Ⓜ/Ⓕ a·for·too·na·do/a lucky

África Ⓕ a·free·ka Africa

agencia Ⓕ **de viajes** a·khen·thya de vya·khes travel agency

agenda Ⓕ a·khen·da diary

A

agente ⓜ **inmobiliario** a·khen·te een·mo·bee·lya·ryo real estate agent

agresivo/a ⓜ/ⓕ a·gre·see·vo/a aggressive

agricultor(a) ⓜ/ⓕ a·gree·kool·tor/ a·gree·kool·to·ra farmer

agricultura ⓕ a·gree·kool·too·ra agriculture

agua ⓕ a·gwa water

— caliente ka·lyen·te hot water

— mineral mee·ne·ral mineral water

aguacate ⓜ a·gwa·ka·te avocado

aguja ⓕ a·goo·kha needle (sewing)

ahora a·o·ra now

ahorrar a·o·rar save (money)

aire ⓜ ai·re air

— acondicionado a·kon·dee·thyo·na·do air-conditioning

ajedrez ⓜ a·khe·dreth chess

al lado de al la·do de next to

alambre ⓜ a·lam·bre wire

alba ⓕ al·ba dawn

albaricoque ⓜ al·ba·ree·ko·ke apricot

albergue ⓜ **juvenil** al·ber·ge khoo·ve·neel youth hostel

alcachofa ⓕ al·ka·cho·fa artichoke

alcohol ⓜ al·kol alcohol

Alemania ⓕ a·le·ma·nya Germany

alérgia ⓕ a·ler·khya allergy

alérgia ⓕ **al polen** a·ler·khya al po·len hay fever

alfarería ⓕ al·fa·re·ree·a pottery

alfombra ⓕ al·fom·bra rug

algo al·go something

algodón ⓜ al·go·don cotton

alguien al·gyen someone

algún al·goon some

alguno/a ⓜ/ⓕ al·goo·no/a any

almendras ⓕ pl al·men·dras almonds

almohada ⓕ al·mwa·da pillow

almuerzo ⓜ al·mwer·tho lunch

alojamiento ⓜ a·lo·kha·myen·to accommodation

alojarse a·lo·khar·se stay (somewhere)

alpinismo ⓜ al·pee·nees·mo mountaineering

alquilar al·kee·lar hire • rent

alquiler ⓜ al·kee·ler rent

— de coche de ko·che car hire

altar ⓜ al·tar altar

alto/a ⓜ/ⓕ al·to/a high • tall

altura ⓕ al·too·ra altitude

ama ⓕ **de casa** a·ma de ka·sa homemaker

amable a·ma·ble kind

amanecer ⓜ a·ma·ne·ther sunrise

amante ⓜ&ⓕ a·man·te lover

amarillo/a ⓜ/ⓕ a·ma·ree·lyo/a yellow

amigo/a ⓜ/ⓕ a·mee·go/a friend

ampolla ⓕ am·po·lya blister

anacardo ⓜ a·na·kar·do cashew nut

analgésicos ⓜ pl a·nal·khe·see·kos painkillers

análisis de sangre ⓜ a·na·lee·sees de san·gre blood test

anarquista ⓜ/ⓕ a·nar·kees·ta anarchist

ancho/a ⓜ/ⓕ an·cho/a wide

andar an·dar walk

animal ⓜ a·nee·mal animal

Año ⓜ **Nuevo** a·nyo nwe·vo New Year

antes an·tes before

antibióticos ⓜ pl an·tee·byo·tee·kos antibiotics

anticonceptivos ⓜ pl an·tee·kon·thep·tee·vos contraceptives

antigüedad ⓕ an·tee·gwe·da antique

antiguo/a ⓜ/ⓕ an·tee·gwo/a ancient

antiséptico ⓜ an·tee·sep·tee·ko antiseptic

antología ⓕ an·to·lo·khee·a anthology

anuncio ⓜ a·noon·thyo advertisement

aparcamiento ⓜ a·par·ka·myen·to carpark

apellido ⓜ a·pe·lyee·do surname

apéndice ⓜ a·*pen*·dee·the the appendix
apodo ⓜ a·*po*·do nickname
aprender a·*pren*·der learn
apretado/a ⓜ/ⓕ a·pre·*ta*·do/a tight
apuesta ⓕ a·*pwes*·ta bet
apuntar a·poon·*tar* point
aquí a·*kee* here
araña ⓕ a·*ra*·nya spider
árbitro ⓜ *ar*·bee·tro referee
árbol ⓜ *ar*·bol tree
arena ⓕ a·*re*·na sand
armario ⓜ ar·*ma*·ryo cupboard
arqueológico/a ⓜ/ⓕ ar·ke·o·lo·*khee*·ko/a archaeological
arquitecto/a ⓜ/ⓕ ar·kee·*tek*·to/a architect
arquitectura ⓕ ar·kee·tek·*too*·ra architecture
arriba a·*rree*·ba above • up
arroyo ⓜ a·*rro*·yo stream
arroz ⓜ a·*roth* rice
arte ⓜ *ar*·te art
— **gráfico** *gra*·fee·ko graphic art
artes ⓕ pl **marciales** *ar*·tes mar·*thya*·les martial arts
artesanía ⓕ ar·te·sa·*nee*·a crafts
artista ⓜ&ⓕ ar·*tees*·ta artist
ascensor ⓜ as·then·*sor* elevator
Asia ⓕ a·sya Asia
asiento ⓜ a·*syen*·to seat
— **de seguridad para bebés** de se·goo·ree·*da* pa·ra be·*bes* child seat
asma ⓜ *as*·ma asthma
aspirina ⓕ as·pee·*ree*·na aspirin
atascado/a ⓜ/ⓕ a·tas·*ka*·do/a blocked
atletismo ⓜ at·le·*tees*·mo athletics
atmósfera ⓕ at·*mos*·fe·ra atmosphere
atún ⓜ a·*toon* tuna
audífono ⓜ ow·*dee*·fo·no hearing aid
Australia ⓕ ow·*stra*·lya Australia
autobús ⓜ ow·to·*boos* bus
autocar ⓜ ow·to·*kar* bus (intercity)
autódromo ⓜ ow·*to*·dro·mo track (car racing)

autoservicio ⓜ ow·to·ser·*vee*·thyo self-service
autovía ⓕ ow·to·*vee*·a motorway
avenida ⓕ a·ve·*nee*·da avenue
avergonzado/a ⓜ/ⓕ a·ver·gon·*tha*·do/a embarrassed
avión ⓜ a·*vyon* plane
ayer a·*yer* yesterday
ayudar a·yoo·*dar* help
azúcar ⓜ a·*thoo*·kar sugar
azul a·*thool* blue

B

bailar bai·*lar* dance
bajo/a ⓜ/ⓕ *ba*·kho/a low • short (height)
balcón ⓜ bal·*kon* balcony
ballet ⓜ ba·*le* ballet
baloncesto ⓜ ba·lon·*thes*·to basketball
bálsamo ⓜ **de aftershave** *bal*·sa·mo de af·ter·*sha*·eev aftershave
bálsamo ⓜ **de labios** *bal*·sa·mo de *la*·byos lip balm
bañador ⓜ ba·nya·*dor* bathing suit
banco ⓜ *ban*·ko bank
bandera ⓕ ban·*de*·ra flag
bañera ⓕ ba·*nye*·ra bath
baño ⓜ *ba*·nyo bathroom
bar ⓜ *bar* bar
barato/a ⓜ/ⓕ ba·*ra*·to/a cheap
barco ⓜ *bar*·ko boat
barrio ⓜ *ba*·ryo suburb
basura ⓕ ba·*soo*·ra rubbish
batería ⓕ ba·te·*ree*·a battery (car) • drums
bebé ⓜ be·*be* baby
béisbol ⓜ *beys*·bol baseball
beneficio ⓜ be·ne·*fee*·thyo profit
berenjenas ⓕ pl be·ren·*khe*·nas aubergine • eggplant
besar be·*sar* kiss
beso ⓜ *be*·so kiss
biblia ⓕ *bee*·blya bible
biblioteca ⓕ bee·blyo·*te*·ka library

C

bicho ⓜ *bee*-cho bug
bici ⓕ *bee*-thee bike
bicicleta ⓕ bee-thee-*kle*-ta bicycle
— de carreras de ka-*re*-ras racing bike
— de montaña de mon-*ta*-nya mountain bike
bien byen well
bienestar ⓜ byen-es-*tar* welfare
bienvenida ⓕ byen-*ve*-nee-da welcome
billete ⓜ bee-*lye*-te ticket
— de ida y vuelta de ee-da ee vwel-ta return ticket
— de lista de espera de lees-ta de es-*pe*-ra standby ticket
billetes ⓜ pl **de banco** bee-*lye*-tes de *ban*-ko banknotes
biografía ⓕ bee-o-gra-*fee*-a biography
bistec ⓜ bees-*tek* steak (beef)
blanco y negro *blan*-ko ee ne-gro B&W (film)
blanco/a ⓜ/ⓕ *blan*-ko/a white
boca ⓕ *bo*-ka mouth
bocado ⓜ bo-*ka*-do bite (food)
boda ⓕ *bo*-da wedding
bodega ⓕ bo-*de*-ga winery • liquor store
bol ⓜ bol bowl
bolas ⓕ pl **de algodón** *bo*-las de al-go-*don* cotton balls
bolígrafo ⓜ bo-*lee*-gra-fo pen
bollos ⓜ pl bo-*lyos* rolls (bread)
bolo ⓜ *bo*-lo gig
bolsillo ⓜ bol-*see*-lyo pocket
bolso ⓜ *bol*-so bag • handbag
bomba ⓕ *bom*-ba bomb • pump
bombilla ⓕ bom-*bee*-lya light bulb
bondadoso/a ⓜ/ⓕ bon-da-*do*-so/a caring
bonito/a ⓜ/ⓕ bo-*nee*-to/a pretty
bordo ⓜ *bor*-do edge
a bordo a *bor*-do aboard
borracho/a ⓜ/ⓕ bo-*ra*-cho/a drunk
bosque ⓜ *bos*-ke forest
botas ⓕ pl *bo*-tas boots
— de montaña de mon-*ta*-nya hiking boots

botella ⓕ bo-*te*-lya bottle
botones ⓜ pl bo-*to*-nes buttons
boxeo ⓜ bo-*kse*-o boxing
bragas ⓕ pl *bra*-gas underpants (women)
brazo ⓜ *bra*-tho arm
broma ⓕ *bro*-ma joke
bronceador ⓜ bron-the-a-*dor* tanning lotion
bronquitis ⓜ bron-*kee*-tees bronchitis
brotes ⓜ pl **de soja** *bro*-tes de so-*kha* bean sprouts
brújula ⓕ *broo*-khoo-la compass
brumoso broo-*mo*-so foggy
buceo ⓜ boo-*the*-o snorkelling
budista ⓜ&ⓕ boo-*dees*-ta Buddhist
bueno/a ⓜ/ⓕ *bwe*-no/a good
bufanda ⓕ boo-*fan*-da scarf
buffet ⓜ boo-*fe* buffet
bulto ⓜ *bool*-to lump
burlarse de boor-*lar*-se de make fun of
burro ⓜ *boo*-ro donkey
buscar boos-*kar* look for
buzón ⓜ boo-*thon* mailbox

C

caballo ⓜ ka-*ba*-lyo horse
cabeza ⓕ ka-*be*-tha head
cabina ⓕ **telefónica** ka-*bee*-na te-le-fo-nee-ka phone box
cable ⓜ *ka*-ble cable
cables ⓜ pl **de arranque** *ka*-bles de a-*ran*-ke jumper leads
cabra ⓕ *ka*-bra goat
cacahuetes ⓜ pl ka-ka-*we*-tes peanuts
cacao ⓜ ka-*kow* cocoa
cachorro ⓜ ka-*cho*-ro puppy
cada *ka*-da each
cadena ⓕ **de bici** ka-*de*-na de *bee*-thee bike chain
café ⓜ ka-*fe* coffee • cafe
caída ⓕ ka-*ee*-da fall

caja ① *ka*·kha box • cashier
— fuerte *fwer*·te safe
— registradora re·khees·tra·*do*·ra cash register
cajero ① automático ka·*khe*·ro ow·to·ma·tee·ko automatic teller machine
calabacín ① ka·la·ba·*theen* zucchini • courgette
calabaza ① ka·la·*ba*·tha pumpkin
calcetines ⑩ pl kal·the·*tee*·nes socks
calculadora ① kal·koo·la·*do*·ra calculator
caldo ⑩ *kal*·do stock
calefacción ① **central** ka·le·fak·*thyon* *then·tral* central heating
calendario ⑩ ka·len·*da*·ryo calendar
calidad ① ka·lee·*da* quality
caliente ka·*lyen*·te hot
calle ① *ka*·lye street
calor ⑩ ka·*lor* heat
calzoncillos ⑩ pl kal·thon·*thee*·lyos underpants (men)
calzones ⑩ pl kal·*tho*·nes boxer shorts
cama ① *ka*·ma bed
— de matrimonio de ma·tree·*mo*·nyo double bed
cámara ① **(fotográfica)** *ka*·ma·ra (fo·to·gra·fee·ka) camera
cámara ① **de aire** *ka*·ma·ra de *ai*·re tube (tyre)
camarero/a ⑩/① ka·ma·*re*·ro/a waiter
cambiar kam·*byar* change • exchange (money)
cambio *kam*·byo ⑩ loose change
— de dinero de dee·*ne*·ro currency exchange
caminar ka·mee·*nar* walk
camino ⑩ ka·*mee*·no trail • way
caminos ⑩ pl **rurales** ka·*mee*·nos roo·*ra*·les hiking routes
camión ⑩ ka·*myon* truck
camisa ① ka·*mee*·sa shirt

camiseta ① ka·mee·*se*·ta singlet • T-shirt
cámping ⑩ *kam*·peen campsite
campo ⑩ *kam*·po countryside • field
Canadá ① ka·na·*da* Canada
canasta ① ka·*nas*·ta basket
cancelar kan·the·*lar* cancel
cáncer ⑩ *kan*·ther cancer
canción ① kan·*thyon* song
candado ⑩ kan·*da*·do padlock
cangrejo ⑩ kan·*gre*·kho crab
canguro ⑩ kan·*goo*·ro babysitter
cansado/a ⑩/① kan·*sa*·do/a tired
cantalupo ⑩ kan·ta·*loo*·po cantaloupe
cantante ⑩&① kan·*tan*·te singer
cantar kan·*tar* sing
cantimplora ① kan·teem·*plo*·ra water bottle
capa ① **de ozono** *ka*·pa de o·*tho*·no ozone layer
capilla ① ka·*pee*·lya shrine
capote ⑩ ka·*po*·te cloak
cara ① *ka*·ra face
caracol ⑩ ka·ra·*kol* snail
caramelos ⑩ pl ka·ra·*me*·los lollies
caravana ① ka·ra·*va*·na caravan • van • traffic jam
cárcel ① *kar*·thel prison
cardenal ⑩ kar·de·*nal* bruise
carne ① *kar*·ne meat
— de vaca de *va*·ka beef
— molida mo·*lee*·da mince meat
carnet ⑩ kar·*ne* licence
— de identidad de ee·den·tee·*da* identification card
— de conducir de kon·doo·*theer* drivers licence
carnicería ① kar·nee·the·*ree*·a butcher's shop
caro/a ⑩/① *ka*·ro/a expensive
carpintero ⑩ kar·peen·*te*·ro carpenter
carrera ① ka·*re*·ra race (sport)
carta ① *kar*·ta letter

C

cartas ① pl *kar*·tas cards
cartón ⓜ kar·*ton* carton • cardboard
casa ① *ka*·sa house
(en) casa (en) *ka*·sa (at) home
casarse ka·*sar*·se marry
cascada ① kas·*ka*·da waterfall
casco ⓜ *kas*·ko helmet
casete ⓜ ka·*se*·te cassette
casi *ka*·see almost
casino ⓜ ka·*see*·no casino
castigar kas·tee·*gar* punish
castillo ⓜ kas·*tee*·lyo castle
catedral ① ka·te·*dral* cathedral
católico/a ⓜ/① ka·to·*lee*·ko/a Catholic
caza ① *ka*·tha hunting
cazuela ① ka·*thwe*·la pot (kitchen)
cebolla ① the·*bo*·lya onion
celebración ① the·le·bra·*thyon* celebration
celebrar the·le·*brar* celebrate (an event)
celoso/a the·*lo*·so/a jealous
cementerio ⓜ the·men·*te*·ryo cemetery
cena ① *the*·na dinner
cenicero ⓜ the·nee·*the*·ro ashtray
centavo ⓜ then·*ta*·vo cent
centímetro ⓜ then·*tee*·me·tro centimetre
central ① **telefónica** then·*tral* te·le·fo·nee·ka telephone centre
centro ⓜ *then*·tro centre
— comercial ko·mer·*thyal* shopping centre
— de la ciudad de la thyu·*da* city centre
cepillo ⓜ the·*pee*·lyo hairbrush
— de dientes de *dyen*·tes toothbrush
cerámica ① the·*ra*·mee·ka ceramic
cerca ① *ther*·ka fence
cerca *ther*·ka near • nearby
cerdo ⓜ *ther*·do pork • pig
cereales ⓜ pl the·re·*a*·les cereal
cerillas ① pl las the·*ree*·lyas matches
cerrado/a ⓜ/① the·*ra*·do/a closed
— con llave kon *lya*·ve locked

cerradura ① the·ra·*doo*·ra lock (padlock)
cerrar the·*rar* close • lock • shut
certificado ⓜ ther·tee·fee·*ka*·do certificate
cerveza ① ther·*ve*·tha beer
— rubia *roo*·bya lager
chaleco ⓜ **salvavidas** cha·le·ko sal·va·vee·das lifejacket
champán ⓜ cham·*pan* Champagne
champiñón ⓜ cham·pee·*nyon* mushrooms
champú ⓜ cham·*poo* shampoo
chaqueta ① cha·*ke*·ta jacket
cheque ⓜ *che*·ke check (bank)
cheques ⓜ pl **de viajero** *che*·kes de vya·*khe*·ro travellers cheque
chica ① *chee*·ka girl
chicle ⓜ *chee*·kle chewing gum
chico ⓜ *chee*·ko boy
chocolate ⓜ cho·ko·*la*·te chocolate
choque ⓜ *cho*·ke crash
chorizo ⓜ cho·*ree*·tho salami (Spanish sausage)
chupete ⓜ choo·*pe*·te dummy • pacifier
cibercafé ⓜ thee·ber·ka·*fe* internet cafe
ciclismo ⓜ thee·*klees*·mo cycling
ciclista ⓜ&① thee·*klees*·ta cyclist
ciego/a ⓜ/① *thye*·go/a blind
cielo ⓜ *thye*·lo heaven • sky
ciencias ① pl *thyen*·thyas science
científico/a ⓜ/① thyen·*tee*·fee·ko/a scientist
cigarillo ⓜ thee·ga·*ree*·lyo cigarette
cigarro ⓜ thee·*ga*·ro cigarette
cine ⓜ *thee*·ne cinema
cinta ① **de vídeo** *theen*·ta de vee·de·o video tape
cinturón ⓜ **de seguridad** theen·too·*ron* de se·goo·ree·da seatbelt
circuito ⓜ **de carreras** theer·*kwee*·to de ka·*re*·ras racetrack (cars)
ciruela ① thee·*rwe*·la plum
— pasa *pa*·sa prune

C

istitis ① thees·tee·tees cystitis

ita ① thee·ta appointment

itarse thee·tar·se date

itología ① thee·to·lo·khee·a pap
mear

iudad ① thyu·da city

iudadanía ① thyu·da·da·nee·a
tizenship

lase ① **preferente** kla·se
re·fe·ren·te business class

lase ① **turística** kla·se
oo·rees·tee·ka economy class

lásico/a ⓜ/① kla·see·ko/a classical

lienta/e ⓜ/① klee·en·ta/e client

línica ① klee·nee·ka private hospital

obrar (un cheque) ko·brar (oon
he·ke) cash (a cheque)

oca ① ko·ka cocaine

ocaína ① ko·ka·ee·na cocaine

oche ⓜ ko·che car

— cama ka·ma sleeping car

ocina ① ko·thee·na kitchen • stove

ocinar ko·thee·nar cook

ocinero ⓜ ko·thee·ne·ro chef • cook

oco ⓜ ko·ko coconut

odeína ① ko·de·ee·na codeine

ódigo ⓜ **postal** ko·dee·go pos·tal
ost code

ojonudo/a ⓜ/① ko·kho·noo·do/a
antastic

ol ⓜ kol cabbage

ola ① ko·la queue

olchón ⓜ kol·chon mattress

olega ⓜ&① ko·le·ga colleague • mate

oles ⓜ pl **de Bruselas** ko·les de
roo·se·las brussels sprouts

oliflor ⓜ ko·lee·flor cauliflower

olina ① ko·lee·na hill

ollar ⓜ ko·lyar necklace

olor ⓜ ko·lor colour

omedia ① ko·me·dya comedy

omenzar ko·men·thar begin • start

omer ko·mer eat

omerciante ⓜ&① ko·mer·thyan·te
usiness person

comercio ⓜ ko·mer·thyo trade

comezón ⓜ ko·me·thon itch

comida ① ko·mee·da food

— de bebé de be·be baby food

— en el campo en el kam·po picnic

comisaría ① ko·mee·sa·ree·a police
station

cómo ko·mo how

cómodo/a ⓜ/① ko·mo·do/a
comfortable

cómpact ⓜ kom·pak CD

compañero/a ⓜ/① kom·pa·nye·ro/a
companion

compañía ① kom·pa·nyee·a company

compartir kom·par·teer share (with)

comprar kom·prar buy

comprender kom·pren·der
understand

compresas ① pl kom·pre·sas
sanitary napkins

compromiso ⓜ kom·pro·mee·so
engagement

comunión ① ko·moo·nyon
communion

comunista ⓜ&① ko·moo·nees·ta
communist

con kon with

coñac ⓜ ko·nyak brandy

concentración ① kon·then·tra·thyon
rally

concierto ⓜ kon·thyer·to concert

condición ① **cardíaca** kon·dee·thyon
kar·dee·a·ka heart condition

condones ⓜ pl kon·do·nes condoms

conducir kon·doo·theer drive

conejo ⓜ ko·ne·kho rabbit

conexión ① ko·ne·ksyon connection

confesión ① kon·fe·syon confession

confianza ① kon·fee·an·tha trust

confiar kon·fee·ar trust

confirmar kon·feer·mar confirm

conocer ko·no·ther know (someone)

conocido/a ⓜ/① ko·no·thee·do/a
famous

consejo ⓜ kon·se·kho advice

C

conservador(a) ⓜ/ⓕ kon·ser·va·dor/ kon·ser·va·do·ra conservative

consigna ⓕ kon·seeg·na left luggage

— automática ow·to·ma·tee·ka luggage lockers

construir kons·troo·eer build

consulado ⓜ kon·soo·la·do consulate

contaminación ⓕ kon·ta·mee·na·thyon pollution

contar kon·tar count

contestador ⓜ **automático** kon·tes·ta·dor ow·to·ma·tee·ko answering machine

contrato ⓜ kon·tra·to contract

control ⓜ kon·trol checkpoint

convento ⓜ kon·ven·to convent

copa ⓕ ko·pa drink

— de vino de vee·no wineglass

Copa ⓕ **Mundial** ko·pa moon·dyal World Cup

copos de maíz ko·pos de ma·eeth corn flakes

corazón ⓜ ko·ra·thon heart

cordero ⓜ kor·de·ro lamb

cordillera ⓕ kor·dee·lye·ra mountain range

correcto/a ⓜ/ⓕ ko·rek·to/a right (correct)

correo ⓜ ko·re·o mail

— urgente oor·khen·te express mail

correos ko·re·os post office

correr ko·rer run

corrida ⓕ **de toros** ko·ree·da de to·ros bullfight

corriente ⓕ ko·ryen·te current (electricity)

corriente ko·ryen·te ordinary

corrupto/a ⓜ/ⓕ ko·roop·to/a corrupt

cortar kor·tar cut

cortauñas ⓜ pl kor·ta·oo·nyas nail clippers

corto/a ⓜ/ⓕ kor·to/a short (length)

cosecha ⓕ ko·se·cha crop

coser ko·ser sew

costa ⓕ kos·ta coast • seaside

costar kos·tar cost

crecer kre·ther grow

crema ⓕ kre·ma cream

— hidratante ee·dra·tan·te moisturising cream

— solar so·lar sunblock

críquet ⓜ kree·ket cricket

cristiano/a ⓜ/ⓕ krees·tya·no/a Christian

crítica ⓕ kree·tee·ka review

cruce ⓜ kroo·the intersection

crudo/a ⓜ/ⓕ kroo·do/a raw

cuaderno ⓜ kwa·der·no notebook • square

cualificaciones ⓕ pl kwa·lee·fee·ka·thyo·nes qualifications

cuando kwan·do when

cuánto kwan·to how much

cuarentena ⓕ kwa·ren·te·na quarantine

Cuaresma ⓕ kwa·res·ma Lent

cuarto ⓜ kwar·to quarter

cubiertos ⓜ pl koo·byer·tos cutlery

cubo ⓜ koo·bo bucket

cucaracha ⓕ koo·ka·ra·cha cockroach

cuchara ⓕ koo·cha·ra spoon

cucharita ⓕ koo·cha·ree·ta teaspoon

cuchillas ⓕ pl **de afeitar** koo·chee·lyas de a·fey·tar razor blade

cuchillo ⓜ koo·chee·lyo knife

cuenta ⓕ kwen·ta bill

— bancaria ban·ka·rya bank account

cuento ⓜ kwen·to story

cuerda ⓕ kwer·da rope • string

— para tender la ropa pa·ra ten·der la ro·pa clothes line

cuero ⓜ kwe·ro leather

cuerpo ⓜ kwer·po body

cuesta abajo kwes·ta a·ba·kho downhill

cuesta arriba kwes·ta a·ree·ba uphill

cuestionar kwes·tyo·nar question

cuevas ⓕ pl kwe·vas caves

cuidar kwee·*dar* care for • mind (an object)

cuidar de kwee·*dar* de care (for someone)

culo ⓜ *koo*·lo bum (of body)

culpable kool·*pa*·ble guilty

cumbre ⓕ *koom*·bre peak

cumpleaños ⓜ koom·ple·a·*nyos* birthday

currículum ⓜ koo·*ree*·koo·loom resumé

curry ⓜ *koo*·ree curry

cus cus ⓜ koos koos cous cous

D

dados ⓜ pl *da*·dos dice (die)

dañar da·*nyar* hurt

dar dar give

— de comer de ko·*mer* feed

— gracias *gra*·thyas thank

— la bienvenida la byen·ve·*nee*·da welcome

— una patada oo·na pa·*ta*·da kick

darse cuenta de *dar*·se *kwen*·ta de realise

de de from

— (cuatro) estrellas de (*kwa*·tro) es·*tre*·lyas (four-)star

— izquierdas de eeth·*kyer*·das left-wing

— pena de *pe*·na terrible

— primera clase de pree·*me*·ra *kla*·se first-class

— segunda mano de se·*goon*·da *ma*·no second-hand

— vez en cuando de veth en *kwan*·do sometimes

deber de·*ver* owe

débil *de*·beel weak

decidir de·thee·*deer* decide

decir de·*theer* say • tell

dedo ⓜ *de*·do finger

— del pie del pye toe

defectuoso/a ⓜ/ⓕ de·fek·*two*·so/a faulty

deforestación ⓕ de·fo·res·ta·*thyon* deforestation

dejar de·*khar* leave • quit

delgado/a ⓜ/ⓕ del·*ga*·do/a thin

delirante de·lee·*ran*·te delirious

demasiado caro/a ⓜ/ⓕ de·ma·*sya*·do *ka*·ro/a too (expensive)

democracia ⓕ de·mo·*kra*·thya democracy

demora ⓕ de·*mo*·ra delay

dentista ⓜ&ⓕ den·*tees*·ta dentist

dentro de (una hora) *den*·tro de (oo·na o·ra) within (an hour)

deportes ⓜ pl de·*por*·tes sport

deportista ⓜ&ⓕ de·por·*tees*·ta sportsperson

depósito ⓜ de·po·*see*·to deposit

derecha ⓕ de·*re*·cha right (not left)

derechista de·re·*chees*·ta right-wing

derechos ⓜ pl **civiles** de·*re*·chos thee·*vee*·les civil rights

derechos ⓜ pl **humanos** de·*re*·chos oo·*ma*·nos human rights

desayuno ⓜ des·a·*yoo*·no breakfast

descansar des·kan·*sar* rest

descanso ⓜ des·*kan*·so intermission

descendiente ⓜ des·then·*dyen*·te descendant

descomponerse des·kom·po·*ner*·se decompose

descubrir des·koo·*breer* discover

descuento ⓜ des·*kwen*·to discount

desde (mayo) *des*·de (*ma*·yo) since (may)

desear de·se·*ar* wish

desierto ⓜ de·*syer*·to desert

desodorante ⓜ de·so·do·*ran*·te deodorant

despacio des·*pa*·thyo slowly

desperdicios ⓜ pl **nucleares** des·per·*dee*·thyos noo·kle·a·res nuclear waste

despertador ⓜ des·per·ta·*dor* alarm clock

después de des·*pwes* de after

E

destino ⓜ des·*tee*·no destination
destruir des·troo·*eer* destroy
detallado/a ⓜ/ⓕ de·ta·*lya*·do/a itemised
detalle ⓜ de·*ta*·lye detail
detener de·te·*ner* arrest
detrás de de·*tras* de behind
devocionario ⓜ de·vo·thyo·*na*·ryo prayer book
día ⓜ *dee*·a day
— festivo fes·*tee*·vo holiday
diabetes ⓕ dee·a·*be*·tes diabetes
diafragma ⓜ dee·a·*frag*·ma diaphragm
diapositiva ⓕ dya·po·see·*tee*·va slide
diariamente dya·rya·*men*·te daily
diarrea ⓕ dee·a·*re*·a diarrhoea
dieta ⓕ dee·e·ta diet
dibujar dee·boo·*khar* draw
diccionario ⓜ deek·thyo·*na*·ryo dictionary
diente (de ajo) *dyen*·te (de a·kho) clove (garlic)
dientes ⓜ pl *dyen*·tes teeth
diferencia de horas dee·fe·*ren*·thya de o·ras time difference
diferente dee·fe·*ren*·te different
difícil dee·*fee*·theel difficult
dinero ⓜ dee·*ne*·ro money
— en efectivo en e·fek·*tee*·vo cash
Dios dyos god
dirección ⓕ dee·rek·*thyon* address
directo/a ⓜ/ⓕ dee·*rek*·to/a direct
director(a) ⓜ/ⓕ dee·rek·*tor*/dee·rek·*to*·ra director
disco ⓜ *dees*·ko disk
discoteca ⓕ dees·ko·*te*·ka disco
discriminación ⓕ dees·kree·mee·na·*thyon* discrimination
discutir dees·koo·*teer* argue
diseño ⓜ dee·*se*·nyo design
disparar dees·pa·*rar* shoot
DIU ⓜ de·ee·oo IUD
diversión ⓕ dee·ver·*syon* fun
divertirse dee·ver·*teer*·se enjoy (oneself)

doblar do·*blar* turn • bend
doble do·ble double
docena ⓕ do·*the*·na dozen
doctor(a) ⓜ/ⓕ dok·*tor*/dok·*to*·ra doctor
dólar ⓜ *do*·lar dollar
dolor ⓜ do·*lor* pain
— de cabeza de ka·*be*·tha headache
— de estómago de es·*to*·ma·go stomachache
— de muelas de *mwe*·las toothache
— menstrual mens·*trwal* period pain
dolorido/a ⓜ/ⓕ do·lo·*ree*·do/a sore
doloroso/a ⓜ/ⓕ do·lo·*ro*·so/a painful
donde *don*·de where
dormir dor·*meer* sleep
dos ⓜ/ⓕ pl dos two
— camas *ka*·mas twin beds
— veces *ve*·thes twice
drama ⓜ *dra*·ma drama
droga ⓕ *dro*·ga drug • dope
drogadicción ⓕ dro·ga·deek·*thyon* drug addiction
drogas ⓕ pl *dro*·gas drugs
ducha ⓕ *doo*·cha shower
dueño/a ⓜ/ⓕ *dwe*·nyo/a owner
dulce *dool*·the sweet
dulces ⓜ pl *dool*·thes sweets
duro/a ⓜ/ⓕ *doo*·ro/a hard

E

eczema ⓜ ek·*the*·ma eczema
edad ⓕ e·*da* age
edificio ⓜ e·dee·*fee*·thyo building
editor(a) ⓜ/ⓕ e·dee·*tor*/e·dee·*to*·ra editor
educación ⓕ e·doo·ka·*thyon* education
egoísta e·go·*ees*·ta selfish
ejemplo ⓜ e·*khem*·plo example
ejército ⓜ e·*kher*·thee·to military
el ⓜ el the
él ⓜ el he
elecciones ⓕ pl e·lek·*thyo*·nes elections
electricidad ⓕ e·lek·tree·thee·*da* electricity

E

elegir e·le·*kheer* pick • choose
ella ①️ e·lya she
ellos/ellas ⑩/① e·lyos/e·lyas they
embajada ① em·ba·*kha*·da embassy
embajador(a) ⑩/① em·ba·kha·*dor*/
em·ba·kha·*do*·ra ambassador
embarazada em·ba·ra·*tha*·da
pregnant
embarcarse em·bar·*kar*·se board
(ship etc)
embrague ⑩ em·*bra*·ge clutch
emergencia ① e·mer·*khen*·thya
emergency
emocional e·mo·thyo·*nal* emotional
empleado/a ⑩/① em·ple·a·do/a
employee
empujar em·poo·*khar* push
en en on
— el extranjero el eks·tran·*khe*·ro
abroad
— el paro el *pa*·ro unemployed
encaje ⑩ en·*ka*·khe lace
encantador(a) ⑩/① en·kan·ta·*dor*/
en·kan·ta·*do*·ra charming
encendedor ⑩ en·then·de·*dor* lighter
encontrar en·kon·*trar* find • meet
encurtidos ⑩ pl en·koor·*tee*·dos
pickles
energía ① **nuclear** e·ner·*khee*·a
noo·*kle*·ar nuclear energy
enfadado/a ⑩/① en·fa·*da*·do/a
angry
enfermedad ① en·fer·me·*da* disease
— venérea ve·*ne*·re·a venereal disease
enfermero/a ⑩/① en·fer·*me*·ro/a
nurse
enfermo/a ⑩/① en·*fer*·mo/a sick
enfrente de en·*fren*·te de in front of
enorme e·*nor*·me huge
ensalada en·sa·*la*·da salad
enseñar en·se·*nyar* show • teach
entrar en·*trar* enter
entre *en*·tre among • between
entregar en·tre·*gar* deliver
entrenador(a) ⑩/① en·tre·na·*dor*/
en·tre·na·*do*·ra coach

entreno ⑩ en·*tre*·no workout
entrevista ① en·tre·*vees*·ta interview
enviar en·vee·*ar* send • ship off
epilepsia ① e·pee·*lep*·sya epilepsy
equipaje ⑩ e·kee·*pa*·khe luggage
equipo ⑩ e·*kee*·po equipment • team
— de inmersión de een·mer·*syon*
diving equipment
— de música de *moo*·see·ka stereo
equitación ① e·kee·ta·*thyon* horse
riding
equivocado/a ⑩/① e·kee·vo·*ka*·do/a
wrong
error ⑩ e·*ror* mistake
escalada ① es·ka·*la*·da rock climbing
escalera ① es·ka·*le*·ra stairway
escaleras ① pl **mecánicas**
es·ka·*le*·ras me·*kan*·icas escalator
escarcha ① es·*kar*·cha frost
escarpado/a ⑩/① es·kar·*pa*·do/a
steep
escasez ① es·ka·*seth* shortage
escenario ⑩ es·the·*na*·ryo stage
Escocia ① es·*ko*·thya Scotland
escoger es·ko·*kher* choose
escribir es·kree·*beer* write
— a máquina a *ma*·kee·na type
escritor(a) ⑩/① es·kree·*tor*/
es·kree·*to*·ra writer
escuchar es·koo·*char* listen
escuela ① es·*kwe*·la school
— de párvulos de *par*·voo·los
kindergarten
escultura ① es·kool·*too*·ra sculpture
espacio ⑩ es·*pa*·thyo space
espalda ① es·*pal*·da back (body)
España ① es·*pa*·nya Spain
especial es·pe·*thyal* special
especialista ⑩&① es·pe·thya·*lees*·ta
specialist
especies ① pl **en peligro de
extinción** es·pe·*thyes* en pe·*lee*·gro de
eks·teen·*thyon* endangered species
espectáculo ⑩ es·pek·*ta*·koo·lo show
espejo ⑩ es·*pe*·kho mirror
esperar es·pe·*rar* wait

F

espinaca ① es·pee·na·ka spinach
esposa ① es·po·sa wife
espuma ① **de afeitar** es·poo·ma de a·fey·tar shaving cream
espumoso/a ⓜ/① es·poo·mo·so/a sparkling • foamy
esquí ⓜ es·kee skiing
— acuático a·kwa·tee·ko waterskiing
esquiar es·kee·ar ski
esquina ① es·kee·na corner
esta noche es·ta no·che tonight
éste/a ⓜ/① es·te/a this
estación ① es·ta·thyon season • station
— de autobuses de ow·to·boo·ses bus station
— de metro de me·tro metro station
— de tren de tren railway station
estacionar es·ta·thyo·nar park (car)
estadio ⓜ es·ta·dyo stadium
estado ⓜ **civil** es·ta·do thee·veel marital status
estado ⓜ **del bienestar** es·ta·do del byen·es·tar social welfare • wellbeing
Estados ⓜ pl **Unidos** es·ta·dos oo·nee·dos USA
estafa ① es·ta·fa rip-off
estanquero es·tan·ke·ro tobacconist
estante ⓜ es·tan·te shelf
estar es·tar to be
— constipado/a ⓜ/① kons·tee·pa·do/a have a cold
— de acuerdo de a·kwer·do agree
estatua ① es·ta·twa statue
este es·te east
esterilla ① es·te·ree·lya mat
estilo ⓜ es·tee·lo style
estómago ⓜ es·to·ma·go stomach
estrellas ① pl es·tre·lyas stars
estreñimiento ⓜ es·tre·nyee·myen·to constipation
estudiante ⓜ&① es·too·dyan·te student
estudio ⓜ es·too·dyo studio
estufa ① es·too·fa heater

estúpido/a ⓜ/① es·too·pee·do/a stupid
etiqueta ① **de equipaje** e·tee·ke·ta de e·kee·pa·khe luggage tag
euro ⓜ e·oo·ro euro
Europa ① e·oo·ro·pa Europe
eutanasia ① e·oo·ta·na·sya euthanasia
excelente eks·the·len·te excellent
excursión ① eks·koor·syon tour
excursionismo ⓜ eks·koor·syo·nees·mo hiking
experiencia ① eks·pe·ryen·thya experience
— laboral ① la·bo·ral work experience
exponer eks·po·ner exhibit
exposición ① eks·po·see·thyon exhibition
expreso eks·pre·so express
exterior ⓜ eks·te·ryor outside
extrañar eks·tra·nyar miss (feel sad)
extranjero/a ⓜ/① eks·tran·khe·ro/a foreign

F

fábrica ① fa·bree·ka factory
fácil fa·theel easy
facturación ① **de equipajes** fak·too·ra·thyon de e·kee·pa·khes check-in
falda ① fal·da skirt
falta ① fal·ta fault
familia ① fa·mee·lya family
fantástico/a ⓜ/① fan·tas·tee·ko/a great
farmacia ① far·ma·thya chemist (shop) • pharmacy
farmacéutico ⓜ far·ma·thee·oo·tee·ko chemist (person)
faros ⓜ pl fa·ros headlights
fecha ① fe·cha date (time)
— de nacimiento de na·thee·myen·to date of birth
feliz fe·leeth happy

ferretería ① fe·re·te·*ree*·a hardware store

festival ⓜ fes·tee·*val* festival

ficción ① feek·*thyon* fiction

fideos ⓜ pl fee·*de*·os noodles

fiebre ① *fye*·bre fever

— glandular glan·doo·*lar* glandular fever

fiesta ① *fyes*·ta party

filete ⓜ fee·*le*·te fillet

film ⓜ feelm film

fin ⓜ feen end

— de semana de se·*ma*·na weekend

final ⓜ fee·*nal* end

firma ① *feer*·ma signature

firmar feer·*mar* sign

flor ① flor flower

florista ⓜ&① flo·*rees*·ta florist

folleto ⓜ fo·*lye*·to brochure

footing ⓜ *foo*·teen jogging

forma ① *for*·ma shape

fotografía ① fo·to·gra·*fee*·a photograph

fotógrafo/a ⓜ/① fo·*to*·gra·fo/a photographer

fotómetro ⓜ fo·*to*·me·tro light meter

frágil *fra*·kheel fragile

frambuesa ① fram·*bwe*·sa raspberry

franela ① fra·*ne*·la flannel

franqueo ⓜ fran·*ke*·o postage

freír fre·*eer* fry

frenos ⓜ pl *fre*·nos brakes

frente a *fren*·te a opposite

fresa ① *fre*·sa strawberry

frío/a ⓜ/① *free*·o/a cold

frontera ① fron·*te*·ra border

fruta ① *froo*·ta fruit

fruto ⓜ **seco** froo·to se·*ko* dried fruit

fuego ⓜ *fwe*·go fire

fuera de juego *fwe*·ra de *khwe*·go offside

fuerte *fwer*·te strong

fumar foo·*mar* smoke

funda ① **de almohada** *foon*·da de al·*mwa*·da pillowcase

funeral ⓜ foo·ne·*ral* funeral

fútbol ⓜ *foot*·bol football • soccer

— australiano ow·stra·*lya*·no Australian Rules football

futuro ⓜ foo·*too*·ro future

G

gafas ① pl *ga*·fas glasses

— de sol de sol sunglasses

— de submarinismo de soob·ma·ree·*nees*·mo goggles

galleta ① ga·*lye*·ta biscuit • cookie

galletas ① pl **saladas** ga·*lye*·tas sa·*la*·das biscuits • crackers

gambas ① pl *gam*·bas prawns

ganador(a) ⓜ/① ga·na·*dor*/ ga·na·*do*·ra winner

ganar ga·*nar* earn • win

garbanzos ⓜ pl gar·*ban*·thos chickpeas

garganta ① gar·*gan*·ta throat

gasolina ① ga·so·*lee*·na petrol

gasolinera ① ga·so·lee·*ne*·ra service station

gatito/a ⓜ/① ga·*tee*·to/a kitten

gato/a ⓜ/① *ga*·to/a cat

gay gai gay

gemelos ⓜ pl khe·*me*·los twins

general khe·ne·*ral* general

gente ① *khen*·te people

gimnasia ① **rítmica** kheem·*na*·sya *reet*·mee·ka gymnastics

ginebra ① khee·*ne*·bra gin

ginecólogo ⓜ khee·ne·*ko*·lo·go gynaecologist

gobierno ⓜ go·*byer*·no government

gol ⓜ gol goal

goma ① *go*·ma condom • rubber

gordo/a ⓜ/① *gor*·do/a fat

grabación ① gra·ba·*thyon* recording

gracioso/a ⓜ/① gra·*thyo*·so/a funny

gramo ⓜ *gra*·mo gram

grande *gran*·de big • large

grande almacene ⓜ *gran*·de al·ma·*the*·ne department store

granja ① *gran*·kha farm

gratis *gra*·tees free (of charge)

H

grifo ⓜ *gree*·fo tap
gripe ⓕ *gree*·pe influenza
gris grees grey
gritar gree·*tar* shout
grupo ⓜ *groo*·po group
— **de rock** de rok rock band
— **sanguíneo** san·*gee*·ne·o blood group
guantes ⓜ pl *gwan*·tes gloves
guardarropa ⓜ gwar·da·*ro*·pa cloakroom
guardería ⓕ gwar·de·*ree*·a childminding service • creche
guerra ⓕ *ge*·ra war
guía ⓜ&ⓕ *gee*·a guide (person)
guía ⓕ *gee*·a guidebook
— **audio** *ow*·dyo audioguide
— **del ocio** del o·*thyo* entertainment guide
— **telefónica** te·le·*fo*·nee·ka phone book
guindilla ⓕ geen·*dee*·lya chilli
guión ⓜ gee·*on* script
guiri ⓕ *gee*·ree tourist (slang)
guisantes gee·*san*·tes peas
güisqui *gwees*·kee whiskey
guitarra ⓕ gee·*ta*·ra guitar
gustar(le) goos·*tar*(·le) like

H

habitación ⓕ a·bee·ta·*thyon* bedroom • room
— **doble** *do*·ble double room
— **individual** een·dee·vee·*dwal* single room
hablar a·*blar* speak • talk
hace sol a·the sol sunny
hacer a·*ther* do • make
— **dedo** de·do hitchhike
— **surf** soorf surf
— **windsurf** ween·soorf windsurfing
hachís ⓜ a·*chees* hash
hacia a·thya towards
— **abajo** a·ba·kho down
halal a·*lal* halal

hamaca ⓕ a·*ma*·ka hammock
hambriento/a ⓜ/ⓕ am·*bryen*·to/a hungry
harina ⓕ a·*ree*·na flour
hasta (junio) as·ta (*khoo*·nyo) until (June)
hecho/a ⓜ/ⓕ e·*cho*/a made
— **a mano** a *ma*·no handmade
— **de (algodón)** de (al·go·*don*) made of (cotton)
heladería ⓕ e·la·de·*ree*·a ice cream parlour
helado ⓜ e·*la*·do ice cream
helar e·*lar* freeze
hepatitis ⓕ e·pa·*tee*·tees hepatitis
herbolario ⓜ er·bo·*la*·ryo herbalist (shop)
herida ⓕ e·*ree*·da injury
hermana ⓕ er·*ma*·na sister
hermano ⓜ er·*ma*·no brother
hermoso/a ⓜ/ⓕ er·*mo*·so/a beautiful
heroína ⓕ e·ro·*ee*·na heroin
hielo ⓜ *ye*·lo ice
hierba ⓕ *yer*·ba grass
hierbas ⓕ pl *yer*·bas herbs
hígado ⓜ *ee*·ga·do liver
higos ⓜ pl *ee*·gos figs
hija ⓕ *ee*·kha daughter
hijo ⓜ *ee*·kho son
hijos ⓜ pl *ee*·khos children
hilo ⓜ thread *ee*·lo
— **dental** den·*tal* dental floss
hinchas ⓜ&ⓕ pl *een*·chas supporters
hindú een·*doo* Hindu
hipódromo ⓜ ee·*po*·dro·mo racetrack (horses)
historial ⓜ **profesional** ees·to·*ryal* pro·fe·syo·*nal* CV
histórico/a ⓜ/ⓕ ees·*to*·ree·ko/a historical
hockey ⓜ *kho*·kee hockey
— **sobre hielo** so·bre *ye*·lo ice hockey
hoja ⓕ *o*·kha leaf • sheet (of paper)

I

hojalata ① o·kha·*la*·ta tin
Holanda ① o·*lan*·da Netherlands
hombre ⓜ *om*·bre man
hombros ⓜ pl *om*·bros shoulders
homosexual ⓜ&① o·mo·se·*kswal* homosexual
hora ① *o*·ra time
horario ⓜ o·*ra*·ryo timetable
horas ① pl **de abrir** *o*·ras de a·*breer* opening hours
hormiga ① or·*mee*·ga ant
horno ⓜ *or*·no oven
horóscopo ⓜ o·*ros*·ko·po horoscope
hospital ⓜ os·pee·*tal* hospital
hostelería ① os·te·le·*ree*·a hospitality
hotel ⓜ o·*tel* hotel
hoy oy today
hueso ⓜ *we*·so bone
huevo ⓜ *we*·vo egg
humanidades ① pl oo·ma·nee·*da*·des humanities

I

identificación ①
ee·den·tee·fee·ka·*thyon* identification
idiomas ⓜ pl ee·*dyo*·mas languages
idiota ⓜ/① ee·*dyo*·ta idiot
iglesia ① ee·*gle*·sya church
igual ee·*gwal* same
igualdad ① ee·gwal·*da* equality
impermeable ⓜ eem·per·me·*a*·ble raincoat
impermeable eem·per·me·*a*·ble waterproof
importante eem·por·*tan*·te important
impuesto ⓜ eem·*pwes*·to tax
— sobre la renta *so*·bre la *ren*·ta income tax
incluido een·kloo·*ee*·do included
incómodo/a ⓜ/① een·*ko*·mo·do/a uncomfortable
India ① *een*·dya India
indicador ⓜ een·dee·ka·*dor* indicator
indigestión ① een·dee·khes·*tyon* indigestion

industria ① een·*doos*·trya industry
infección ① een·fek·*thyon* infection
inflamación ① een·fla·ma·*thyon* inflammation
informática ① een·for·*ma*·tee·ka IT
ingeniería ① een·khe·nye·*ree*·a engineering
ingeniero/a ⓜ/① een·khe·*nye*·ro/a engineer
Inglaterra ① een·gla·*te*·ra England
inglés ⓜ een·*gles* English • English language
ingrediente ⓜ een·gre·*dyen*·te ingredient
injusto/a ⓜ/① een·*khoos*·to/a unfair
inmigración ① een·mee·gra·*thyon* immigration
inocente ee·no·*then*·te innocent
inseguro/a ⓜ/① een·se·*goo*·ro/a unsafe
instituto ⓜ eens·tee·*too*·to high school
intentar (hacer algo) een·ten·*tar* (a·*ther* al·go) try (to do something)
interesante een·te·re·*san*·te interesting
internacional een·ter·na·thyo·*nal* international
Internet ⓜ een·ter·*net* Internet
intérprete ⓜ&① een·*ter*·pre·te interpreter
inundación ① ee·noon·da·*thyon* flooding
invierno ⓜ een·*vyer*·no winter
invitar een·vee·*tar* invite
inyección ① een·yek·*thyon* injection
inyectar(se) een·yek·*tar*(·se) inject (oneself)
ir eer go
— de compras de *kom*·pras go shopping
— de excursión de eks·koor·*syon* hike
— en tobogán en to·bo·*gan* tobogganing
Irlanda ① eer·*lan*·da Ireland

J

irritación ① ee·ree·ta·*thyon* rash
— de pañal de pa·*nyal* nappy rash
isla ① *ees*·la island
itinerario ⓜ ee·tee·ne·*ra*·ryo
itinerary
IVA ⓜ *ee*·va sales tax
izquierda ① eeth·*kyer*·da left

J

jabón ⓜ kha·*bon* soap
jamón ⓜ kha·*mon* ham
Japón ⓜ kha·*pon* Japan
jarabe ⓜ kha·*ra*·be cough medicine
jardín ⓜ **botánico** khar·*deen*
bo·*ta*·nee·ko botanic garden
jarra ① *kha*·ra jar
jefe/a ⓜ/① *khe*·fe/a boss • leader
— de sección de sek·*thyon*
manager
jengibre ⓜ khen·*khee*·bre ginger
jeringa ① khe·*reen*·ga syringe
jersey ⓜ kher·*sey* jumper • sweater
jet lag ⓜ dyet lag jet lag
jockey ⓜ dyo·*kee* jockey
joven *kho*·ven young
joyería ① kho·ye·*ree*·a jeweller
(shop)
jubilado/a ⓜ/① khoo·bee·*la*·do/a
retired
judías ① pl khoo·*dee*·as beans
judío/a ⓜ/① khoo·*dee*·o/a Jewish
juegos ⓜ pl **de ordenador** *khwe*·gos
de or·de·na·*dor* computer games
juegos ⓜ pl **olímpicos** *khwe*·gos
o·*leem*·pee·kos Olympic Games
juez ⓜ&① khweth judge
jugar khoo·*gar* play (sport/games)
jugo ⓜ *khoo*·go juice
juguetería ① khoo·ge·te·*ree*·a
toyshop
juntos/as ⓜ/① pl *khoon*·tos/as
together

K

kilogramo ⓜ kee·lo·*gra*·mo kilogram
kilómetro ⓜ kee·*lo*·me·tro kilometre

kiwi ⓜ *kee*·wee kiwifruit
kosher *ko*·sher Kosher

L

labios ⓜ pl *la*·byos lips
lado ⓜ *la*·do side
ladrón ⓜ la·*dron* thief
lagartija ① la·gar·*tee*·kha lizard
lago ⓜ *la*·go lake
lamentar la·men·*tar* regret
lana ① *la*·na wool
lápiz ⓜ *la*·peeth pencil
— de labios de *la*·byos lipstick
largo/a ⓜ/① *lar*·go/a long
lata ① *la*·ta can
lavadero ⓜ la·va·de·ro laundry
lavadora ① la·va·*do*·ra washing
machine
lavandería ① la·van·de·*ree*·a
laundrette
lavar la·*var* wash (something)
lavarse la·*var*·se wash (oneself)
leche ① *le*·che milk
— de soja de *so*·kha soy milk
— desnatada des·na·*ta*·da skimmed
milk
lechuga ① le·*choo*·ga lettuce
leer le·*er* read
legal le·*gal* legal
legislación ① le·khees·la·*thyon*
legislation
legumbre ① le·*goom*·bre legume
lejos le·khos far
leña ① *le*·nya firewood
lentejas ① pl len·*te*·khas lentils
lentes ⓜ pl **de contacto** *len*·tes de
kon·*tak*·to contact lenses
lento/a ⓜ/① *len*·to/a slow
lesbiana ① les·bee·*a*·na lesbian
leve *le*·ve light
ley ① ley law
libra ① *lee*·bra pound (money)
libre *lee*·bre free (not bound)
librería ① lee·bre·*ree*·a bookshop
libro ⓜ *lee*·bro book
— de frases de *fra*·ses phrasebook

M

bros ⓜ pl **de viajes** lee·bros de
va·khes travel books
der ⓜ lee·der leader
gar lee·gar pick up
la lee·la purple
ma lee·ma lime
mite ⓜ **de equipaje** lee·mee·te de
kee·pa·khe baggage allowance
món ⓜ lee·mon lemon
monada ⓕ lee·mo·na·da lemonade
mpio/a ⓜ/ⓕ leem·pyo/a clean
nea ⓕ lee·ne·a line
nterna ⓕ leen·ter·na flashlight •
orch
sto/a ⓜ/ⓕ lees·to/a ready
amada ⓕ lya·ma·da phone call
- a cobro revertido a ko·bro
e·ver·tee·do collect call
amar por telefono lya·mar por
e·le·fo·no to make a phone call
ano/a ⓜ/ⓕ lya·no/a flat
ave ⓕ lya·ve key
egadas ⓕ pl lye·ga·das arrivals
egar lye·gar arrive
enar lye·nar fill
eno/a ⓜ/ⓕ lye·no/a full
evar lye·var carry • wear
luvia ⓕ lyoo·vya rain
o que lo ke what
ocal ⓜ lo·kal venue
ocal lo·kal local
oco/a ⓜ/ⓕ lo·ko/a crazy
odo ⓜ lo·do mud
ombrices ⓕ pl lom·bree·thes worms
s dos los dos both
ubricante ⓜ loo·bree·kan·te
ubricant
uces ⓕ pl loo·thes lights
uchar contra loo·char kon·tra fight
gainst
ugar ⓜ loo·gar place
- de nacimiento de na·thee·myen·to
lace of birth
ujo ⓜ loo·kho luxury

luna ⓕ loo·na moon
— llena lye·na full moon
— de miel de myel honeymoon
luz ⓕ looth light

M

machismo ⓜ ma·chees·mo sexism
madera ⓕ ma·de·ra wood
madre ⓕ ma·dre mother
madrugada ⓕ ma·droo·ga·da early
morning
mago/a ⓜ/ⓕ ma·go/a magician
maíz ⓜ ma·eeth corn
maleta ⓕ ma·le·ta suitcase
maletín ⓜ ma·le·teen briefcase
— de primeros auxilios ⓜ de
pree·me·ros ow·ksee·lyos first-aid kit
malo/a ⓜ/ⓕ ma·lo/a bad
mamá ⓕ ma·ma mum
mamograma ⓜ ma·mo·gra·ma
mammogram
mañana ⓕ ma·nya·na tomorrow •
morning (6am–1pm)
— por la mañana por la ma·nya·na
tomorrow morning
— por la noche por la no·che
tomorrow evening
— por la tarde por la tar·de tomorrow
afternoon
mandarina ⓕ man·da·ree·na mandarin
mandíbula ⓕ man·dee·boo·la jaw
mando ⓜ **a distancia** man·do a
dees·tan·thya remote control
mango ⓜ man·go mango
manifestación ⓕ
ma·nee·fes·ta·thyon demonstration
manillar ⓜ ma·nee·lyar handlebar
mano ⓕ ma·no hand
manta ⓕ man·ta blanket
manteca ⓕ man·te·ka lard
mantel ⓜ man·tel tablecloth
mantequilla ⓕ man·te·kee·lya butter
manzana ⓕ man·tha·na apple
mapa ⓜ ma·pa map

maquillaje ⓜ ma·kee·*lya*·khe make-up

máquina ⓕ *ma*·kee·na machine

— de billetes de bee·*lye*·tes ticket machine

— de tabaco de ta·*ba*·ko cigarette machine

mar ⓜ mar sea

marido ⓜ ma·*ree*·do husband

maravilloso/a ⓜ/ⓕ ma·ra·vee·*lyo*·so/a wonderful

marcador ⓜ mar·ka·*dor* scoreboard

marcapasos ⓜ mar·ka·*pa*·sos pacemaker

marcar mar·*kar* score

marea ⓕ ma·*re*·a tide

mareado/a ⓜ/ⓕ ma·re·a·do/a dizzy • seasick

mareo ⓜ ma·*re*·o travel sickness

margarina ⓕ mar·ga·*ree*·na margarine

marihuana ⓕ ma·ree·*wa*·na marijuana

mariposa ⓕ ma·ree·*po*·sa butterfly

marrón ma·*ron* brown

martillo ⓜ mar·*tee*·lyo hammer

más cercano/a ⓜ/ⓕ mas ther·*ka*·no/a nearest

masaje ⓜ ma·*sa*·khe massage

masajista ⓜ&ⓕ ma·sa·*khees*·ta masseur

matar ma·*tar* kill

matrícula ⓕ ma·*tree*·koo·la license plate number

matrimonio ⓜ ma·tree·*mo*·nyo marriage

mayonesa ⓕ ma·yo·*ne*·sa mayonnaise

mecánico ⓜ me·*ka*·nee·ko mechanic

mechero ⓜ me·*che*·ro lighter

medianoche ⓕ me·dya·*no*·che midnight

medias ⓕ pl *me*·dyas stockings • pantyhose

medicina ⓕ me·dee·*thee*·na medicine

medico/a ⓜ/ⓕ *me*·dee·co/a doctor

medio ambiente *me*·dyo am·*byen*·te environment

medio/a ⓜ/ⓕ *me*·dyo/a half

mediodía ⓜ me·dyo·*dee*·a noon

medios ⓜ pl **de comunicación** *me*·dyos de ko·moo·nee·ka·*thyon* media

medios ⓜ pl **de transporte** *me*·dyo de trans·*por*·te means of transport

meditación ⓕ meditation me·dee·ta·*thyon*

mejillones ⓜ pl me·khee·*lyo*·nes mussels

mejor me·*khor* better • best

melocotón ⓜ me·lo·ko·*ton* peach

melodía ⓕ me·lo·*dee*·a tune

melón ⓜ me·*lon* melon

mendigo/a ⓜ/ⓕ men·*dee*·go/a beggar

menos *me*·nos less

mensaje ⓜ men·*sa*·khe message

menstruación ⓕ mens·trwa·*thyon* menstruation

mentiroso/a ⓜ/ⓕ men·tee·ro·so/a liar

menú ⓜ me·*noo* menu

menudo/a ⓜ/ⓕ me·*noo*·do/a little

a menudo a me·*noo*·do often

mercado ⓜ mer·*ka*·do market

mermelada ⓕ mer·me·*la*·da jam • marmalade

mes ⓜ mes month

mesa ⓕ *me*·sa table

meseta ⓕ me·*se*·ta plateau

metal ⓜ me·*tal* metal

meter (un gol) me·*ter* (oon gol) kick (a goal)

metro ⓜ *me*·tro metre

mezclar meth·*klar* mix

mezquita ⓕ meth·*kee*·ta mosque

mi mee my

microondas ⓜ mee·kro·*on*·das microwave

miel ⓕ myel honey

miembro ⓜ *myem*·bro member

migraña ⓕ mee·*gra*·nya migraine

milímetro ⓜ mee·*lee*·me·tro millimetre

millón ⓜ mee·*lyon* million

minusválido/a ⓜ/ⓕ
mee·noos·*va*·lee·do/a disabled

minuto ⓜ mee·*noo*·to minute

mirador ⓜ mee·ra·*dor* lookout

mirar mee·*rar* look • watch

— los escaparates los es·ka·pa·*ra*·tes window-shopping

misa ⓕ *mee*·sa mass

mochila ⓕ mo·*chee*·la backpack

módem ⓜ *mo*·dem modem

(carne) molida (*kar*·ne) mo·*lee*·da mince (meat)

mojado/a ⓜ/ⓕ mo·*kha*·do/a wet

monasterio ⓜ mo·nas·*te*·ryo monastery

monedas ⓕ pl mo·*ne*·das coins

monja ⓕ *mon*·kha nun

monopatinaje ⓜ
mo·no·pa·tee·*na*·khe skateboarding

montaña ⓕ mon·*ta*·nya mountain

montar mon·*tar* ride

— en bicicleta en bee·thee·*kle*·ta cycle

monumento ⓜ mo·noo·*men*·to monument

mordedura ⓕ mor·de·*doo*·ra bite (dog)

morir mo·*reer* die

mosquitera ⓕ mos·kee·*te*·ra mosquito net

mosquito ⓜ mos·*kee*·to mosquito

mostaza ⓕ mos·*ta*·tha mustard

mostrador ⓜ mos·tra·*dor* counter

mostrar mos·*trar* show

motocicleta ⓕ mo·to·thee·*kle*·ta motorcycle

motor ⓜ mo·*tor* engine

motora ⓕ mo·*to*·ra motorboat

muchas/os ⓜ/ⓕ pl *moo*·chas/os many

mudo/a ⓜ/ⓕ *moo*·do/a mute

muebles ⓜ pl *mwe*·bles furniture

muela ⓕ *mwe*·la tooth (back)

muelle ⓜ *mwe*·lye spring

muerto/a ⓜ/ⓕ *mwer*·to/a dead

muesli ⓜ *mwes*·lee muesli

mujer ⓕ moo·*kher* woman

multa ⓕ *mool*·ta fine

mundo ⓜ *moon*·do world

muñeca ⓕ moo·*nye*·ka doll • wrist

murallas ⓕ pl moo·*ra*·lyas city walls

músculo ⓜ *moos*·koo·lo muscle

museo ⓜ moo·*se*·o museum

— de arte de *ar*·te art gallery

música ⓕ *moo*·see·ka music

músico/a ⓜ/ⓕ *moo*·see·ko/a musician

— ambulante am·boo·*lan*·te busker

muslo ⓜ *moos*·lo drumstick (chicken)

musulmán(a) ⓜ/ⓕ moo·sool·*man*/ moo·sool·*ma*·na Muslim

muy mooy very

N

nacionalidad ⓕ na·thyo·na·lee·*da* nationality

nada *na*·da none • nothing

nadar na·*dar* swim

naranja ⓕ na·*ran*·kha orange

nariz ⓕ na·*reeth* nose

nata ⓕ **agria** *na*·ta a·*grya* sour cream

naturaleza ⓕ na·too·ra·*le*·tha nature

naturopatía ⓕ na·too·ro·pa·*tee*·a naturopathy

náusea ⓕ *now*·se·a nausea

náuseas ⓕ pl **del embarazo** *now*·se·as del em·ba·*ra*·tho morning sickness

navaja ⓕ na·*va*·kha penknife

Navidad ⓕ na·vee·*da* Christmas

necesario/a ⓜ/ⓕ ne·the·*sa*·ryo/a necessary

necesitar ne·the·see·*tar* need

negar ne·*gar* deny

negar ne·*gar* refuse

negocio Ⓜ ne·*go*·thyo business

— de artículos básicos de ar·*tee*·koo·los ba·*see*·kos convenience store

negro/a Ⓜ/Ⓕ *ne*·gro/a black

neumático Ⓜ ne·oo·*ma*·tee·ko tyre

nevera Ⓕ ne·*ve*·ra refrigerator

nieto/a Ⓜ/Ⓕ *nye*·to/a grandchild

nieve Ⓕ *nye*·ve snow

niño/a Ⓜ/Ⓕ *nee*·nyo/a child

no no no

— fumadores foo·ma·*do*·res non-smoking

— incluido een·kloo·*ee*·do excluded

noche Ⓕ *no*·che evening • night

Nochebuena Ⓕ no·che·*bwe*·na Christmas Eve

Nochevieja Ⓕ no·che·*vye*·kha New Year's Eve

nombre Ⓜ *nom*·bre name

— de pila de *pee*·la Christian name

norte Ⓜ *nor*·te north

nosotros/as Ⓜ/Ⓕ pl no·*so*·tros/no·*so*·tras we

noticias Ⓕ pl no·*tee*·thyas news

— de actualidad de ak·twal·ee·*da* current affairs

novia Ⓕ *no*·vya girlfriend

novio Ⓜ *no*·vyo boyfriend

nube Ⓕ *noo*·be cloud

nublado noo·*bla*·do cloudy

nueces *nwe*·thes nuts

— crudas *kroo*·das raw nuts

— tostadas tos·*ta*·das roasted nuts

nuestro/a Ⓜ/Ⓕ *nwes*·tro/a our

Nueva Zelanda Ⓕ *nwe*·va the·*lan*·da New Zealand

nuevo/a Ⓜ/Ⓕ *nwe*·vo/a new

número Ⓜ *noo*·me·ro number

— de la habitación de la a·bee·ta·*thyon* room number

— de pasaporte de pa·sa·*por*·te passport number

nunca *noon*·ka never

O

o o or

obra Ⓕ *o*·bra play • building site

obrero/a Ⓜ/Ⓕ o·*bre*·ro/a factory worker • labourer

océano Ⓜ o·*the*·a·no ocean

ocupado/a Ⓜ/Ⓕ o·koo·*pa*·do/a busy

ocupar o·koo·*par* live (somewhere)

oeste Ⓜ o·*es*·te west

oficina Ⓕ o·fee·*thee*·na office

— de objetos perdidos de ob·*khe*·tos per·*dee*·dos lost property office

— de turismo de too·*rees*·mo tourist office

oír o·*eer* hear

ojo Ⓜ *o*·kho eye

ola Ⓕ *o*·la wave

olor Ⓜ o·*lor* smell

olvidar ol·vee·*dar* forget

ópera Ⓕ *o*·pe·ra opera

operación Ⓕ o·pe·ra·*thyon* operation

opinión Ⓕ o·pee·*nyon* opinion

oporto Ⓜ o·*por*·to port (wine)

oportunidad Ⓕ o·por·too·nee·*da* chance

oración Ⓕ o·ra·*thyon* prayer

orden Ⓜ *or*·den order (placement)

ordenador Ⓜ or·de·na·*dor* computer

— portátil por·ta·*teel* laptop

ordenar or·de·*nar* order

oreja Ⓕ o·*re*·kha ear

orgasmo Ⓜ or·*gas*·mo orgasm

original o·ree·khee·*nal* original

orquesta Ⓕ or·*kes*·ta orchestra

oscuro/a Ⓜ/Ⓕ os·*koo*·ro/a dark

ostra Ⓕ *os*·tra oyster

otoño Ⓜ o·*to*·nyo autumn

otra vez *o*·tra veth again

otro/a Ⓜ/Ⓕ *o*·tro/a other • another

oveja Ⓕ o·*ve*·kha sheep

oxígeno Ⓜ o·*ksee*·khe·no oxygen

P

padre Ⓜ *pa*·dre father

padres Ⓜ pl *pa*·dres parents

pagar pa·*gar* pay

página ① pa·*khee*·na page

pago ⓜ *pa*·go payment

país ⓜ pa·*ees* country

pájaro ⓜ *pa*·kha·ro bird

palabra ① pa·*la*·bra word

palacio ⓜ pa·*la*·thyo palace

palillo ⓜ pa·*lee*·lyo toothpick

pan ⓜ pan bread

— integral in·te·*gral* wholemeal bread

— moreno mo·*re*·no brown bread

panadería ① pa·na·de·*ree*·a bakery

pañal ⓜ pa·*nyal* diaper • nappy

pantalla ① pan·*ta*·lya screen

pantalones ⓜ pl pan·ta·*lo*·nes pants • trousers

— cortos kor·*tos* shorts

pañuelos ⓜ pl **de papel** pa·*nywe*·los de pa·*pel* tissues

papá ⓜ pa·*pa* dad

papel ⓜ pa·*pel* paper

— de fumar de foo·*mar* cigarette papers

— higiénico ee·*khye*·nee·ko toilet paper

paquete ⓜ pa·*ke*·te packet • package

para llevar pa·ra lye·*var* to take away

parabrisas ⓜ pa·ra·*bree*·sas windscreen

paracaidismo ⓜ pa·ra·kai·*dees*·mo skydiving

parada ① pa·*ra*·da stop

— de autobús de ow·to·*boos* bus stop

— de taxis de *ta*·ksees taxi stand

paraguas ⓜ pa·ra·*gwas* umbrella

parapléjico/a ⓜ/① pa·ra·*ple*·khee·ko/a paraplegic

parar pa·*rar* stop

pared ① pa·*re* wall (inside)

pareja ① pa·*re*·kha pair (couple)

parlamento ⓜ par·la·*men*·to parliament

paro ⓜ *pa*·ro dole

parque ⓜ *par*·ke park

— nacional na·thyo·*nal* national park

parte ① *par*·te part

partida ① **de nacimiento** par·*tee*·da de na·thee·*myen*·to birth certificate

partido ⓜ par·*tee*·do match (sport) • (political) party

pasado ⓜ pa·*sa*·do past

pasado mañana pa·*sa*·do ma·*nya*·na day after tomorrow

pasado/a ⓜ/① pa·*sa*·do/a off (food)

pasajero ⓜ pa·sa·*khe*·ro passenger

pasaporte ⓜ pa·sa·*por*·te passport

Pascua ① *pas*·kwa Easter

pase ⓜ *pa*·se pass

paseo ⓜ pa·*se*·o street

paso ⓜ *pa*·so step

— de cebra de *the*·bra pedestrian crossing

pasta ① *pas*·ta pasta

— dentífrica den·*tee*·free·ka toothpaste

pastel ⓜ pas·*tel* cake • pie

— de cumpleaños de koom·ple·a·*nyos* birthday cake

pastelería ① pas·te·le·*ree*·a cake shop

pastilla ① pas·*tee*·lya pill

pastillas ① pl **de menta** pas·*tee*·lyas de *men*·ta mints

pastillas ① pl **para dormir** pas·*tee*·lyas *pa*·ra dor·*meer* sleeping pills

patata ① pa·*ta*·ta potato

paté ⓜ pa·*te* pate (food)

patinar pa·*tee*·nar rollerblading • ice skating

pato ⓜ *pa*·to duck

pavo ⓜ *pa*·vo turkey

paz ① path peace

peatón ⓜ&① pe·a·*ton* pedestrian

pecho ⓜ *pe*·cho chest

pechuga ① pe·*choo*·ga breast (poultry)

pedal ⓜ pe·*dal* pedal

pedazo ⓜ pe·*da*·tho piece

pedir pe·*deer* ask (for something)

P

peine ⓜ *pey*·ne comb
pelea ⓕ pe·*le*·a fight
película ⓕ pe·*lee*·koo·la movie • film (camera)
— **en color** en ko·*lor* colour film
peligroso/a ⓜ/ⓕ pe·lee·*gro*·so/a dangerous
pelo ⓜ *pe*·lo hair
pelota ⓕ pe·*lo*·ta ball
— **de golf** de golf golf ball
peluquero/a ⓜ/ⓕ pe·loo·*ke*·ro/a hairdresser
pendientes ⓜ pl pen·*dyen*·tes earrings
pene ⓜ *pe*·ne penis
pensar pen·*sar* think
pensión ⓕ pen·*syon* boarding house
pensionista ⓜ&ⓕ pen·syo·*nees*·ta pensioner
pepino ⓜ pe·*pee*·no cucumber
pequeñito/a ⓜ/ⓕ pe·ke·*nyee*·to/a tiny
pequeño/a ⓜ/ⓕ pe·*ke*·nyo/a small
pera ⓕ *pe*·ra pear
perder per·*der* lose
perdido/a ⓜ/ⓕ per·*dee*·do/a lost
perdonar per·do·*nar* forgive
perejil ⓜ pe·re·*kheel* parsley
perfume ⓜ per·*foo*·me perfume
periódico ⓜ pe·*ryo*·dee·ko newspaper
periodista ⓜ&ⓕ pe·ryo·*dees*·ta journalist
permiso ⓜ per·*mee*·so permission • permit
— **de trabajo** ⓜ de tra·*ba*·kho work permit
permitir per·mee·*teer* allow • permit
pero *pe*·ro but
perro/a ⓜ/ⓕ *pe*·ro/a dog
perro lazarillo *pe*·ro la·tha·*ree*·lyo guide dog
persona ⓕ per·*so*·na person
pesado/a ⓜ/ⓕ pe·*sa*·do/a heavy
pesar pe·*sar* weigh

pesas ⓕ pl *pe*·sas weights
pesca ⓕ *pes*·ka fishing
pescadería ⓕ pes·ka·de·*ree*·a fish shop
pescado ⓜ pes·*ka*·do fish (as food)
peso ⓜ *pe*·so weight
petición ⓕ pe·tee·*thyon* petition
pez ⓜ peth fish
picadura ⓕ pee·ka·*doo*·ra bite (insect)
picazón ⓕ pee·ka·*thon* itch
pie ⓜ pye foot
piedra ⓕ *pye*·dra stone
piel ⓕ pyel skin
pierna ⓕ *pyer*·na leg
pila ⓕ *pee*·la battery (small)
píldora ⓕ *peel*·do·ra the Pill
pimienta ⓕ pee·*myen*·ta pepper
pimiento ⓜ pee·*myen*·to capsicum • bell pepper
— **rojo** *ro*·kho red capsicum
— **verde** *ver*·de green capsicum
piña ⓕ *pee*·nya pineapple
pinchar peen·*char* puncture
ping pong ⓜ peeng pong table tennis
pintar peen·*tar* paint
pintor(a) ⓜ/ⓕ peen·*tor*/peen·*to*·ra painter
pintura ⓕ peen·*too*·ra painting
pinzas ⓕ pl *peen*·thas tweezers
piojos ⓜ pl *pyo*·khos lice
piqueta ⓕ pee·*ke*·ta pickaxe
piquetas ⓕ pl pee·*ke*·tas tent pegs
piscina ⓕ pees·*thee*·na swimming pool
pista ⓕ *pees*·ta court (tennis)
— **de tenis** de *te*·nees tennis court
pistacho ⓜ pees·*ta*·cho pistachio
plancha ⓕ *plan*·cha iron
planeta ⓜ pla·*ne*·ta planet
planta ⓕ *plan*·ta plant
plástico ⓜ *plas*·tee·ko plastic
plata ⓕ *pla*·ta silver
plataforma ⓕ pla·ta·*for*·ma platform
plátano ⓜ *pla*·ta·no banana

plateado/a ⓜ/ⓕ pla·te·a·do/a silver
plato ⓜ pla·to plate
playa ⓕ pla·ya beach
plaza ⓕ pla·tha square
— de toros de to·ros bullring
pobre po·bre poor
pobreza ⓕ po·bre·tha poverty
pocos po·kos few
poder po·der can (be able)
poder ⓜ po·der power
poesía ⓕ po·e·see·a poetry
polen ⓜ po·len pollen
policía ⓕ po·lee·thee·a police
política ⓕ po·lee·tee·ka policy ·
politics
político ⓜ po·lee·tee·ko politician
póliza ⓕ po·lee·tha policy (insurance)
pollo ⓜ po·lyo chicken
pomelo ⓜ po·me·lo grapefruit
poner po·ner put
popular po·poo·lar popular
póquer ⓜ po·ker poker
por (día) por (dee·a) per (day)
por ciento por thyen·to percent
por qué por ke why
por vía aérea por vee·a a·e·re·a air
mail
por vía terrestre por vee·a te·res·tre
surface mail
porque por·ke because
portero/a ⓜ/ⓕ por·te·ro/a
goalkeeper
posible po·see·ble possible
postal ⓕ pos·tal postcard
póster ⓜ pos·ter poster
potro ⓜ po·tro foal
pozo ⓜ po·tho well
precio ⓜ pre·thyo price
— de entrada de en·tra·da admission
price
— del cubierto del koo·byer·to cover
charge
preferir pre·fe·reer prefer
pregunta ⓕ pre·goon·ta question
preguntar pre·goon·tar ask
(a question)

preocupado/a ⓜ/ⓕ
pre·o·koo·pa·do/a worried
preocuparse por pre·o·koo·par·se por
care (about something)
preparar pre·pa·rar prepare
presidente/a ⓜ/ⓕ pre·see·den·te/a
president
presión ⓕ pre·syon pressure
— arterial ar·te·ryal blood pressure
prevenir pre·ve·neer prevent
primavera ⓕ pree·ma·ve·ra spring
(season)
primer ministro ⓜ pree·mer
mee·nees·tro prime minister
primera ministra ⓕ pree·me·ra
mee·nees·tra prime minister
primero/a ⓜ/ⓕ pree·me·ro/a first
principal preen·thee·pal main
prisa ⓕ pree·sa hurry
prisionero/a ⓜ/ⓕ pree·syon·ne·ro/a
prisoner
privado/a ⓜ/ⓕ pree·va·do/a private
probar pro·bar try
producir pro·doo·theer produce
productos ⓜ pl **congelados**
pro·dook·tos kon·khe·la·dos frozen
foods
profesor(a) ⓜ/ⓕ pro·fe·sor/
pro·fe·so·ra lecturer · instructor ·
teacher
profundo/a ⓜ/ⓕ pro·foon·do/a deep
programa ⓜ pro·gra·ma programme
prolongación ⓕ pro·lon·ga·thyon
extension (visa)
promesa ⓕ pro·me·sa promise
prometida ⓕ pro·me·tee·da fiancee
prometido ⓜ pro·me·tee·do fiance
pronto pron·to soon
propietaria ⓕ pro·pye·ta·rya landlady
propietario ⓜ pro·pye·ta·ryo landlord
propina ⓕ pro·pee·na tip
proteger pro·te·kher protect
protegido/a ⓜ/ⓕ pro·te·khee·do/a
protected
protesta ⓕ pro·tes·ta protest

provisiones ① pl pro·bee·syo·nes provisions

proyector ⓜ pro·yek·tor projector

prudente proo·den·te sensible

prueba ① prwe·ba test

— del embarazo del em·ba·ra·tho pregnancy test kit

pruebas ① pl **nucleares** prwe·bas noo·kle·a·res nuclear testing

pub ⓜ poob bar (with music) • pub

pueblo ⓜ pwe·blo village

puente ⓜ pwen·te bridge

puerro ⓜ pwe·ro leek

puerta ① pwer·ta door

puerto ⓜ pwer·to port • harbour

puesta ① **del sol** pwes·ta del sol sunset

pulga ① pool·ga flea

pulmones ⓜ pl pool·mo·nes lungs

punto ⓜ poon·to point (tip/score)

puro ⓜ poo·ro cigar

puro/a ⓜ/① poo·ro/a pure

(el mes) que viene (el mes) ke vye·ne next (month)

quedar ke·dar leave (behind)

quedarse ke·dar·se stay (remain)

quedarse sin ke·dar·se seen run out of

quejarse ke·khar·se complain

quemadura ① ke·ma·doo·ra burn

— de sol de sol sunburn

querer ke·rer love • want

queso ⓜ ke·so cheese

— crema kre·ma cream cheese

— de cabra de ka·bra goat's cheese

quien kyen who

quincena ① keen·the·na fortnight

quiosco ⓜ kyos·ko news stand • newsagency

quiste ⓜ **ovárico** kees·te o·va·ree·ko ovarian cyst

quizás kee·thas maybe

R

rábano ⓜ ra·ba·no radish

— picante pee·kan·te horseradish

rápido/a ⓜ/① ra·pee·do/a fast

raqueta ① ra·ke·ta racquet

raro/a ⓜ/① ra·ro/a rare (item)

rastro ⓜ ras·tro track (footprints)

rata ① ra·ta rat

ratón ⓜ ra·ton mouse

raza ① ra·tha race (people)

razón ① ra·thon reason

realista re·a·lees·ta realistic

recibir re·thee·beer receive

recibo ⓜ re·thee·bo receipt

reciclable re·thee·kla·ble recyclable

reciclar re·thee·klar recycle

recientemente re·thyen·te·men·te recently

recogida ① **de equipajes** re·ko·khee·da de e·kee·pa·khes baggage claim

recolección ① **de fruta** re·ko·lek·thyon de froo·ta fruit picking

recomendar re·ko·men·dar recommend

reconocer re·ko·no·ther recognise

recordar re·kor·dar remember

recorrido ⓜ **guiado** re·ko·ree·do gee·a·do guided tour

recto/a ⓜ/① rek·to/a straight

recuerdo ⓜ re·kwer·do souvenir

red ① red net

redondo/a ⓜ/① re·don·do/a round

reembolsar re·em·bol·sar refund

reembolso ⓜ re·em·bol·so refund

referencias ① pl re·fe·ren·thyas references

refresco ⓜ re·fres·ko soft drink

refugiado/a ⓜ/① re·foo·khya·do/a refugee

regalar re·ga·lar exchange (gifts)

regalo ⓜ re·ga·lo gift

— de bodas de bo·das wedding present

régimen ⓜ re·khee·men diet

reglas ① pl re·glas rules

reina ① rey·na queen

reírse re·eer·se laugh

elación ① re·la·*thyon* relationship

elajarse re·la·*khar*·se relax

elegión ① re·lee·*khyon* religion

eligioso/a ⓜ/① re·lee·*khyo*·so/a religious

eliquia ① re·lee·*kya* relic

eloj ⓜ re·*lokh* clock

– de pulsera de pool·*se*·ra watch

emo ⓜ *re*·mo rowing

emolacha ① re·mo·*la*·cha beetroot

emoto/a ⓜ/① re·*mo*·to/a remote

eparar re·pa·*rar* repair

epartir re·par·*teer* divide up (share)

epetir re·pe·*teer* repeat

epública ① re·poo·*blee*·ka republic

equesón ⓜ re·ke·*son* cottage cheese

eserva ① re·*ser*·va reservation

eservar re·ser·*var* book (make a reservation)

esfriado ⓜ res·*free*·a·do cold

esidencia ① **de estudiantes** e·see·*den*·thya de es·too·*dyan*·tes college

esiduos ⓜ pl **tóxicos** re·*see*·dwos *o*·ksee·kos toxic waste

espirar res·pee·*rar* breathe

espuesta ① res·*pwes*·ta answer

estaurante ⓜ res·tow·*ran*·te restaurant

evisar re·vee·*sar* check

evisor(a) ⓜ/① re·vee·*sor*/ e·vee·*so*·ra ticket collector

evista ① re·*vees*·ta magazine

ey ⓜ rey king

ico/a ⓜ/① *ree*·ko/a rich

iesgo ⓜ *ryes*·go risk

ío ⓜ *ree*·o river

itmo ⓜ *reet*·mo rhythm

obar ro·*bar* rob • steal

oca ① *ro*·ka rock

ock ⓜ rok rock (music)

odilla ① ro·*dee*·lya knee

ojo/a ⓜ/① *ro*·kho/a red

ollo ⓜ **repelente contra mosquitos** *o*·lyo re·pe·*len*·te *kon*·tra mos·*kee*·tos mosquito coil

romántico/a ⓜ/① ro·*man*·tee·ko/a romantic

romper rom·*per* break

ron ⓜ ron rum

ropa ① *ro*·pa clothing

– de cama de *ka*·ma bedding

– interior een·te·*ryor* underwear

rosa *ro*·sa pink

roto/a ⓜ/① *ro*·to/a broken

rueda ① *rwe*·da wheel

rugby ⓜ roog·*bee* rugby

ruidoso/a ⓜ/① rwee·*do*·so/a loud

ruinas ① pl *rwee*·nas ruins

ruta ① *roo*·ta route

S

S

sábado ⓜ *sa*·ba·do Saturday

sábana ① *sa*·ba·na sheet (bed)

saber sa·*ber* know (something)

sabroso/a ⓜ/① sa·*bro*·so/a tasty

sacar sa·*kar* take out • take (photo)

sacerdote ⓜ sa·ther·*do*·te priest

saco ⓜ **de dormir** *sa*·ko de dor·*meer* sleeping bag

sal ① sal salt

sala ① **de espera** *sa*·la de es·*pe*·ra waiting room

sala ① **de tránsito** *sa*·la de *tran*·see·to transit lounge

salario ⓜ sa·*la*·ryo rate of pay • salary

salchicha ① sal·*chee*·cha sausage

saldo ⓜ *sal*·do balance (account)

salida ① sa·*lee*·da departure • exit

saliente ⓜ sa·*lyen*·te ledge

salir con sa·*leer* kon go out with

salir de sa·*leer* de depart

salmón ⓜ sal·*mon* salmon

salón de belleza ⓜ sa·*lon* de be·*lye*·tha beauty salon

salsa ① *sal*·sa sauce

– de guindilla de geen·*dee*·lya chilli sauce

– de soja de *so*·kha soy sauce

– de tomate de to·*ma*·te tomato sauce • ketchup

S

saltar sal·*tar* jump

salud ⓕ sa·*loo* health

salvaeslips ⓜ pl sal·va·e·*sleeps* panty liners

salvar sal·*var* save

sandalias ⓕ pl san·*da*·lyas sandals

sandía ⓕ san·*dee*·a watermelon

sangrar san·*grar* bleed

sangre ⓕ san·gre blood

santo/a ⓜ/ⓕ san·to/a saint

sarampión ⓜ sa·ram·*pyon* measles

sartén ⓕ sar·*ten* frying pan

sastre ⓜ *sas*·tre tailor

sauna ⓕ *sow*·na sauna

secar se·*kar* dry

secretario/a ⓜ/ⓕ se·kre·*ta*·ryo/a secretary

sed ⓕ se·da thirst

seda ⓕ se·da silk

seguir se·*geer* follow

segundo/a ⓜ/ⓕ se·*goon*·do/a second

seguro ⓜ se·*goo*·ro insurance

seguro/a ⓜ/ⓕ se·*goo*·ro/a safe

sello ⓜ se·lyo stamp

semáforos ⓜ pl se·*ma*·fo·ros traffic lights

Semana ⓕ **Santa** se·*ma*·na san·ta Easter Week

sembrar sem·*brar* plant

semidirecto/a ⓜ/ⓕ se·mee·dee·*rek*·to/a non-direct

señal ⓕ se·*nyal* sign

sencillo/a ⓜ/ⓕ sen·*thee*·lyo/a simple

(un billete) sencillo ⓜ (oon bee·*lye*·te) sen·*thee*·lyo one-way (ticket)

sendero ⓜ sen·*de*·ro mountain path · path

senos ⓜ pl se·nos breasts

sensibilidad ⓕ sen·see·bee·lee·*da* sensitivity · film speed

sensual sen·*swal* sensual

sentarse sen·*tar*·se sit

sentimientos ⓜ pl sen·tee·*myen*·tos feelings

sentir sen·*teer* feel

separado/a ⓜ/ⓕ se·pa·*ra*·do/a separate

separar se·pa·*rar* separate

ser ser be

serie ⓕ se·rye series

serio/a ⓜ/ⓕ se·ryo/a serious

seropositivo/a ⓜ/ⓕ se·ro·po·see·*tee*·vo/a HIV positive

serpiente ⓕ ser·*pyen*·te snake

servicio ⓜ ser·*vee*·thyo service charge

— militar mee·lee·*tar* military service

— telefónico automático te·le·fo·nee·ko ow·to·ma·tee·ko direct-dial

servicios ⓜ pl ser·*vee*·thyos toilets

servilleta ⓕ ser·vee·*lye*·ta napkin

sexo ⓜ sek·so sex

— seguro se·goo·ro safe sex

sexy sek·see sexy

si see if

sí see yes

SIDA ⓜ see·da AIDS

sidra ⓕ see·dra cider

siempre *syem*·pre always

silla ⓕ see·lya chair

— de ruedas de rwe·das wheelchair

sillín ⓜ see·*lyeen* saddle

similar see·mee·*lar* similar

simpático/a ⓜ/ⓕ seem·*pa*·tee·ko/a nice

sin seen without

— hogar o·*gar* homeless

— plomo *plo*·mo unleaded

sinagoga ⓕ see·na·go·ga synagogue

Singapur ⓜ seen·ga·*poor* Singapore

sintético/a ⓜ/ⓕ seen·*te*·tee·ko/a synthetic

soborno ⓜ so·*bor*·no bribe

sobre so·bre about · on top of

sobre ⓜ so·bre envelope

sobredosis ⓕ so·bre·*do*·sees overdose

sobrevivir so·bre·vee·*veer* survive

socialista m&① so·thya·*lees*·ta socialist

sol m sol sun

soldado m sol·*da*·do soldier

sólo so·lo only

solo/a m/① so·lo/a alone

soltero/a m/① sol·*te*·ro/a single

sombra ① *som*·bra shadow

sombrero m som·*bre*·ro hat

soñar so·*nyar* dream

sondeos m pl son·*de*·os polls

sonreír son·re·*eer* smile

sopa ① *so*·pa soup

sordo/a m/① *sor*·do/a deaf

sorpresa ① sor·*pre*·sa surprise

su soo her • his • their

subir soo·*beer* climb

submarinismo m soob·ma·ree·*nees*·mo diving

subtítulos m pl soob·*tee*·too·los subtitles

sucio/a m/① soo·thyo/a dirty

sucursal ① soo·koor·*sal* branch office

sudar soo·*dar* perspire

suegra ① *swe*·gra mother-in-law

suegro m *swe*·gro father-in-law

sueldo m *swel*·do wage

suelo m *swe*·lo floor

suerte ① *swer*·te luck

suficiente soo·fee·*thyen*·te enough

sufrir soo·*freer* suffer

sujetador m soo·khe·ta·*dor* bra

supermercado m soo·per·mer·*ka*·do supermarket

superstición ① soo·pers·tee·*thyon* superstition

sur m soor south

surf m **sobre la nieve** soorf so·bre la nye·ve snowboarding

T

tabaco m ta·*ba*·ko tobacco

tabla ① **de surf** *ta*·bla de soorf surfboard

tablero m **de ajedrez** ta·*ble*·ro de a·khe·*dreth* chess board

tacaño/a m/① ta·*ka*·nyo/a stingy

talco m *tal*·ko baby powder

talla ① *ta*·lya size (clothes)

taller m ta·*lyer* workshop

también tam·*byen* also

tampoco tam·po·ko neither

tampones m pl tam·po·nes tampons

tanga ① *tan*·ga g-string

tapones m pl **para los oídos** ta·po·nes pa·ra los o·ee·dos earplugs

taquilla ① ta·kee·lya ticket office

tarde *tar*·de late

tarjeta tar·*khe*·ta card

— **de crédito** de *kre*·dee·to credit card

— **de embarque** de em·*bar*·ke boarding pass

— **de teléfono** de te·*le*·fo·no phone card

tarta ① **nupcial** *tar*·ta noop·*thyal* wedding cake

tasa ① **del aeropuerto** *ta*·sa del ay·ro·*pwer*·to airport tax

taxi m *ta*·ksee taxi

taza ① *ta*·tha cup

té m te tea

teatro m te·*a*·tro theatre

teclado m te·*kla*·do keyboard

técnica ① *tek*·nee·ka technique

tela ① *te*·la fabric

tele ① *te*·le TV

teleférico m te·le·*fe*·ree·ko cable car

teléfono m te·*le*·fo·no telephone

— **móvil** mo·veel mobile phone

— **público** *poo*·blee·ko public telephone

telegrama m te·le·*gra*·ma telegram

telenovela ① te·le·no·ve·la soap opera

telescopio m te·les·ko·pyo telescope

televisión ① te·le·vee·*syon* television

temperatura ① tem·pe·ra·*too*·ra temperature (weather)

templado/a m/① tem·*pla*·do/a warm

T

templo ⓜ *tem*·plo temple
temporada ⓕ tem·po·*ra*·da season (in sport)
temprano tem·*pra*·no early
tenedor te·ne·*dor* fork
tener te·*ner* have
— **hambre** *am*·bre to be hungry
— **prisa** *pree*·sa to be in a hurry
— **sed** seth to be thirsty
— **sueño** *swe*·nyo to be sleepy
tenis ⓜ *te*·nees tennis
tensión ⓕ **premenstrual** ten·*syon* pre·mens·*trwal* premenstrual tension
tentempié ⓜ ten·tem·*pye* snack
tercio ⓜ *ter*·thyo third
terminar ter·mee·*nar* finish
ternera ⓕ ter·*ne*·ra veal
ternero ⓜ ter·*ne*·ro calf
terremoto ⓜ te·re·*mo*·to earthquake
testarudo/a ⓜ/ⓕ tes·ta·roo·do/a stubborn
tía ⓕ *tee*·a aunt
tiempo ⓜ *tyem*·po time • weather
a— a *tyem*·po on time
a— completo/parcial a *tyem*·po kom·*ple*·to/par·*thyal* full-time/part-time
tienda ⓕ **(de campaña)** *tyen*·da (de kam·*pa*·nya) tent
tienda ⓕ *tyen*·da shop
— **de comestibles** de ko·mes·*tee*·bles grocery
— **de fotografía** de fo·to·gra·*fee*·a camera shop
— **de eléctrodomésticos** de e·lek·tro·do·mes·*tee*·kos electrical store
— **de cámping** de *kam*·peen camping store
— **de recuerdos** de re·*kwer*·dos souvenir shop
— **de ropa** de *ro*·pa clothing store
— **deportiva** de·por·*tee*·va sports store
Tierra ⓕ *tye*·ra Earth

tierra ⓕ *tye*·ra land
tiesto ⓜ *tyes*·to pot (plant)
tijeras ⓕ pl tee·*khe*·ras scissors
tímido/a ⓜ/ⓕ tee·mee·do/a shy
típico/a ⓜ/ⓕ tee·pee·ko/a typical
tipo ⓜ *tee*·po type
— **de cambio** de *kam*·byo exchange rate
tirar tee·*rar* pull
tiritas ⓕ pl tee·*ree*·tas band-aids
título ⓜ *tee*·too·lo degree
toalla ⓕ to·a·lya towel
toallita ⓕ to·a·lyee·ta face cloth
tobillo ⓜ to·bee·lyo ankle
tocar to·*kar* touch
— **la guitarra** la gee·*ta*·ra play guitar
tocino ⓜ to·*thee*·no bacon
todavía (no) to·da·*vee*·a (no) (not) yet
todo *to*·do all • everything
tofu ⓜ to·*foo* tofu
tomar to·*mar* take • drink
tomate ⓜ to·*ma*·te tomato
— **secado al sol** se·*ka*·do al sol sun-dried tomato
tono ⓜ *to*·no tone
torcedura ⓕ tor·the·*doo*·ra sprain
tormenta ⓕ tor·*men*·ta storm
toro ⓜ *to*·ro bull
torre ⓕ *to*·re tower
tos ⓕ tos cough
tostada ⓕ tos·*ta*·da toast
tostadora ⓕ tos·ta·*do*·ra toaster
trabajar tra·ba·*khar* work
trabajo ⓜ tra·*ba*·kho job • work
— **administrativo** ad·mee·nees·tra·*tee*·vo paperwork
— **de camarero/a** ⓜ/ⓕ de ka·ma·re·ro/a bar work
— **de casa** de *ka*·sa housework
— **de limpieza** de leem·*pye*·tha cleaning
— **eventual** e·ven·*twal* casual work
traducir tra·doo·*theer* translate
traer tra·*er* bring
traficante ⓜ&ⓕ **de drogas** tra·fee·*kan*·te de *dro*·gas drug dealer

U

tráfico m *tra·fee·ko* traffic

tramposo/a m/f *tram·po·so/a* cheat

tranquilo/a m/f *tran·kee·lo/a* quiet

tranvía m *tran·vee·a* tram

a través a *tra·ves* across

tren m *tren* train

— de cercanías de ther·ka·*nee*·as local train

trepar tre·*par* climb • scale

tres en raya tres en *ra·ya* noughts & crosses

triste *trees*·te sad

tú inf *too* you

tu *too* your

tubo m **de escape** *too*·bo de es·*ka*·pe exhaust

tumba f *toom*·ba grave

tumbarse toom·*bar*·se lie (not stand)

turista m&f *too·rees*·ta tourist

— operador(a) m/f o·pe·ra·*dor*/ o·pe·ra·*do*·ra tourist operator

U

uniforme m oo·nee·*for*·me uniform

universidad f oo·nee·ver·see·*da* university

universo m oo·nee·*ver*·so universe

urgente oor·*khen*·te urgent

Usted pol oos·*te* you

Ustedes pol pl oos·*te*·des you

útil *oo*·teel useful

uvas f pl *oo*·vas grapes

— pasas *pa*·sas raisins

V

vaca f *va*·ka cow

vacaciones f pl va·ka·*thyo*·nes holidays • vacation

vacante va·*kan*·te vacant

vacío/a m/f va·*thee*·o/a empty

vacuna f va·*koo*·na vaccination

vagina f va·*khee*·na vagina

vagón m **restaurante** va·*gon* res·tow·*ran*·te dining car

validar va·lee·*dar* validate

valiente va·*lyen*·te brave

valioso/a m/f va·*lyo*·so/a valuable

valle m *va*·lye valley

valor m va·*lor* value

vaqueros m pl va·*ke*·ros jeans

varios/as m/f pl *va*·ryos/as several

vaso m *va*·so (drinking) glass

vegetariano/a m/f ve·khe·ta·*rya*·no/a vegetarian

vela f *ve*·la candle

velocidad f ve·lo·thee·*da* speed

velocímetro m ve·lo·*thee*·me·tro speedometer

velódromo m ve·*lo*·dro·mo racetrack (bicycles)

vena f *ve*·na vein

vendaje m ven·*da*·khe bandage

vendedor(a) m/f **de flores** ven·de·*dor*/ven·de·*do*·ra de *flo*·res florist

vender ven·*der* sell

venenoso/a m/f ve·ne·*no*·so/a poisonous

venir ve·*neer* come

ventana f ven·*ta*·na window

ventilador m ven·tee·la·*dor* fan (machine)

ver ver see

verano m ve·*ra*·no summer

verde ver·de green

verdulería f ver·doo·le·*ree*·a greengrocery (shop)

verdulero/a m/f ver·doo·*le*·ro/a grocer (shopkeeper)

verduras f pl ver·*doo*·ras vegetables

vestíbulo m ves·*tee*·boo·lo foyer

vestido m ves·*tee*·do dress

vestuario m ves·*twa*·ryo wardrobe

vestuarios m pl ves·*twa*·ryos changing room

vez f veth once

viajar vya·*khar* travel

viaje m *vya*·khe trip

vid f veed vine

Y

vida ⓕ *vee*·da life
vidrio ⓜ *vee*·dryo glass
viejo/a ⓜ/ⓕ *vye*·kho/a old
viento ⓜ *vyen*·to wind
vinagre ⓜ vee·*na*·gre vinegar
viñedo ⓜ vee·*nye*·do vineyard
vino ⓜ *vee*·no wine
violar vyo·*lar* rape
virus ⓜ *vee*·roos virus
visado ⓜ vee·*sa*·do visa
visitar vee·see·*tar* visit
vista ⓕ *vees*·ta view
vitaminas ⓕ pl vee·ta·*mee*·nas vitamins
víveres ⓜ pl *vee*·ve·res food supplies
vivir vee·*veer* live (life)
vodka ⓕ *vod*·ka vodka
volar vo·*lar* fly
volumen ⓜ vo·*loo*·men volume
volver vol·*ver* return
vosotros/as ⓜ/ⓕ pl inf vo·*so*·tros/as you
votar vo·*tar* vote
voz ⓕ voth voice
vuelo doméstico ⓜ *vwe*·lo do·*mes*·tee·ko domestic flight

Y

y ee and
ya ya already
yip ⓜ yeep jeep
yo yo I
yoga ⓜ *yo*·ga yoga
yogur ⓜ yo·*goor* yogurt

Z

zanahoria ⓕ tha·na·o·rya carrot
zapatería ⓕ tha·pa·te·*ree*·a shoe shop
zapatos ⓜ pl tha·*pa*·tos shoes
zodíaco ⓜ tho·*dee*·a·ko zodiac
zoológico ⓜ zo·o·*lo*·khee·ko zoo
zumo ⓜ *thoo*·mo juice
— de naranja de na·*ran*·kha orange juice

Index
índice

For topics that are covered in several sections of this book, we've indicated the most relevant page number in bold.

10 Ways to Start a Sentence

When's (the next flight)?	¿Cuándo sale (el próximo vuelo)?	*kwan·do sa·le (el prok·see·mo vwe·lo)*
Where's (the station)?	¿Dónde está (la estación)?	*don·de es·ta (la es·ta·thyon)*
Where can I (buy a ticket)?	¿Dónde puedo (comprar un billete)?	*don·de pwe·do (kom·prar oon bee·lye·te)*
How much is (a room)?	¿Cuánto cuesta (una habitación)?	*kwan·to kwes·ta (oo·na a·bee·ta·thyon)*
Do you have (a map)?	¿Tiene (un mapa)?	*tye·ne (oon ma·pa)*
Is there (a toilet)?	¿Hay (servicios)?	*ai (ser·vee·thyos)*
I'd like (a coffee).	Quisiera (un café).	*kee·sye·ra (oon ka·fe)*
Can I (enter)?	¿Se puede (entrar)?	*se pwe·de (en·trar)*
Could you please (help me)?	¿Puede (ayudarme), por favor?	*pwe·de (a·yoo·dar·me) por fa·vor*
Do I have to (get a visa)?	¿Necesito (obtener un visado)?	*ne·the·see·to (ob·te·ner oon vee·sa·do)*